Woody After Hours Volume 1:

Live From Downtown Raleigh, North Carolina...

TERRY,
SORRY IN
ADVANCE FOR
THE ART IN
THIS BOOK!
PAUL
WESTOVER
ECCC '14

Written by Ben Carter
Illustrated by Paul Westover

DV

DEPTH VARIES

Woody After Hours, Volume 1:
Live From Downtown Raleigh, North Carolina…

DEPTH VARIES

Grateful acknowledgements are made to the following for their contribution. Characters and art used with the individual copyright holder's permission:

Diablito Del Ring & Jezebelle, from the comic *Diablito Del Ring* (www.diablitodelring.com), are © Jesse Justice.
Chelsea Chattan & Sebastian, from the comic *Clan of the Cats* (clanofthecats.com), are © Jamie Robertson.
Hank Addanac, from the comic *Addanac City* (www.addanaccity.com), is © George Ford.
Edmund Finney, from the comic *Edmund Finney's Quest to Find the Meaning of Life* (eqcomics.com), is © Dan Long.
Andy Lemon & Jeff Katzenburg, from the comic *Lemon Inc.* (laiguyscomics.com/lemoninc), are © Tim Lai.
Crowbar Benson, from the comic *Crowbar Benson* (www.crowbarbenson.com), is © Sandy Debreuil.
Sam, Harry, Jill & Ed, from the comic *Circuit* (unbalancedhumors.com), are © Luke Pola.

First Printing, 2011

Printed in the United States of America.

ISBN-13: 978-0615526317
ISBN-10: 0615526314

For our wives, Lisa & Jennifer.

I really enjoy late-night talk shows (in fact, I've got *Conan* on as I type this). The key for me is the variety. It's fun to watch a charismatic host do topical stand-up, participate in comedy sketches and interview a diverse assortment of people in only 48 minutes. Throw in a mix of videos, stunts, audience participation, musical performances, cooking segments and more stand-up routines and you've got hours of seriously entertaining comedy five nights a week.

My primary goal with *Woody After Hours* is to tap into that late-night energy, tweak it to work in a webcomic format and share it with as many people as possible. I'm very proud of what Paul and I have accomplished so far. With every strip I feel that we're making progress. We still have a long way to go, but we're definitely growing and getting better.

Thank you for reading our book. We hope you find it entertaining.

- Ben

Name: Woody
Age: 38
Job: *WAH* Host

Woody decided to get a head start on his mid-life crisis. Instead of buying a sports car, he quit his job to host his own late-night talk show.

Optimistic: Yes
Funny: Sporadically
Crazy: Possibly

Name: Isabel
Age: 25
Job: *WAH*
Producer

Isabel has sunk everything she has, and then some, into getting *Woody After Hours* off the ground and on its way to success. Her dream is to one day be a producer on Broadway.

Driven: Yes
Naive: Unfortunately
Poor: Mostly

Name: Joseph
Age: 63
Job: *WAH*
Cameraman

Joseph has been behind the camera for the Army during the Vietnam War, the *Tonight Show with Johnny Carson* and the *Late Show with David Letterman*. He has returned to Raleigh to slow down and take it easy.

Tall: Yes
Crotchety: Totally
Retired: Not really

Name: Renee
Age: 38
Job: Consultant

Renee is Woody's wife. She's not enthusiastic about Woody's new career choice but loves and supports him. She is always working on her laptop. For who or what industry she consults is a mystery.

Smart: Yes
Workaholic: Probably
Passive-aggressive: Usually

Name: Timmy
Age: 19
Job: NCSU
    Student &
    WAH Intern

Name: Roger
Age: 35
Job: Agent

Timmy was introduced to *WAH* as a captive audience member. Freed after the show, he admitted that the show had potential and wanted to be a part of it. His interaction with an unknown being has yet to be explained.

Young: Yes
Geek: Unquestionably
Has potential: Questionably

Roger is Woody's best friend. After each show the first thing Woody typically does is call Roger to see if he enjoyed it. Unfortunately, Roger has missed them all, as he is typically neck deep in the middle of his job.

Physically fit: Yes
Multifaceted: Largely
Available: Rarely

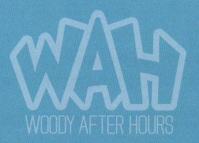

Name: ?
Age: ?
Job: Ghost

Name: Nemesis
Age: 43
Job: Master
    Sommelier

The ghost lives in the Sir Walter Raleigh Theater. Certain people on staff are aware of and friendly with the ghost. Others have yet to meet it, and therefore don't believe it really exists...yet.

Spiritual: Yes
Rational: Nearly
Purpose: Likely

Nemesis and Woody met outside the SWR Theater a few hours before the first *Woody After Hours* show. Nemesis couldn't resist giving Woody a hard time just for fun. Their relationship has been rocky ever since. Nemesis' real name is currently unknown.

Certified: Yes
Dashing: Positively
Smart ass: Occasionally

Comic: *Diablito Del Ring*
Written and illustrated by Jesse Justice
Website: http://www.diablitodelring.com/

Diablito Del Ring, pound-for-pound the world's greatest pro wrestler, travels the world fighting against opponents of all shapes and sizes, in and out of the squared circle. Outside the ring, he is an angel of mercy; once in the ring, he fights like the devil himself. With his valet and close friend, Jezebelle, Diablito fights for glory, honor and justice.

Comic: *Clan of the Cats*
Written and illustrated by: Jamie Robertson
Website: http://clanofthecats.com/

COTC is an urban fantasy about a witch, Chelsea Chattan, who is also afflicted by an ancient family curse. In times of stress she transforms into a black panther. This, coupled by her increasing magical power, makes having an ordinary life rather challenging. The stories deal with supernatural themes mainly, but also creep into the realm of normal everyday life.

Comic: *Addanac City*
Written and illustrated by: George Ford
Website:
http://www.addanaccity.com/wordpress/

Addanac City features seven-year-old Hank Addanac, a rambunctious 2nd-grader who constantly finds himself in hot water with his parents, friends, neighbors and school officials. The series also spotlights several other citizens in town. Addanac City is updated seven days a week.

Comic: *Edmund Finney's Quest to Find the Meaning of Life*
Written and illustrated by: Dan Long
Website: http://eqcomics.com/

Edmund Finney backpacks across the globe in search of life's answers, stumbling across strange civilizations and quirky characters along the way. It is a twice-weekly comic strip with new comics on Tuesdays and Friday.

Comic: *Lemon Inc.*
Written and illustrated by: Tim Lai
Website: http://laiguyscomics.com/lemoninc/

Lemon Inc. is a webcomic about a couple of kids who run a lemonade stand that they treat like an office environment. Andy Lemon, a pompous and ambitious seven-year-old recruits his loyal and hard working best friend, Jeff Katzenburg, as his "business partner" and hires other kids and even stuffed animals as employees for his business.

Comic: *Crowbar Benson*
Written and illustrated by: Sandy Debreuil
Website: http://www.crowbarbenson.com/

Crowbar Benson got his nickname in the rinks of Northern Manitoba, where he played hockey in his youth until he got one to many pucks in the head. He's essentially a good guy, but his competitive spirit and complete disregard for his or anyone else's personal safety tends to get him in trouble. He's a practical joker, and loves to tease his kids, Benny and Eddie.

Comic: *Circuit*
Written and illustrated by: Luke Pola
Website: http://unbalancedhumors.com/

Circuit is a webcomic about two pals, Sam and Harry, who leave their jobs in Central Processing and venture into the Wide Open World. During their travels they forge new friendships, battle annoying and petty enemies and occasionally discuss what it means to be an "Exploding Ninja." They have yet to determine if it involves any actual exploding... or actual ninjas, for that matter.

WAH
WOODY AFTER HOURS

Coming Up Next on the DV
WAH
WOODY AFTER HOURS
OK, WOODY--
--IN TEN SECONDS YOU'RE GOING TO WALK OUT ON THAT STAGE AND START YOUR NEW CAREER.
YOU CAN DO THIS.
LIVE FROM DOWNTOWN RALEIGH, NORTH CAROLINA...
YOU KNOW--
--MAYBE I SHOULDN'T HAVE HAD THE KITCHEN SINK™ BURRITO FOR DINNER.
...IT'S WOODY AFTER HOURS!
OH CRAP!
AND HERE HE IS... WOODY!
MUUUGHAAA!
WELCOME TO THE FIRST EPISODE OF WOODY AFTER HOURS.
I'M REALLY EXCITED TO BE HERE, AND I'M GLAD YOU COULD MAKE IT.
I DECIDED TO QUIT MY JOB AND TRY MY LUCK AT HOSTING MY OWN SHOW--
--SO IF YOU WANT TO WATCH A GUY GO THROUGH HIS MIDLIFE CRISIS NIGHTLY, THEN STAY TUNED.
I'D LIKE TO THANK MY WIFE FOR ALL OF HER SUPPORT.
I THINK SHE'S OUT IN THE AUDIENCE--
--YES, THERE SHE IS, AND IT LOOKS LIKE SHE IS HOLDING UP A SIGN SO THAT IT'S EASIER TO FIND HER.
YOU HAVE BURRITO ON YOUR CHIN!

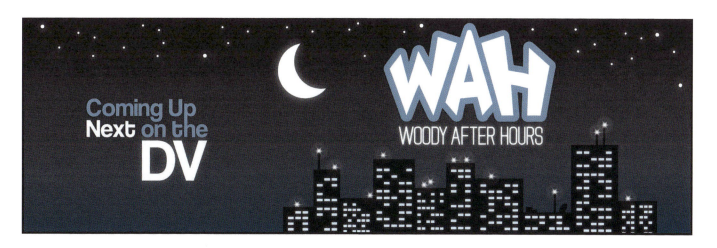

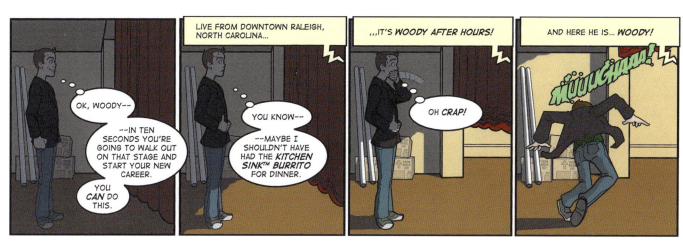

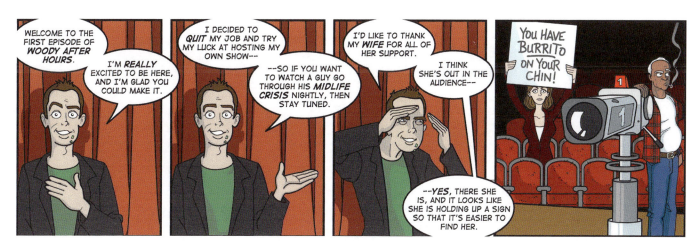

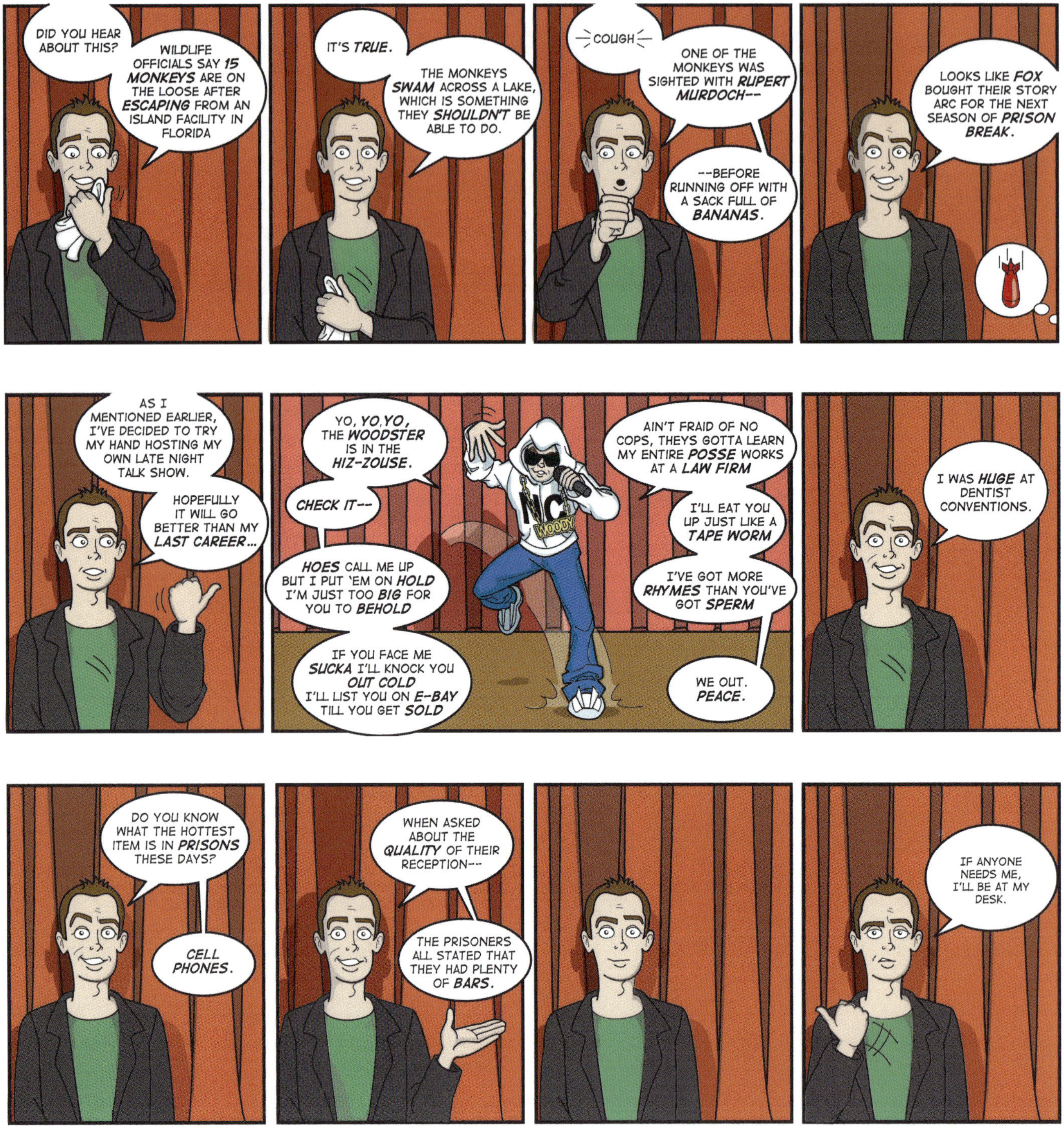
DID YOU HEAR ABOUT THIS?
WILDLIFE OFFICIALS SAY 15 MONKEYS ARE ON THE LOOSE AFTER ESCAPING FROM AN ISLAND FACILITY IN FLORIDA
IT'S TRUE.
THE MONKEYS SWAM ACROSS A LAKE, WHICH IS SOMETHING THEY SHOULDN'T BE ABLE TO DO.
COUGH
ONE OF THE MONKEYS WAS SIGHTED WITH RUPERT MURDOCH--
--BEFORE RUNNING OFF WITH A SACK FULL OF BANANAS.
LOOKS LIKE FOX BOUGHT THEIR STORY ARC FOR THE NEXT SEASON OF PRISON BREAK.
AS I MENTIONED EARLIER, I'VE DECIDED TO TRY MY HAND HOSTING MY OWN LATE NIGHT TALK SHOW.
HOPEFULLY IT WILL GO BETTER THAN MY LAST CAREER...
YO, YO,YO, THE WOODSTER IS IN THE HIZ-ZOUSE.
CHECK IT--
HOES CALL ME UP BUT I PUT 'EM ON HOLD I'M JUST TOO BIG FOR YOU TO BEHOLD
IF YOU FACE ME SUCKA I'LL KNOCK YOU OUT COLD I'LL LIST YOU ON E-BAY TILL YOU GET SOLD
AIN'T FRAID OF NO COPS, THEYS GOTTA LEARN MY ENTIRE POSSE WORKS AT A LAW FIRM
I'LL EAT YOU UP JUST LIKE A TAPE WORM
I'VE GOT MORE RHYMES THAN YOU'VE GOT SPERM
WE OUT. PEACE.
NC WOODY
I WAS HUGE AT DENTIST CONVENTIONS.
DO YOU KNOW WHAT THE HOTTEST ITEM IS IN PRISONS THESE DAYS?
CELL PHONES.
WHEN ASKED ABOUT THE QUALITY OF THEIR RECEPTION--
THE PRISONERS ALL STATED THAT THEY HAD PLENTY OF BARS.
IF ANYONE NEEDS ME, I'LL BE AT MY DESK.

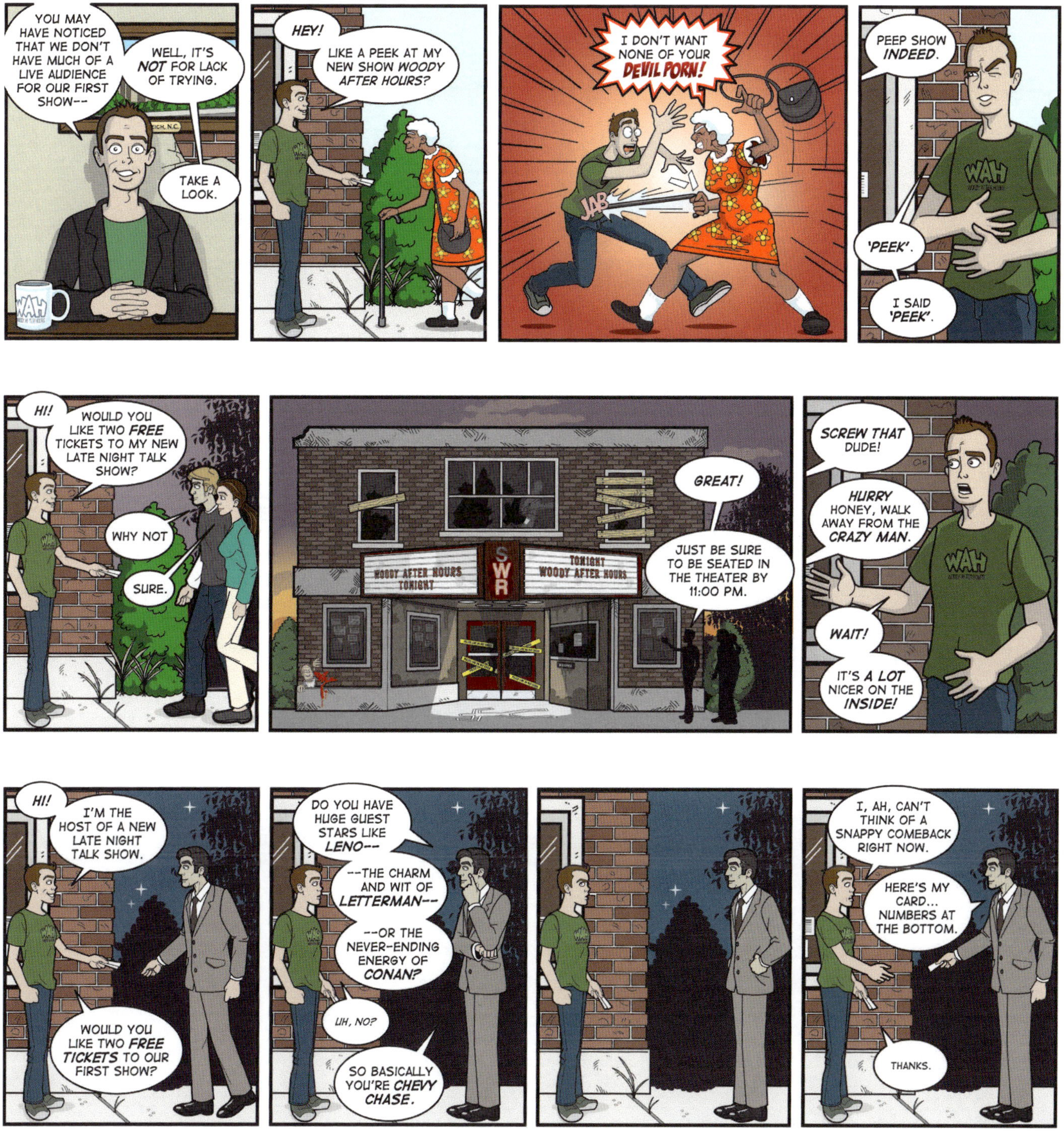
YOU MAY HAVE NOTICED THAT WE DON'T HAVE MUCH OF A LIVE AUDIENCE FOR OUR FIRST SHOW--
WELL, IT'S NOT FOR LACK OF TRYING.
TAKE A LOOK.
HEY!
LIKE A PEEK AT MY NEW SHOW WOODY AFTER HOURS?
I DON'T WANT NONE OF YOUR DEVIL PORN!
JAB
PEEP SHOW INDEED.
'PEEK'.
I SAID 'PEEK'.
HI!
WOULD YOU LIKE TWO FREE TICKETS TO MY NEW LATE NIGHT TALK SHOW?
WHY NOT
SURE.
WOODY AFTER HOURS TONIGHT
SWR
TONIGHT WOODY AFTER HOURS
GREAT!
JUST BE SURE TO BE SEATED IN THE THEATER BY 11:00 PM.
SCREW THAT DUDE!
HURRY HONEY, WALK AWAY FROM THE CRAZY MAN.
WAIT!
IT'S A LOT NICER ON THE INSIDE!
HI!
I'M THE HOST OF A NEW LATE NIGHT TALK SHOW.
WOULD YOU LIKE TWO FREE TICKETS TO OUR FIRST SHOW?
DO YOU HAVE HUGE GUEST STARS LIKE LENO--
--THE CHARM AND WIT OF LETTERMAN--
--OR THE NEVER-ENDING ENERGY OF CONAN?
UH, NO?
SO BASICALLY YOU'RE CHEVY CHASE.
I, AH, CAN'T THINK OF A SNAPPY COMEBACK RIGHT NOW.
HERE'S MY CARD... NUMBERS AT THE BOTTOM.
THANKS.

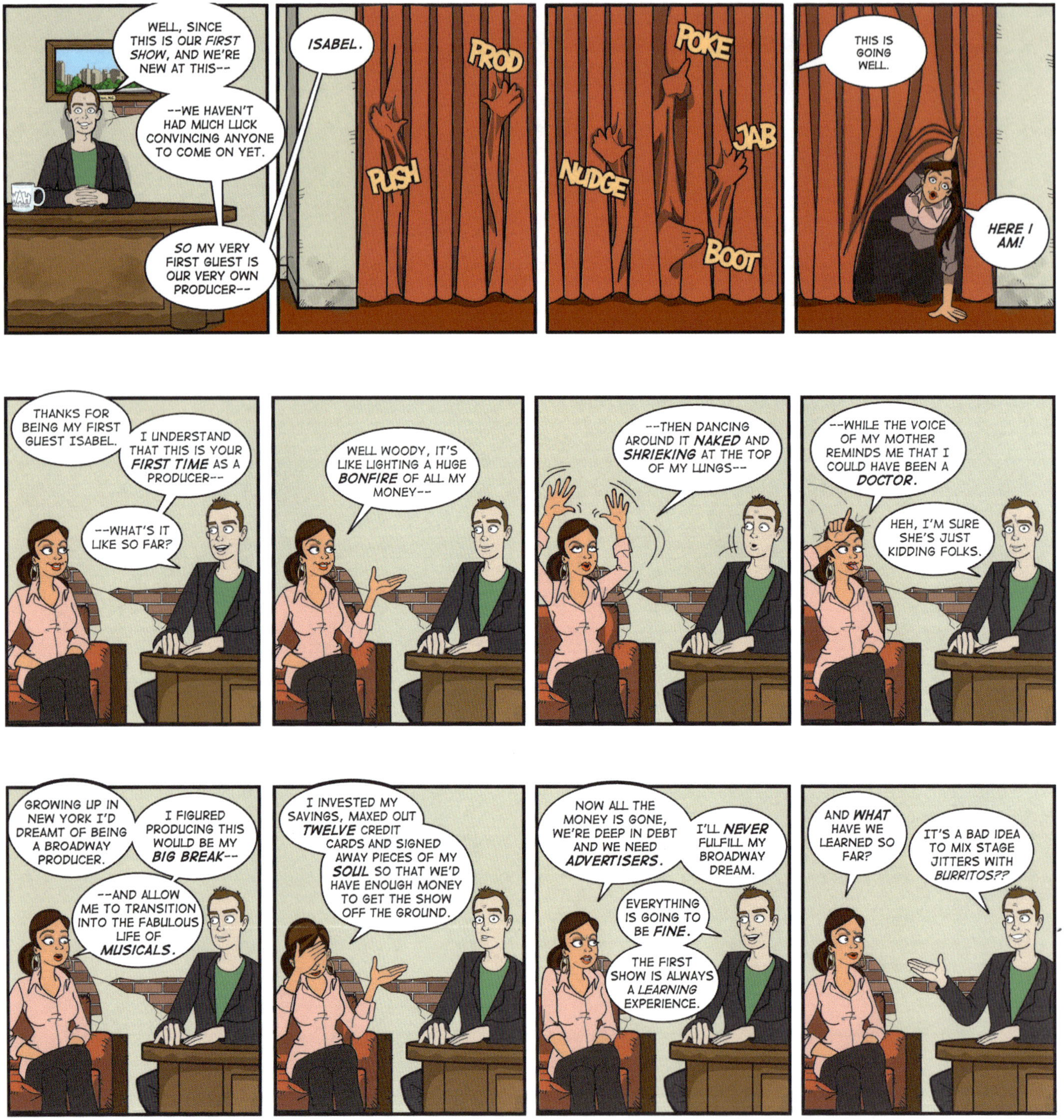
WELL, SINCE THIS IS OUR FIRST SHOW, AND WE'RE NEW AT THIS--
--WE HAVEN'T HAD MUCH LUCK CONVINCING ANYONE TO COME ON YET.
SO MY VERY FIRST GUEST IS OUR VERY OWN PRODUCER--
ISABEL.
PROD
PUSH
POKE
JAB
NUDGE
BOOT
THIS IS GOING WELL.
HERE I AM!
THANKS FOR BEING MY FIRST GUEST ISABEL.
I UNDERSTAND THAT THIS IS YOUR FIRST TIME AS A PRODUCER--
--WHAT'S IT LIKE SO FAR?
WELL WOODY, IT'S LIKE LIGHTING A HUGE BONFIRE OF ALL MY MONEY--
--THEN DANCING AROUND IT NAKED AND SHRIEKING AT THE TOP OF MY LUNGS--
--WHILE THE VOICE OF MY MOTHER REMINDS ME THAT I COULD HAVE BEEN A DOCTOR.
HEH, I'M SURE SHE'S JUST KIDDING FOLKS.
GROWING UP IN NEW YORK I'D DREAMT OF BEING A BROADWAY PRODUCER.
I FIGURED PRODUCING THIS WOULD BE MY BIG BREAK--
--AND ALLOW ME TO TRANSITION INTO THE FABULOUS LIFE OF MUSICALS.
I INVESTED MY SAVINGS, MAXED OUT TWELVE CREDIT CARDS AND SIGNED AWAY PIECES OF MY SOUL SO THAT WE'D HAVE ENOUGH MONEY TO GET THE SHOW OFF THE GROUND.
NOW ALL THE MONEY IS GONE, WE'RE DEEP IN DEBT AND WE NEED ADVERTISERS.
I'LL NEVER FULFILL MY BROADWAY DREAM.
EVERYTHING IS GOING TO BE FINE.
THE FIRST SHOW IS ALWAYS A LEARNING EXPERIENCE.
AND WHAT HAVE WE LEARNED SO FAR?
IT'S A BAD IDEA TO MIX STAGE JITTERS WITH BURRITOS??

I CANNOT BELIEVE I WAS SO NAIVE, TO THINK I COULD PRODUCE THIS BORE. WHAT WAS I THINKING? THIS SHOW IS SINKING, CAUSE NO ONE CAME IN THE FRONT DOOR.
THIS THEATER SUCKS AND IT COSTS BIG BUCKS, AND A GHOST HAUNTS THE SECOND FLOOR. IT'S JUST THE FIRST NIGHT, I'M SO FULL OF FRIGHT, AND THIS SEEMS LIKE SUCH A HARD CHORE.
MY BODY DOTH ACHE MORE THAN I CAN TAKE, THE PAIN CUTS ME DOWN TO THE CORE. SO WITH THIS SHARP KNIFE I WILL TAKE MY OWN LIFE, THEN I WON'T HAVE TO CARE ANYMORE.
ARGGG!
HEY ISABEL, YOU STILL WITH US?
SNAP SNAP
HUH?
OH, SORRY, JUST HAVING A BROADWAY MOMENT.
COME ON ISABEL, THINGS ARE GOING TO PICK UP AND WE'LL BE FINE.
YOU WILL FULFILL YOUR BROADWAY DREAM--
--I PROMISE.
YOU REALLY THINK SO WOODY?
OF COURSE I DO--
--AND THE AUDIENCE THINKS SO TOO.
WE ARE ALL DOOMED!
1
WHERE THE HECK IS SHE GETTING THOSE SIGNS?
AND NOW A WORD FROM OUR SPONSOR...
822

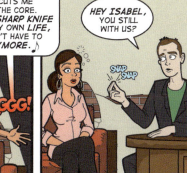

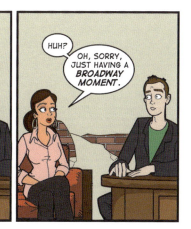

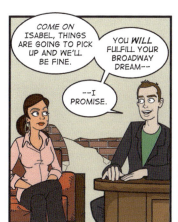

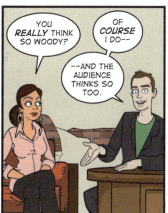

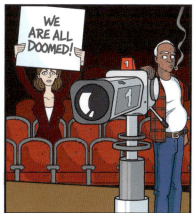

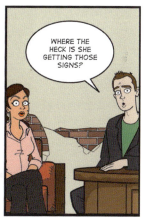

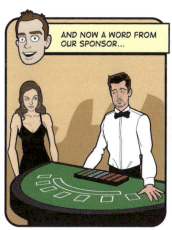

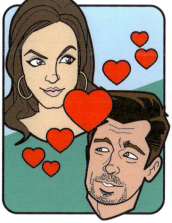

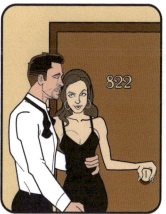

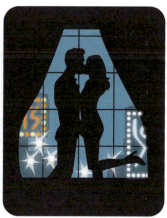

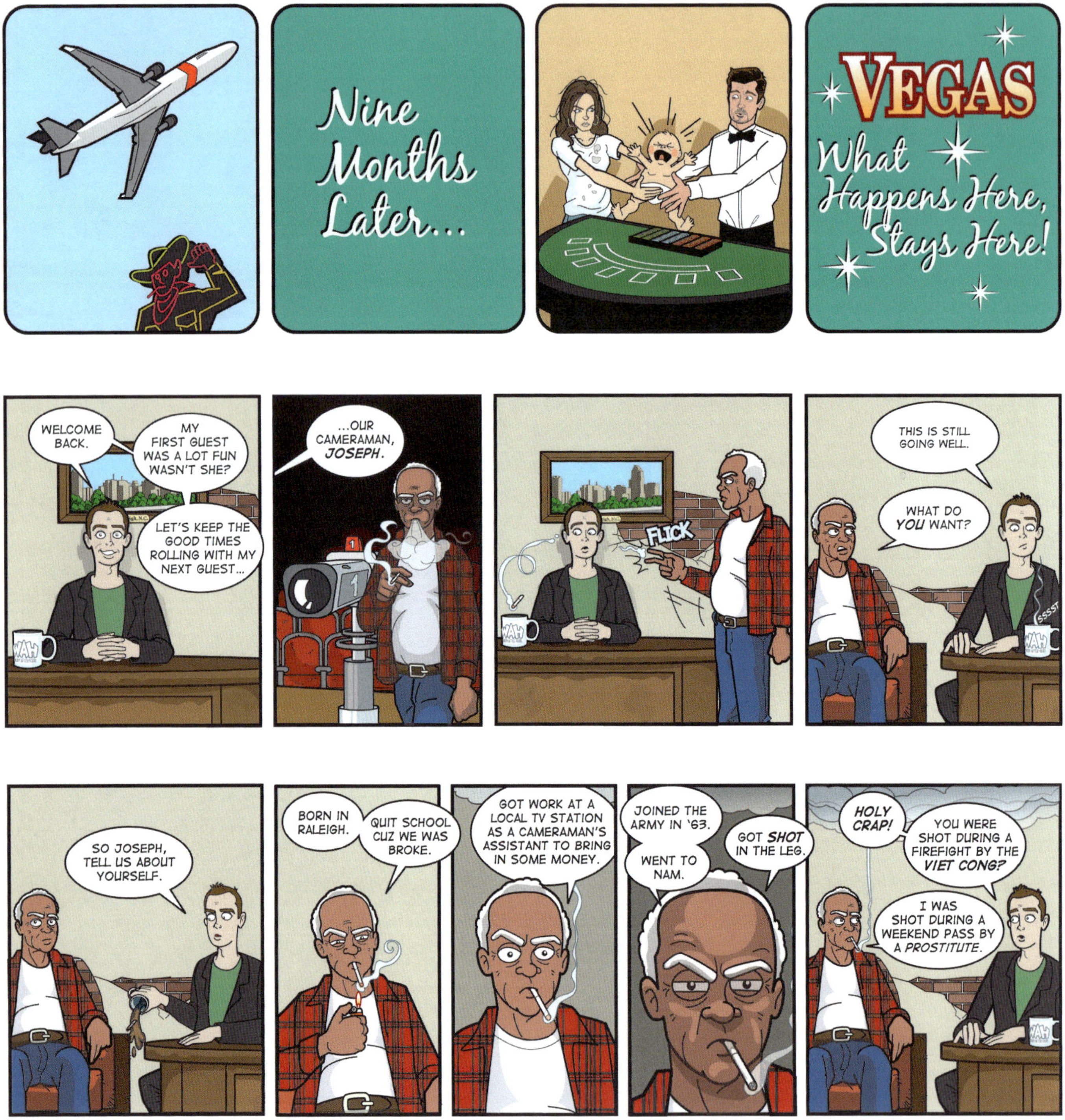
Nine Months Later...
VEGAS
What Happens Here, Stays Here!
WELCOME BACK.
MY FIRST GUEST WAS A LOT FUN WASN'T SHE?
LET'S KEEP THE GOOD TIMES ROLLING WITH MY NEXT GUEST...
...OUR CAMERAMAN, JOSEPH.
FLICK
THIS IS STILL GOING WELL.
WHAT DO YOU WANT?
SSSST
SO JOSEPH, TELL US ABOUT YOURSELF.
BORN IN RALEIGH.
QUIT SCHOOL CUZ WE WAS BROKE.
GOT WORK AT A LOCAL TV STATION AS A CAMERAMAN'S ASSISTANT TO BRING IN SOME MONEY.
JOINED THE ARMY IN '63.
WENT TO NAM.
GOT SHOT IN THE LEG.
HOLY CRAP!
YOU WERE SHOT DURING A FIREFIGHT BY THE VIET CONG?
I WAS SHOT DURING A WEEKEND PASS BY A PROSTITUTE.

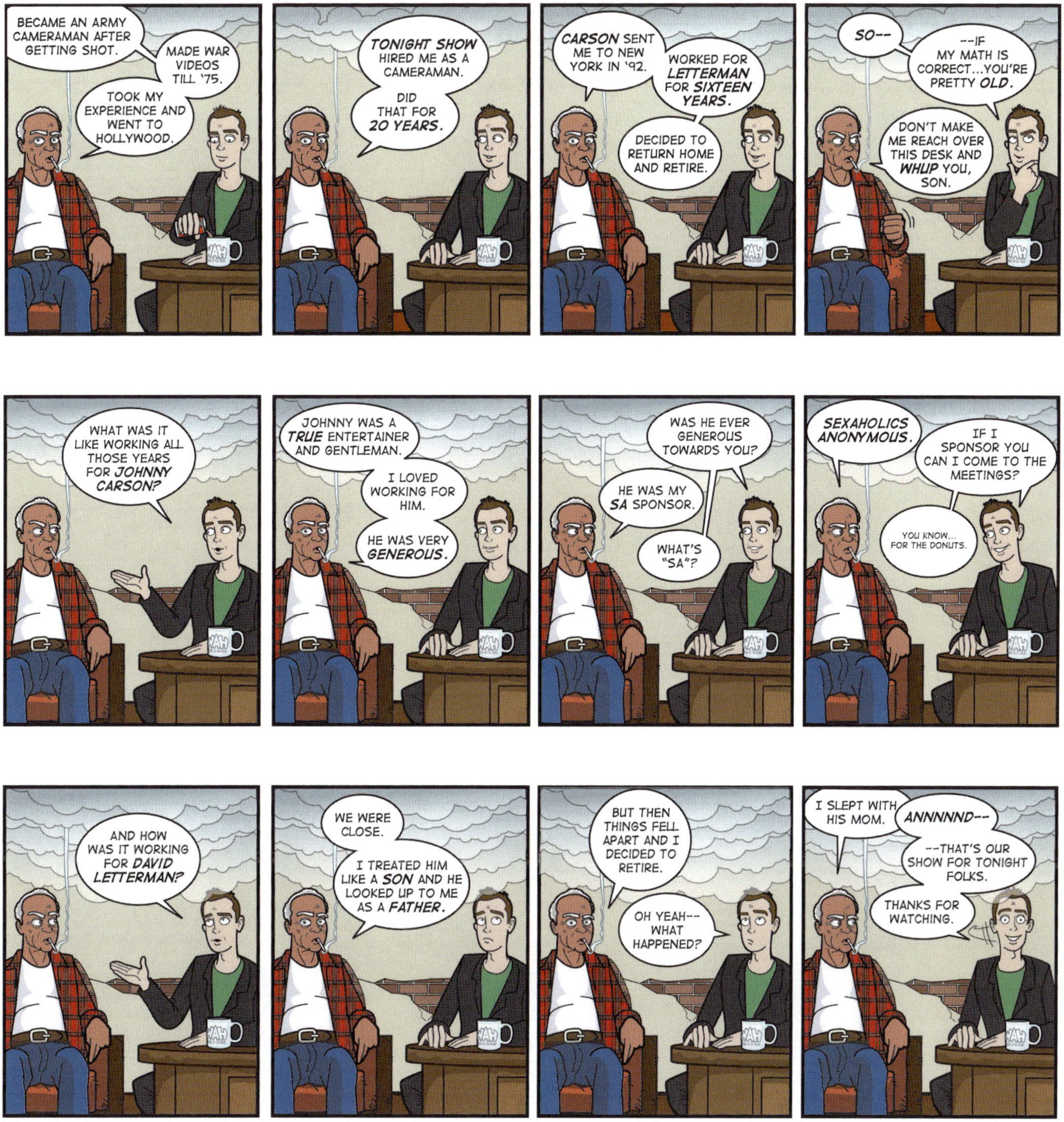
BECAME AN ARMY CAMERAMAN AFTER GETTING SHOT.
MADE WAR VIDEOS TILL '75.
TOOK MY EXPERIENCE AND WENT TO HOLLYWOOD.
TONIGHT SHOW HIRED ME AS A CAMERAMAN.
DID THAT FOR 20 YEARS.
CARSON SENT ME TO NEW YORK IN '92.
WORKED FOR LETTERMAN FOR SIXTEEN YEARS.
DECIDED TO RETURN HOME AND RETIRE.
SO--
--IF MY MATH IS CORRECT...YOU'RE PRETTY OLD.
DON'T MAKE ME REACH OVER THIS DESK AND WHUP YOU, SON.
WHAT WAS IT LIKE WORKING ALL THOSE YEARS FOR JOHNNY CARSON?
JOHNNY WAS A TRUE ENTERTAINER AND GENTLEMAN.
I LOVED WORKING FOR HIM.
HE WAS VERY GENEROUS.
WAS HE EVER GENEROUS TOWARDS YOU?
HE WAS MY SA SPONSOR.
WHAT'S "SA"?
SEXAHOLICS ANONYMOUS.
IF I SPONSOR YOU CAN I COME TO THE MEETINGS?
YOU KNOW... FOR THE DONUTS.
AND HOW WAS IT WORKING FOR DAVID LETTERMAN?
WE WERE CLOSE.
I TREATED HIM LIKE A SON AND HE LOOKED UP TO ME AS A FATHER.
BUT THEN THINGS FELL APART AND I DECIDED TO RETIRE.
OH YEAH-- WHAT HAPPENED?
I SLEPT WITH HIS MOM.
ANNNNND--
--THAT'S OUR SHOW FOR TONIGHT FOLKS.
THANKS FOR WATCHING.

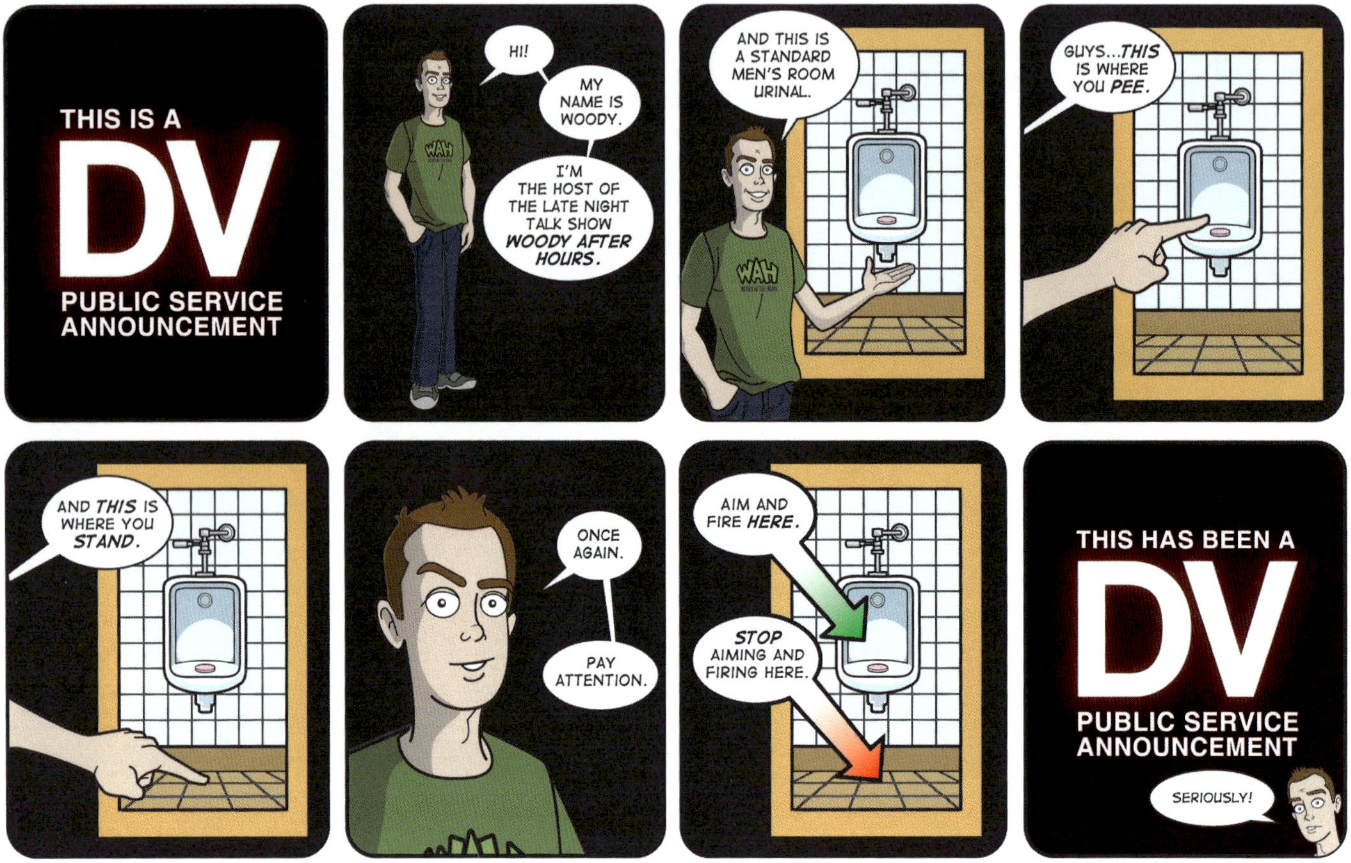
THIS IS A
DV
PUBLIC SERVICE ANNOUNCEMENT
HI!
MY NAME IS WOODY.
I'M THE HOST OF THE LATE NIGHT TALK SHOW *WOODY AFTER HOURS.*
AND THIS IS A STANDARD MEN'S ROOM URINAL.
GUYS...*THIS* IS WHERE YOU *PEE.*
AND *THIS* IS WHERE YOU *STAND.*
ONCE AGAIN.
PAY ATTENTION.
AIM AND FIRE *HERE.*
STOP AIMING AND FIRING HERE.
THIS HAS BEEN A
DV
PUBLIC SERVICE ANNOUNCEMENT
SERIOUSLY!

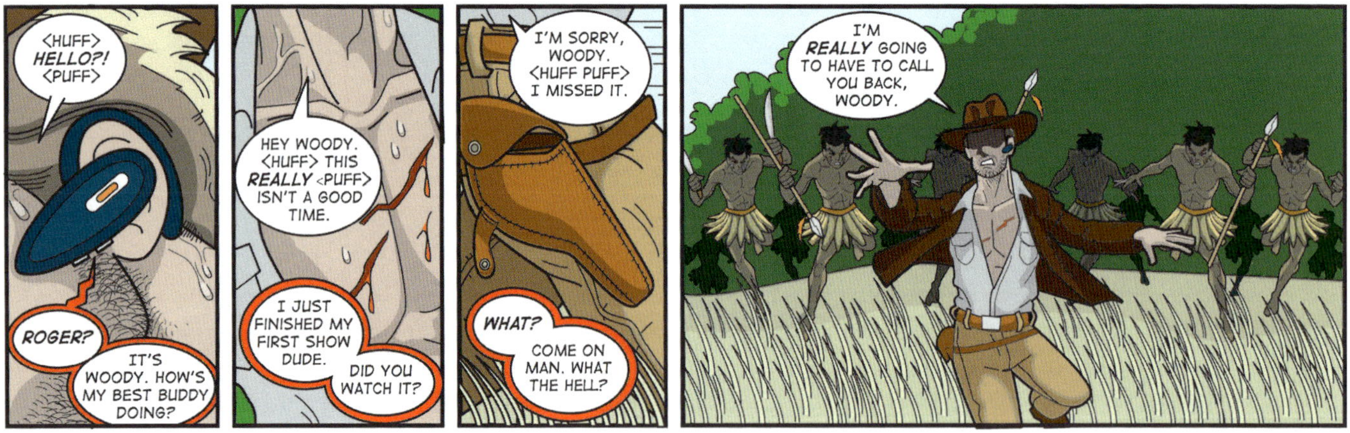
<HUFF> *HELLO?!* <PUFF>
ROGER?
IT'S WOODY. HOW'S MY BEST BUDDY DOING?
HEY WOODY. <HUFF> THIS *REALLY* <PUFF> ISN'T A GOOD TIME.
I JUST FINISHED MY FIRST SHOW DUDE.
DID YOU WATCH IT?
I'M SORRY, WOODY. <HUFF PUFF> I MISSED IT.
WHAT?
COME ON MAN. WHAT THE HELL?
I'M *REALLY* GOING TO HAVE TO CALL YOU BACK, WOODY.

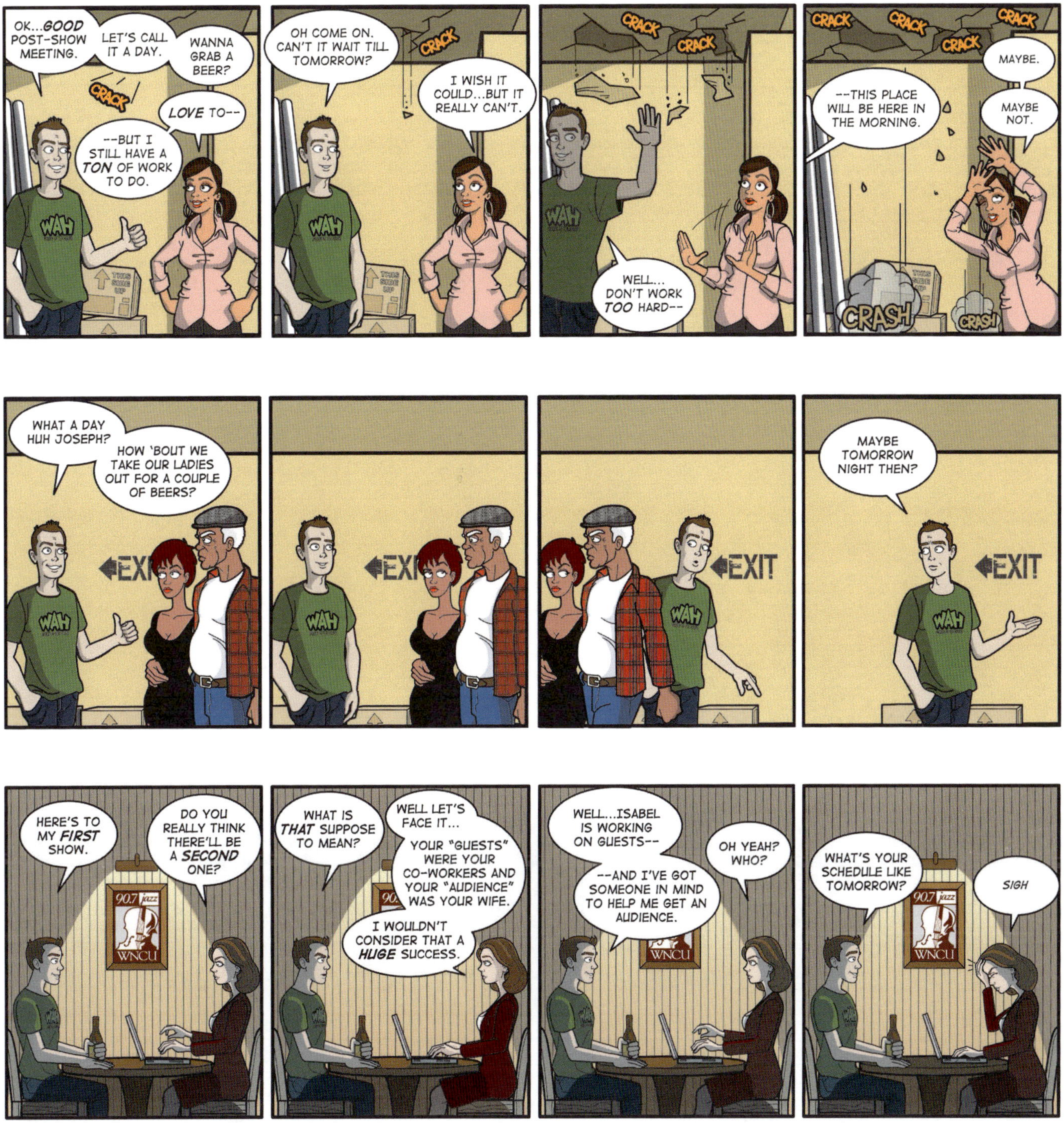
OK...GOOD POST-SHOW MEETING.
LET'S CALL IT A DAY.
WANNA GRAB A BEER?
CRACK
LOVE TO--
--BUT I STILL HAVE A TON OF WORK TO DO.
OH COME ON. CAN'T IT WAIT TILL TOMORROW?
CRACK
I WISH IT COULD...BUT IT REALLY CAN'T.
CRACK
CRACK
WELL... DON'T WORK TOO HARD--
CRACK
CRACK
CRACK
CRACK
--THIS PLACE WILL BE HERE IN THE MORNING.
MAYBE.
MAYBE NOT.
CRASH
CRASH
WHAT A DAY HUH JOSEPH?
HOW 'BOUT WE TAKE OUR LADIES OUT FOR A COUPLE OF BEERS?
EXIT
MAYBE TOMORROW NIGHT THEN?
HERE'S TO MY FIRST SHOW.
DO YOU REALLY THINK THERE'LL BE A SECOND ONE?
90.7 jazz WNCU
WHAT IS THAT SUPPOSE TO MEAN?
WELL LET'S FACE IT...
YOUR "GUESTS" WERE YOUR CO-WORKERS AND YOUR "AUDIENCE" WAS YOUR WIFE.
I WOULDN'T CONSIDER THAT A HUGE SUCCESS.
WELL...ISABEL IS WORKING ON GUESTS--
--AND I'VE GOT SOMEONE IN MIND TO HELP ME GET AN AUDIENCE.
OH YEAH? WHO?
WHAT'S YOUR SCHEDULE LIKE TOMORROW?
SIGH

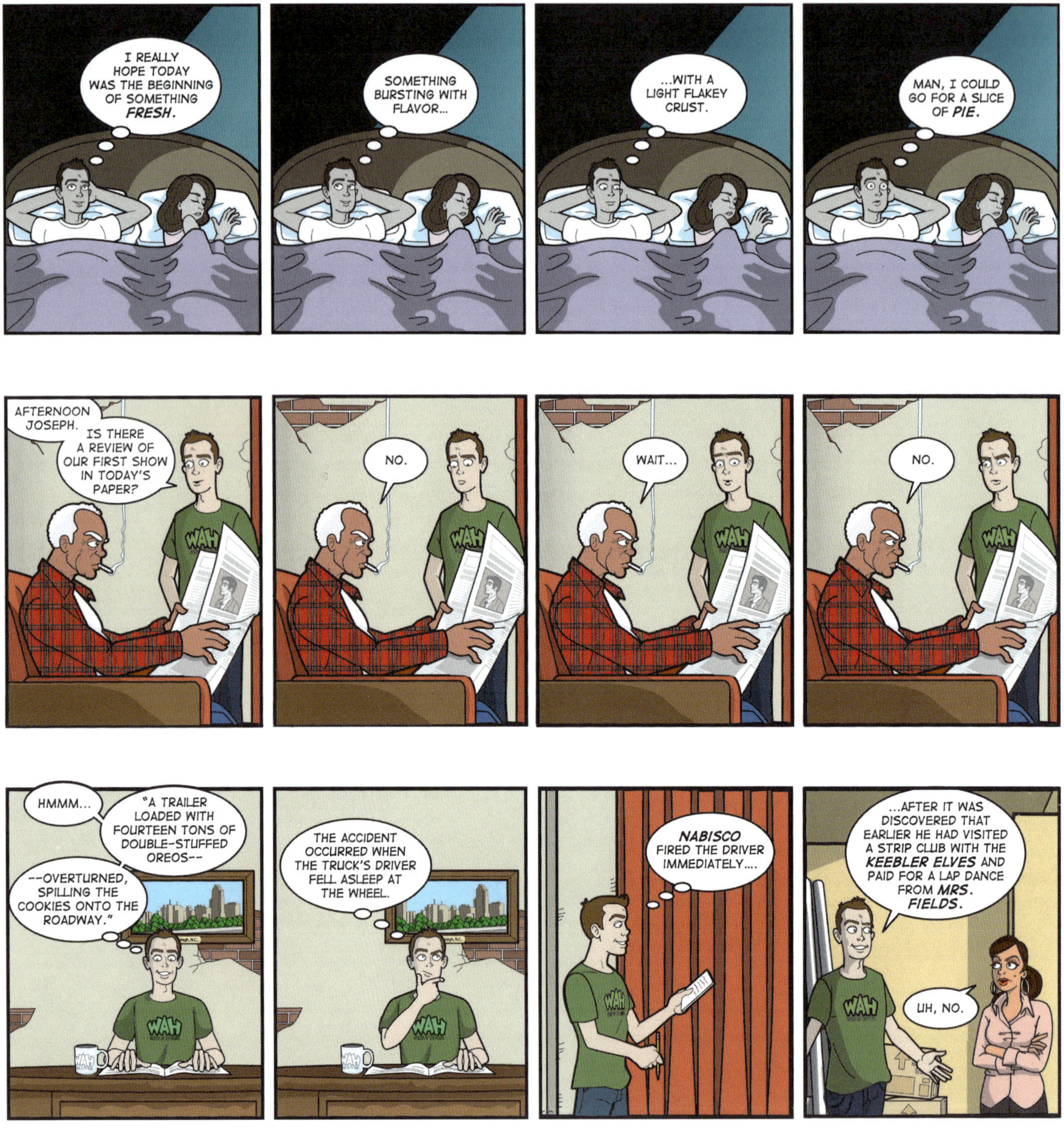
I REALLY HOPE TODAY WAS THE BEGINNING OF SOMETHING ***FRESH***.
SOMETHING BURSTING WITH FLAVOR...
...WITH A LIGHT FLAKEY CRUST.
MAN, I COULD GO FOR A SLICE OF ***PIE***.
AFTERNOON JOSEPH.
IS THERE A REVIEW OF OUR FIRST SHOW IN TODAY'S PAPER?
NO.
WAIT...
NO.
HMMM...
"A TRAILER LOADED WITH FOURTEEN TONS OF DOUBLE-STUFFED OREOS--
--OVERTURNED, SPILLING THE COOKIES ONTO THE ROADWAY."
THE ACCIDENT OCCURRED WHEN THE TRUCK'S DRIVER FELL ASLEEP AT THE WHEEL.
NABISCO FIRED THE DRIVER IMMEDIATELY....
...AFTER IT WAS DISCOVERED THAT EARLIER HE HAD VISITED A STRIP CLUB WITH THE ***KEEBLER ELVES*** AND PAID FOR A LAP DANCE FROM ***MRS. FIELDS***.
UH, NO.

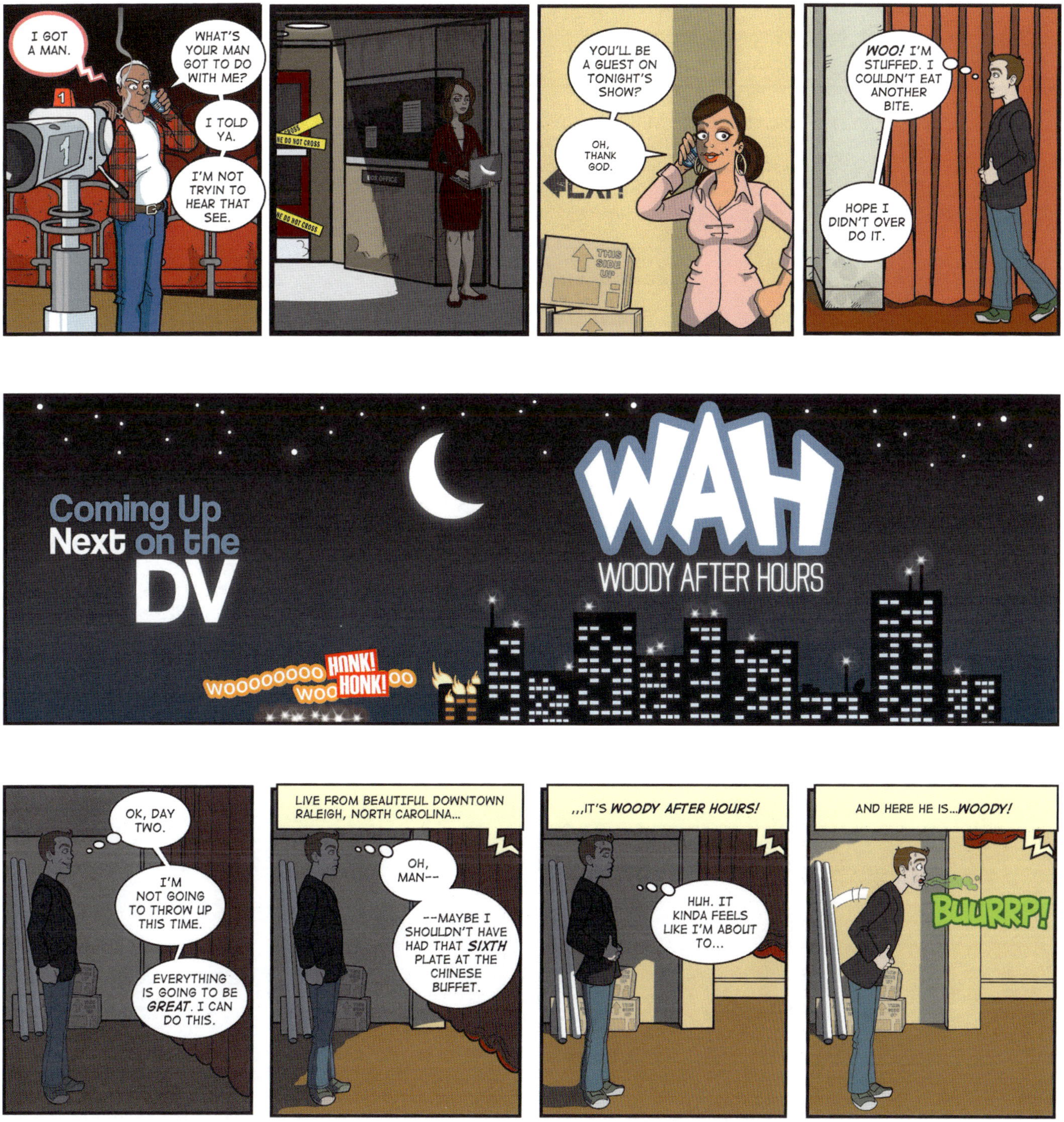
I GOT A MAN.
WHAT'S YOUR MAN GOT TO DO WITH ME?
I TOLD YA.
I'M NOT TRYIN TO HEAR THAT SEE.
DO NOT CROSS
BOX OFFICE
YOU'LL BE A GUEST ON TONIGHT'S SHOW?
OH, THANK GOD.
THIS SIDE UP
WOO! I'M STUFFED. I COULDN'T EAT ANOTHER BITE.
HOPE I DIDN'T OVER DO IT.
Coming Up Next on the DV
WAH
WOODY AFTER HOURS
WOOOOOOOO HONK! WOO HONK! OO
OK, DAY TWO.
I'M NOT GOING TO THROW UP THIS TIME.
EVERYTHING IS GOING TO BE GREAT. I CAN DO THIS.
LIVE FROM BEAUTIFUL DOWNTOWN RALEIGH, NORTH CAROLINA...
OH, MAN--
--MAYBE I SHOULDN'T HAVE HAD THAT SIXTH PLATE AT THE CHINESE BUFFET.
...IT'S WOODY AFTER HOURS!
HUH. IT KINDA FEELS LIKE I'M ABOUT TO...
AND HERE HE IS...WOODY!
BUURRP!

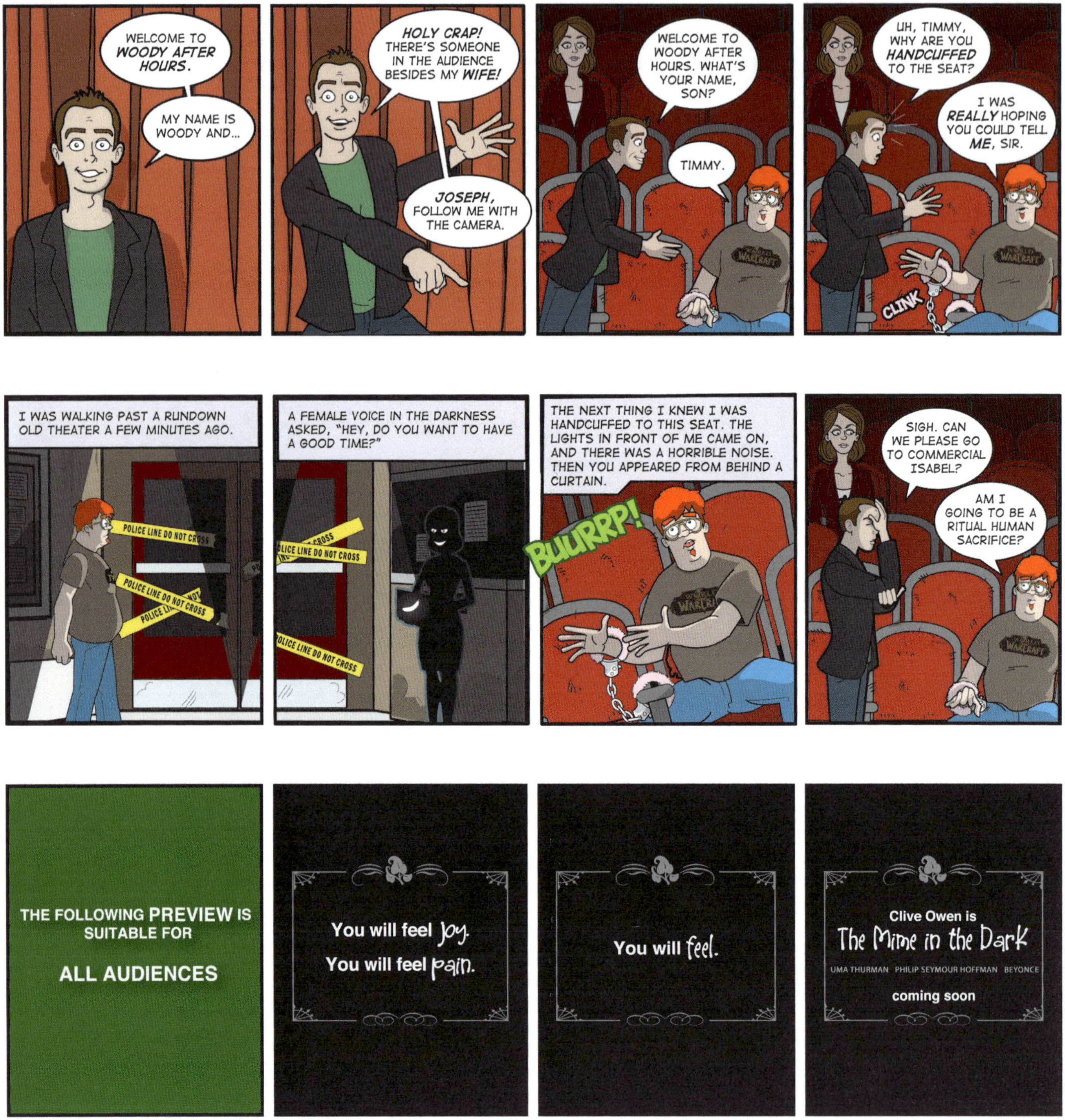
WELCOME TO WOODY AFTER HOURS.
MY NAME IS WOODY AND...
HOLY CRAP! THERE'S SOMEONE IN THE AUDIENCE BESIDES MY WIFE!
JOSEPH, FOLLOW ME WITH THE CAMERA.
WELCOME TO WOODY AFTER HOURS. WHAT'S YOUR NAME, SON?
TIMMY.
UH, TIMMY, WHY ARE YOU HANDCUFFED TO THE SEAT?
I WAS REALLY HOPING YOU COULD TELL ME, SIR.
CLINK
I WAS WALKING PAST A RUNDOWN OLD THEATER A FEW MINUTES AGO.
POLICE LINE DO NOT CROSS
A FEMALE VOICE IN THE DARKNESS ASKED, "HEY, DO YOU WANT TO HAVE A GOOD TIME?"
THE NEXT THING I KNEW I WAS HANDCUFFED TO THIS SEAT. THE LIGHTS IN FRONT OF ME CAME ON, AND THERE WAS A HORRIBLE NOISE. THEN YOU APPEARED FROM BEHIND A CURTAIN.
BUURRP!
SIGH. CAN WE PLEASE GO TO COMMERCIAL ISABEL?
AM I GOING TO BE A RITUAL HUMAN SACRIFICE?
THE FOLLOWING PREVIEW IS SUITABLE FOR
ALL AUDIENCES
You will feel joy.
You will feel pain.
You will feel.
Clive Owen is
The Mime in the Dark
UMA THURMAN PHILIP SEYMOUR HOFFMAN BEYONCE
coming soon

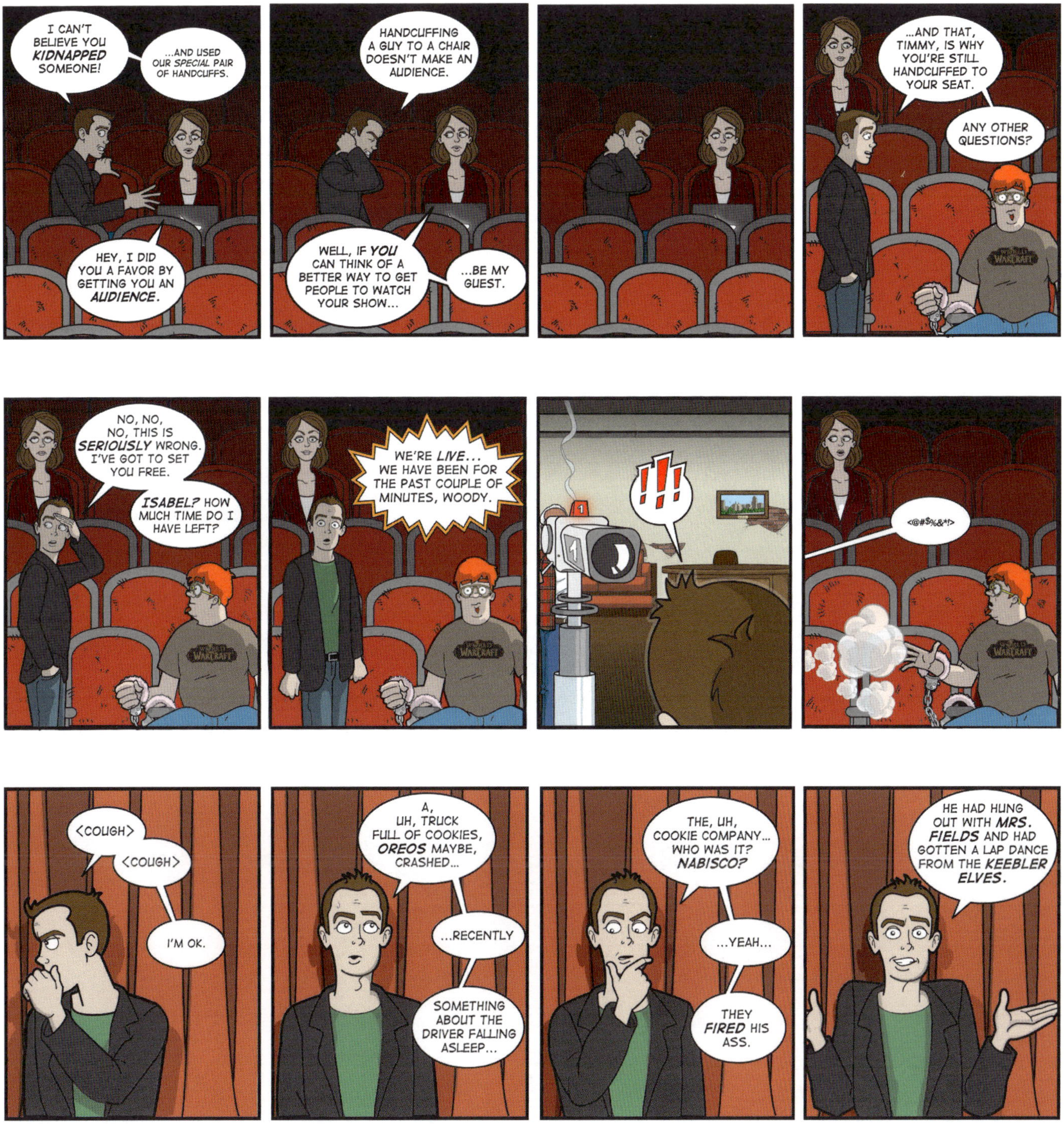
I CAN'T BELIEVE YOU KIDNAPPED SOMEONE!
...AND USED OUR SPECIAL PAIR OF HANDCUFFS.
HEY, I DID YOU A FAVOR BY GETTING YOU AN AUDIENCE.
HANDCUFFING A GUY TO A CHAIR DOESN'T MAKE AN AUDIENCE.
WELL, IF YOU CAN THINK OF A BETTER WAY TO GET PEOPLE TO WATCH YOUR SHOW...
...BE MY GUEST.
...AND THAT, TIMMY, IS WHY YOU'RE STILL HANDCUFFED TO YOUR SEAT.
ANY OTHER QUESTIONS?
WORLD OF WARCRAFT
NO, NO, NO, THIS IS SERIOUSLY WRONG. I'VE GOT TO SET YOU FREE.
ISABEL? HOW MUCH TIME DO I HAVE LEFT?
WE'RE LIVE... WE HAVE BEEN FOR THE PAST COUPLE OF MINUTES, WOODY.
!!!
1
<@#$%&*!>
<COUGH>
<COUGH>
I'M OK.
A, UH, TRUCK FULL OF COOKIES, OREOS MAYBE, CRASHED...
...RECENTLY
SOMETHING ABOUT THE DRIVER FALLING ASLEEP...
THE, UH, COOKIE COMPANY... WHO WAS IT? NABISCO?
...YEAH...
THEY FIRED HIS ASS.
HE HAD HUNG OUT WITH MRS. FIELDS AND HAD GOTTEN A LAP DANCE FROM THE KEEBLER ELVES.

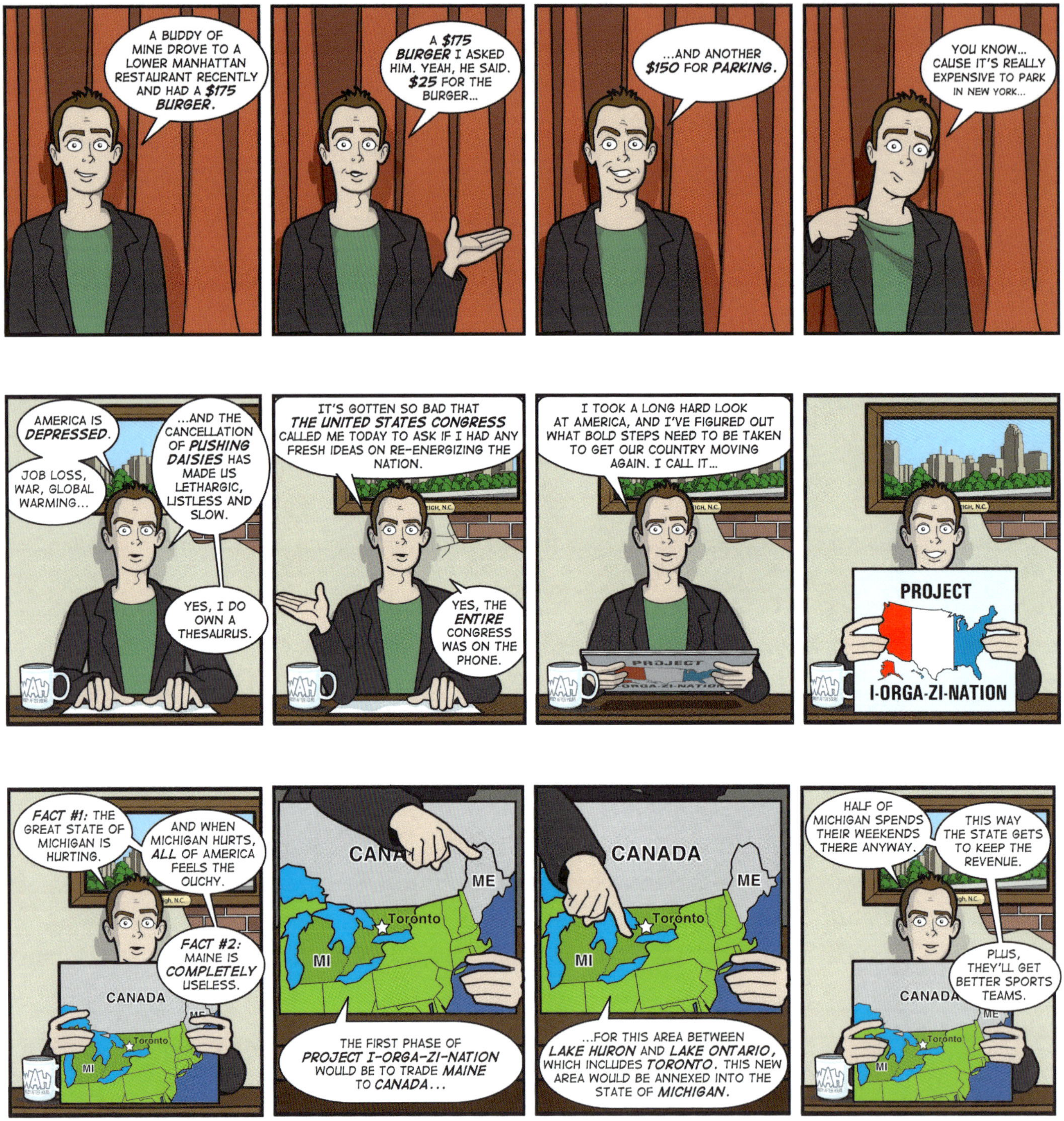
A BUDDY OF MINE DROVE TO A LOWER MANHATTAN RESTAURANT RECENTLY AND HAD A $175 BURGER.
A $175 BURGER I ASKED HIM. YEAH, HE SAID. $25 FOR THE BURGER...
...AND ANOTHER $150 FOR PARKING.
YOU KNOW... CAUSE IT'S REALLY EXPENSIVE TO PARK IN NEW YORK...
AMERICA IS DEPRESSED.
JOB LOSS, WAR, GLOBAL WARMING...
...AND THE CANCELLATION OF PUSHING DAISIES HAS MADE US LETHARGIC, LISTLESS AND SLOW.
YES, I DO OWN A THESAURUS.
IT'S GOTTEN SO BAD THAT THE UNITED STATES CONGRESS CALLED ME TODAY TO ASK IF I HAD ANY FRESH IDEAS ON RE-ENERGIZING THE NATION.
YES, THE ENTIRE CONGRESS WAS ON THE PHONE.
I TOOK A LONG HARD LOOK AT AMERICA, AND I'VE FIGURED OUT WHAT BOLD STEPS NEED TO BE TAKEN TO GET OUR COUNTRY MOVING AGAIN. I CALL IT...
PROJECT I-ORGA-ZI-NATION
FACT #1: THE GREAT STATE OF MICHIGAN IS HURTING.
AND WHEN MICHIGAN HURTS, ALL OF AMERICA FEELS THE OUCHY.
FACT #2: MAINE IS COMPLETELY USELESS.
CANADA
Toronto
MI
ME
THE FIRST PHASE OF PROJECT I-ORGA-ZI-NATION WOULD BE TO TRADE MAINE TO CANADA...
...FOR THIS AREA BETWEEN LAKE HURON AND LAKE ONTARIO, WHICH INCLUDES TORONTO. THIS NEW AREA WOULD BE ANNEXED INTO THE STATE OF MICHIGAN.
HALF OF MICHIGAN SPENDS THEIR WEEKENDS THERE ANYWAY.
THIS WAY THE STATE GETS TO KEEP THE REVENUE.
PLUS, THEY'LL GET BETTER SPORTS TEAMS.

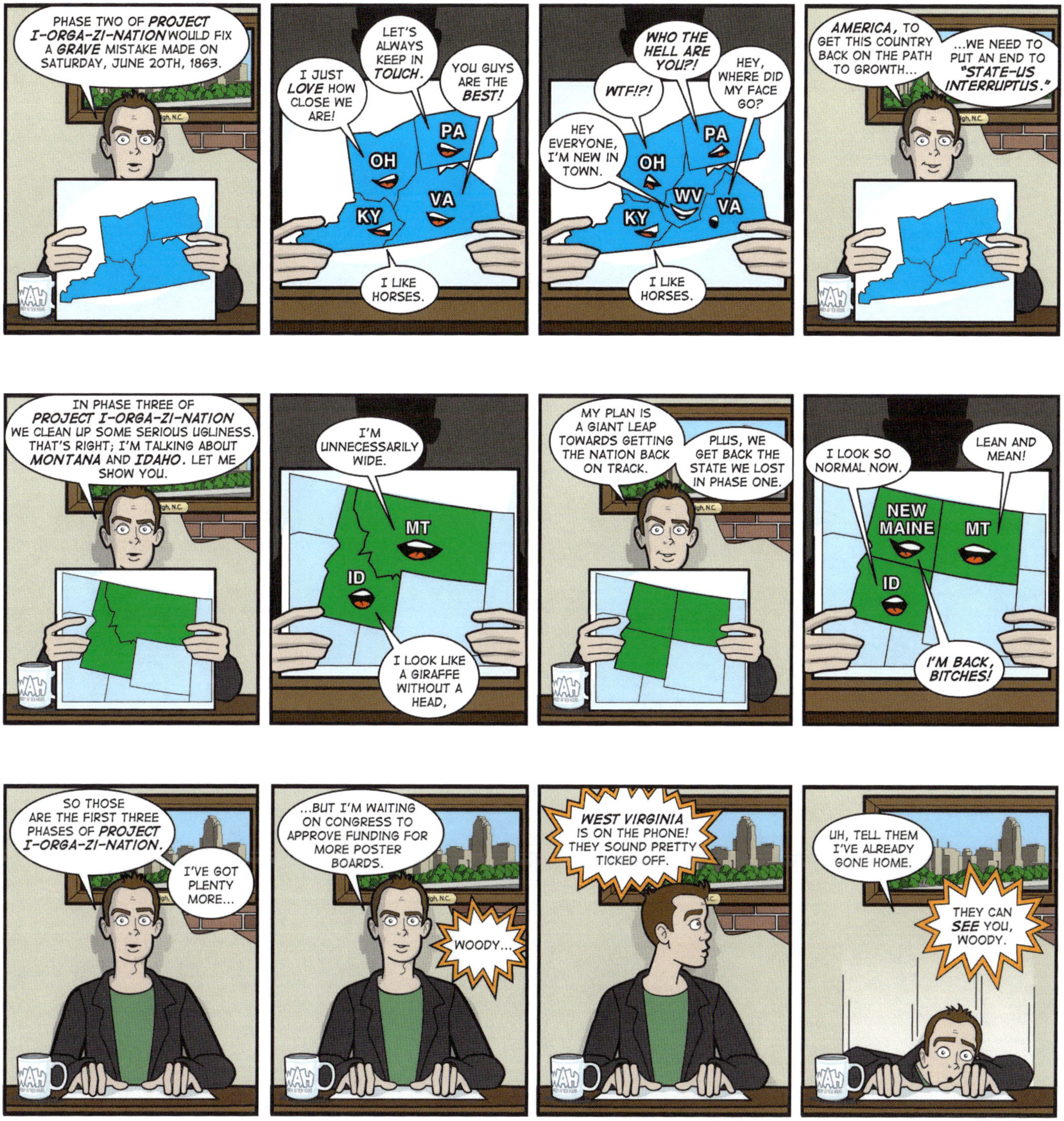
PHASE TWO OF PROJECT I-ORGA-ZI-NATION WOULD FIX A GRAVE MISTAKE MADE ON SATURDAY, JUNE 20TH, 1863.
I JUST LOVE HOW CLOSE WE ARE!
LET'S ALWAYS KEEP IN TOUCH.
YOU GUYS ARE THE BEST!
PA
OH
VA
KY
I LIKE HORSES.
WTF!?!
WHO THE HELL ARE YOU?!
HEY, WHERE DID MY FACE GO?
HEY EVERYONE, I'M NEW IN TOWN.
PA
OH
WV
VA
KY
I LIKE HORSES.
AMERICA, TO GET THIS COUNTRY BACK ON THE PATH TO GROWTH...
...WE NEED TO PUT AN END TO "STATE-US INTERRUPTUS."
IN PHASE THREE OF PROJECT I-ORGA-ZI-NATION WE CLEAN UP SOME SERIOUS UGLINESS. THAT'S RIGHT; I'M TALKING ABOUT MONTANA AND IDAHO. LET ME SHOW YOU.
I'M UNNECESSARILY WIDE.
MT
ID
I LOOK LIKE A GIRAFFE WITHOUT A HEAD,
MY PLAN IS A GIANT LEAP TOWARDS GETTING THE NATION BACK ON TRACK.
PLUS, WE GET BACK THE STATE WE LOST IN PHASE ONE.
I LOOK SO NORMAL NOW.
LEAN AND MEAN!
NEW MAINE
MT
ID
I'M BACK, BITCHES!
SO THOSE ARE THE FIRST THREE PHASES OF PROJECT I-ORGA-ZI-NATION.
I'VE GOT PLENTY MORE...
...BUT I'M WAITING ON CONGRESS TO APPROVE FUNDING FOR MORE POSTER BOARDS.
WOODY...
WEST VIRGINIA IS ON THE PHONE! THEY SOUND PRETTY TICKED OFF.
UH, TELL THEM I'VE ALREADY GONE HOME.
THEY CAN SEE YOU, WOODY.

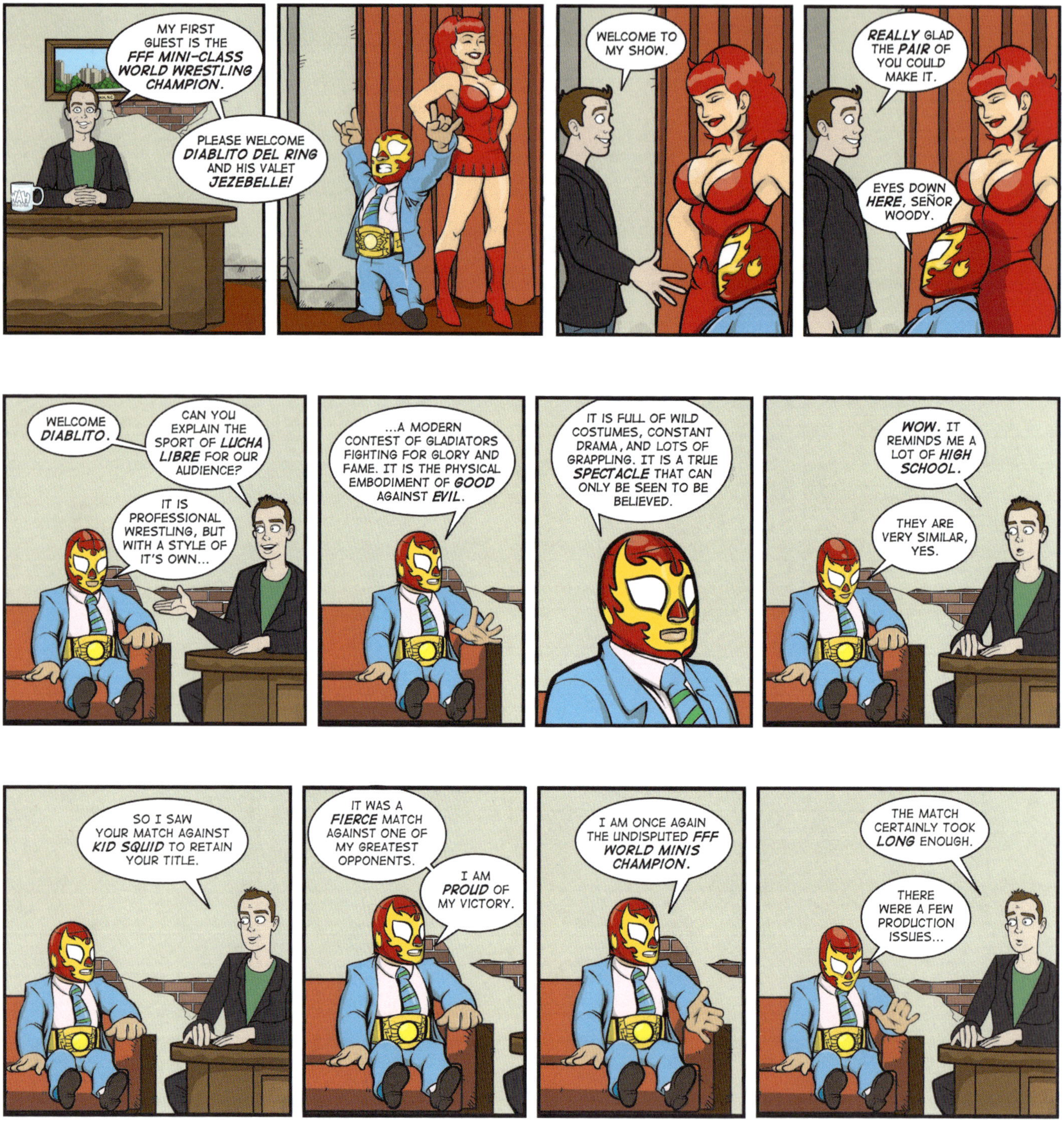

MY FIRST GUEST IS THE FFF MINI-CLASS WORLD WRESTLING CHAMPION.
PLEASE WELCOME DIABLITO DEL RING AND HIS VALET JEZEBELLE!
WELCOME TO MY SHOW.
REALLY GLAD THE PAIR OF YOU COULD MAKE IT.
EYES DOWN HERE, SEÑOR WOODY.
WELCOME DIABLITO.
CAN YOU EXPLAIN THE SPORT OF LUCHA LIBRE FOR OUR AUDIENCE?
IT IS PROFESSIONAL WRESTLING, BUT WITH A STYLE OF IT'S OWN...
...A MODERN CONTEST OF GLADIATORS FIGHTING FOR GLORY AND FAME. IT IS THE PHYSICAL EMBODIMENT OF GOOD AGAINST EVIL.
IT IS FULL OF WILD COSTUMES, CONSTANT DRAMA, AND LOTS OF GRAPPLING. IT IS A TRUE SPECTACLE THAT CAN ONLY BE SEEN TO BE BELIEVED.
WOW. IT REMINDS ME A LOT OF HIGH SCHOOL.
THEY ARE VERY SIMILAR, YES.
SO I SAW YOUR MATCH AGAINST KID SQUID TO RETAIN YOUR TITLE.
IT WAS A FIERCE MATCH AGAINST ONE OF MY GREATEST OPPONENTS.
I AM PROUD OF MY VICTORY.
I AM ONCE AGAIN THE UNDISPUTED FFF WORLD MINIS CHAMPION.
THE MATCH CERTAINLY TOOK LONG ENOUGH.
THERE WERE A FEW PRODUCTION ISSUES...

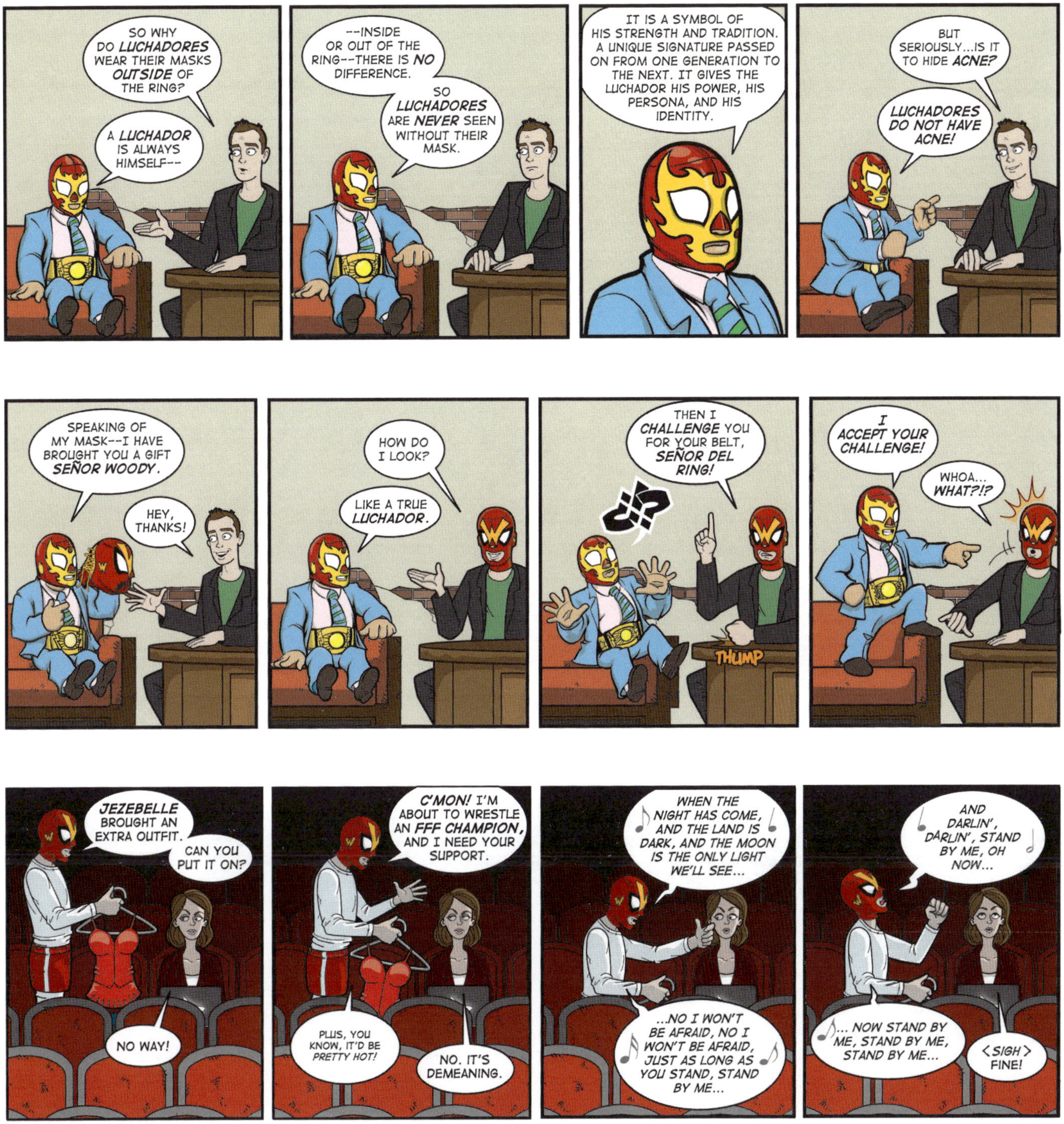

SO WHY DO LUCHADORES WEAR THEIR MASKS OUTSIDE OF THE RING?
A LUCHADOR IS ALWAYS HIMSELF--
--INSIDE OR OUT OF THE RING--THERE IS NO DIFFERENCE.
SO LUCHADORES ARE NEVER SEEN WITHOUT THEIR MASK.
IT IS A SYMBOL OF HIS STRENGTH AND TRADITION. A UNIQUE SIGNATURE PASSED ON FROM ONE GENERATION TO THE NEXT. IT GIVES THE LUCHADOR HIS POWER, HIS PERSONA, AND HIS IDENTITY.
BUT SERIOUSLY...IS IT TO HIDE ACNE?
LUCHADORES DO NOT HAVE ACNE!
SPEAKING OF MY MASK--I HAVE BROUGHT YOU A GIFT SEÑOR WOODY.
HEY, THANKS!
HOW DO I LOOK?
LIKE A TRUE LUCHADOR.
THEN I CHALLENGE YOU FOR YOUR BELT, SEÑOR DEL RING!
THUMP
I ACCEPT YOUR CHALLENGE!
WHOA... WHAT?!?
JEZEBELLE BROUGHT AN EXTRA OUTFIT.
CAN YOU PUT IT ON?
NO WAY!
C'MON! I'M ABOUT TO WRESTLE AN FFF CHAMPION, AND I NEED YOUR SUPPORT.
PLUS, YOU KNOW, IT'D BE PRETTY HOT!
NO. IT'S DEMEANING.
WHEN THE NIGHT HAS COME, AND THE LAND IS DARK, AND THE MOON IS THE ONLY LIGHT WE'LL SEE...
...NO I WON'T BE AFRAID, NO I WON'T BE AFRAID, JUST AS LONG AS YOU STAND, STAND BY ME...
AND DARLIN', DARLIN', STAND BY ME, OH NOW...
... NOW STAND BY ME, STAND BY ME, STAND BY ME...
<SIGH> FINE!

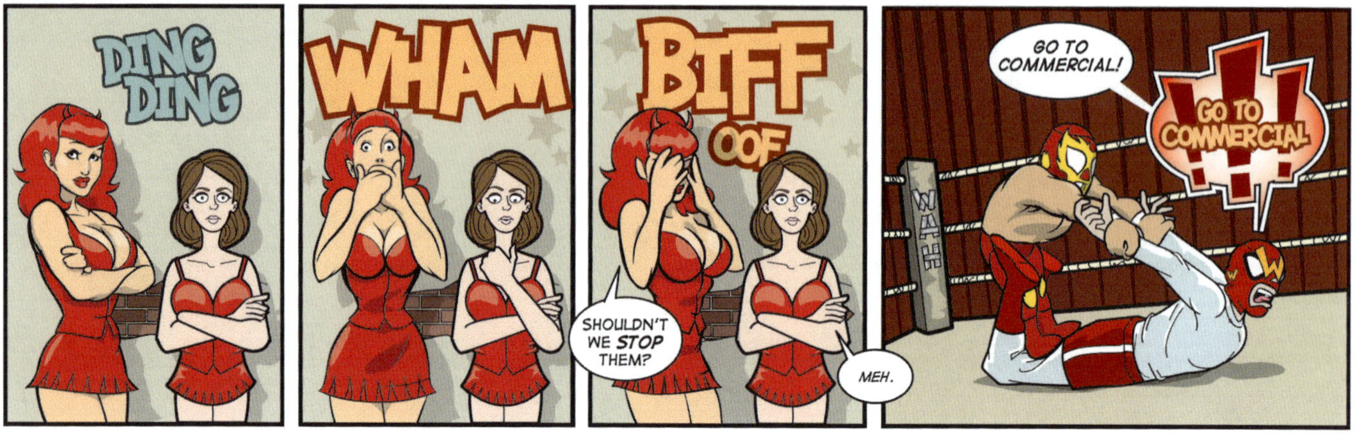
DING DING
WHAM
BIFF
OOF
SHOULDN'T WE STOP THEM?
MEH.
GO TO COMMERCIAL!
GO TO COMMERCIAL

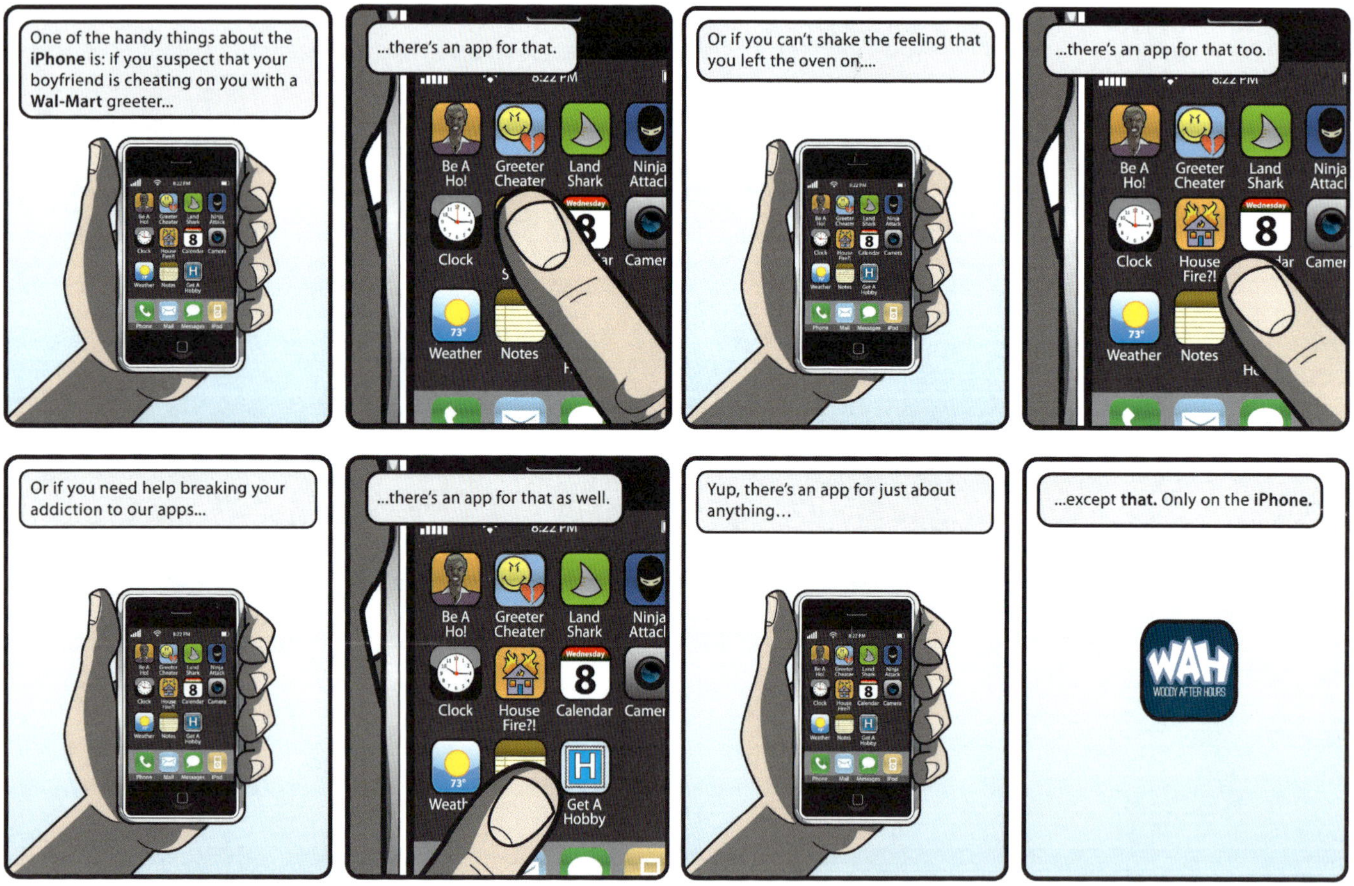
One of the handy things about the **iPhone** is: if you suspect that your boyfriend is cheating on you with a **Wal-Mart** greeter...
...there's an app for that.
Be A Ho!
Greeter Cheater
Land Shark
Clock
Weather
Notes
Or if you can't shake the feeling that you left the oven on....
...there's an app for that too.
Be A Ho!
Greeter Cheater
Land Shark
Clock
House Fire?!
Weather
Notes
Or if you need help breaking your addiction to our apps...
...there's an app for that as well.
Be A Ho!
Greeter Cheater
Land Shark
Clock
House Fire?!
Calendar
Get A Hobby
Yup, there's an app for just about anything...
...except **that.** Only on the **iPhone.**
WAH
WOODY AFTER HOURS

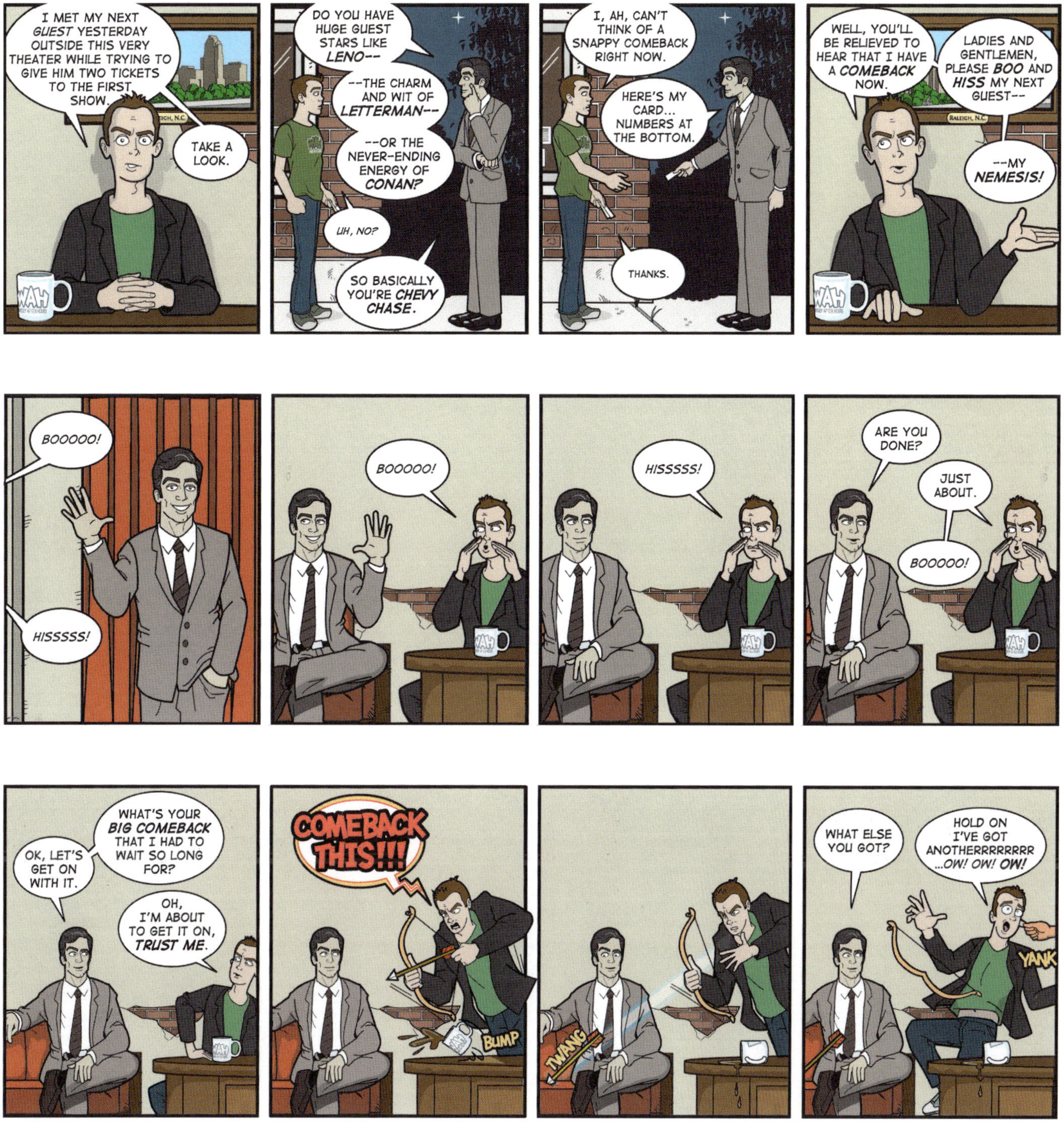
I MET MY NEXT GUEST YESTERDAY OUTSIDE THIS VERY THEATER WHILE TRYING TO GIVE HIM TWO TICKETS TO THE FIRST SHOW.
TAKE A LOOK.
RALEIGH, N.C.
WAH
DO YOU HAVE HUGE GUEST STARS LIKE LENO--
--THE CHARM AND WIT OF LETTERMAN--
--OR THE NEVER-ENDING ENERGY OF CONAN?
UH, NO?
SO BASICALLY YOU'RE CHEVY CHASE.
I, AH, CAN'T THINK OF A SNAPPY COMEBACK RIGHT NOW.
HERE'S MY CARD... NUMBERS AT THE BOTTOM.
THANKS.
WELL, YOU'LL BE RELIEVED TO HEAR THAT I HAVE A COMEBACK NOW.
LADIES AND GENTLEMEN, PLEASE BOO AND HISS MY NEXT GUEST--
--MY NEMESIS!
RALEIGH, N.C.
BOOOOO!
HISSSSS!
BOOOOO!
HISSSSS!
ARE YOU DONE?
JUST ABOUT.
BOOOOO!
OK, LET'S GET ON WITH IT.
WHAT'S YOUR BIG COMEBACK THAT I HAD TO WAIT SO LONG FOR?
OH, I'M ABOUT TO GET IT ON, TRUST ME.
COMEBACK THIS!!!
BUMP
TWANG
WHAT ELSE YOU GOT?
HOLD ON I'VE GOT ANOTHERRRRRRRR ...OW! OW! OW!
YANK

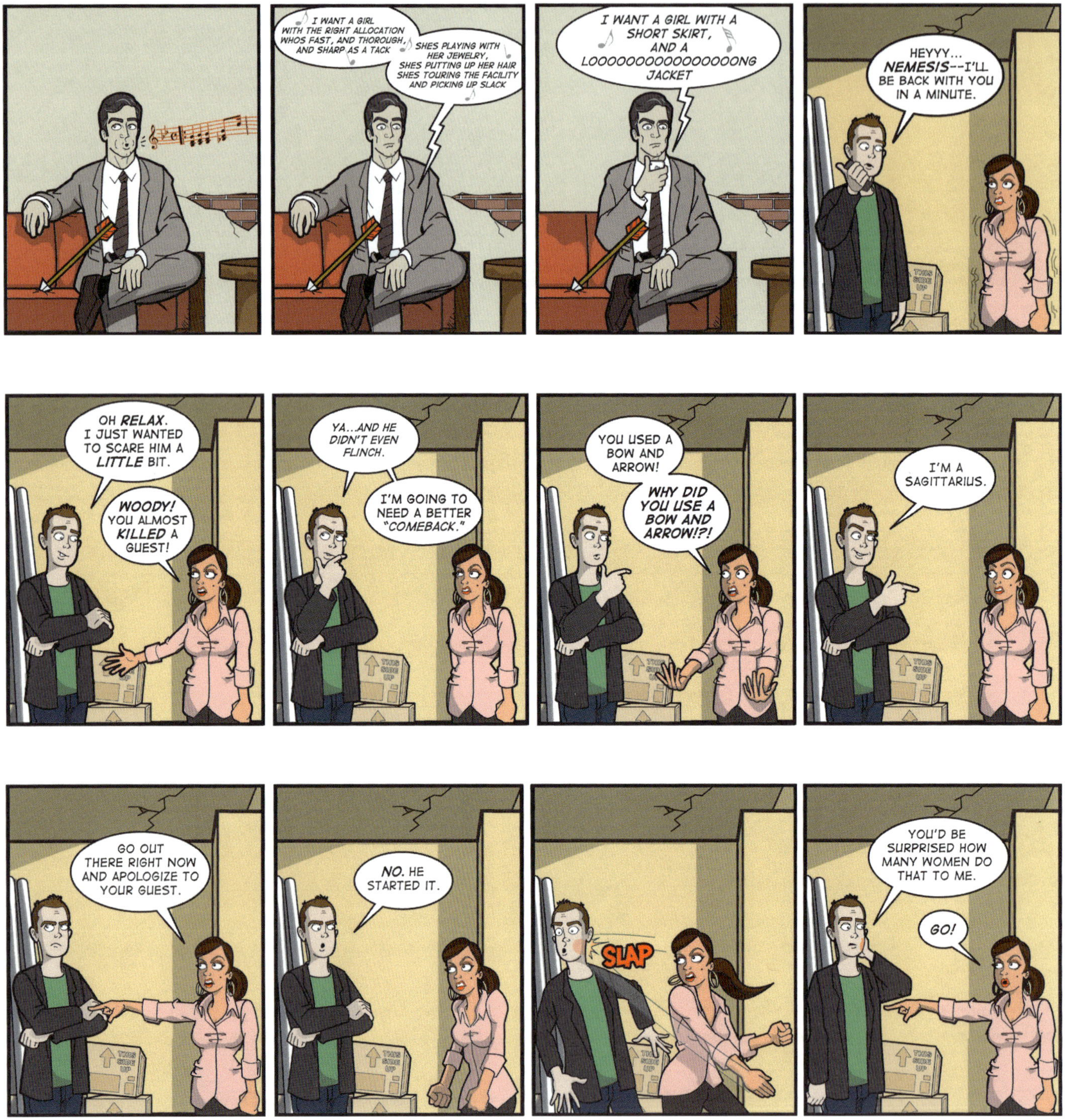

I WANT A GIRL WITH THE RIGHT ALLOCATION WHOS FAST, AND THOROUGH, AND SHARP AS A TACK
SHES PLAYING WITH HER JEWELRY, SHES PUTTING UP HER HAIR SHES TOURING THE FACILITY AND PICKING UP SLACK
I WANT A GIRL WITH A SHORT SKIRT, AND A LOOOOOOOOOOOOOOOONG JACKET
HEYYY... NEMESIS--I'LL BE BACK WITH YOU IN A MINUTE.
OH RELAX. I JUST WANTED TO SCARE HIM A LITTLE BIT.
WOODY! YOU ALMOST KILLED A GUEST!
YA...AND HE DIDN'T EVEN FLINCH.
I'M GOING TO NEED A BETTER "COMEBACK."
YOU USED A BOW AND ARROW!
WHY DID YOU USE A BOW AND ARROW!?!
I'M A SAGITTARIUS.
GO OUT THERE RIGHT NOW AND APOLOGIZE TO YOUR GUEST.
NO. HE STARTED IT.
SLAP
YOU'D BE SURPRISED HOW MANY WOMEN DO THAT TO ME.
GO!

FIRST, RENEE KIDNAPS A COLLEGE KID, AND THEN WOODY SHOOTS AT A GUEST WITH A BOW AND ARROW. WHAT IS WRONG WITH THESE PEOPLE?
LORD--GIVE ME STRENGTH.
CRACK
THUNK
WHICH PART OF "STRENGTH" WAS UNCLEAR TO YOU LORD?

SIGH
NEMESIS, I'M SORRY THAT I SHOT AN ARROW AT YOU.
I WAS ONLY KIDDING.
I OWE YOU AN APOLOGY AS WELL.
IT LOOKS LIKE YOU'RE NOT CHEVY CHASE AFTER ALL.
YEAH?
YEAH...I'M PRETTY SURE CHEVY WAS A BETTER SHOT.
SWELL.
I'D LIKE TO THANK MY GUESTS, DIABLITO DEL RING AND NEMESIS.
I HAVE A NAME YOU KNOW. IT'S
GOOD NIGHT!

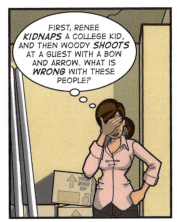

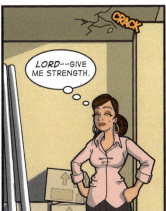

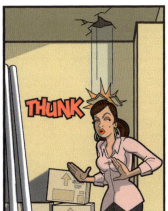

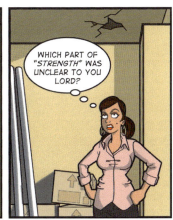

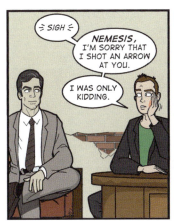

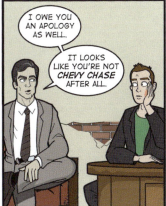

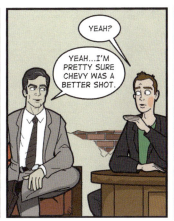

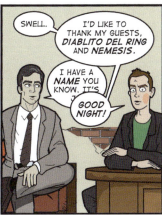

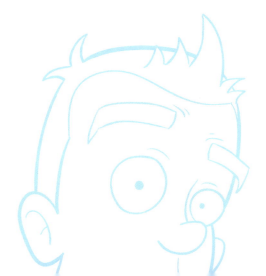

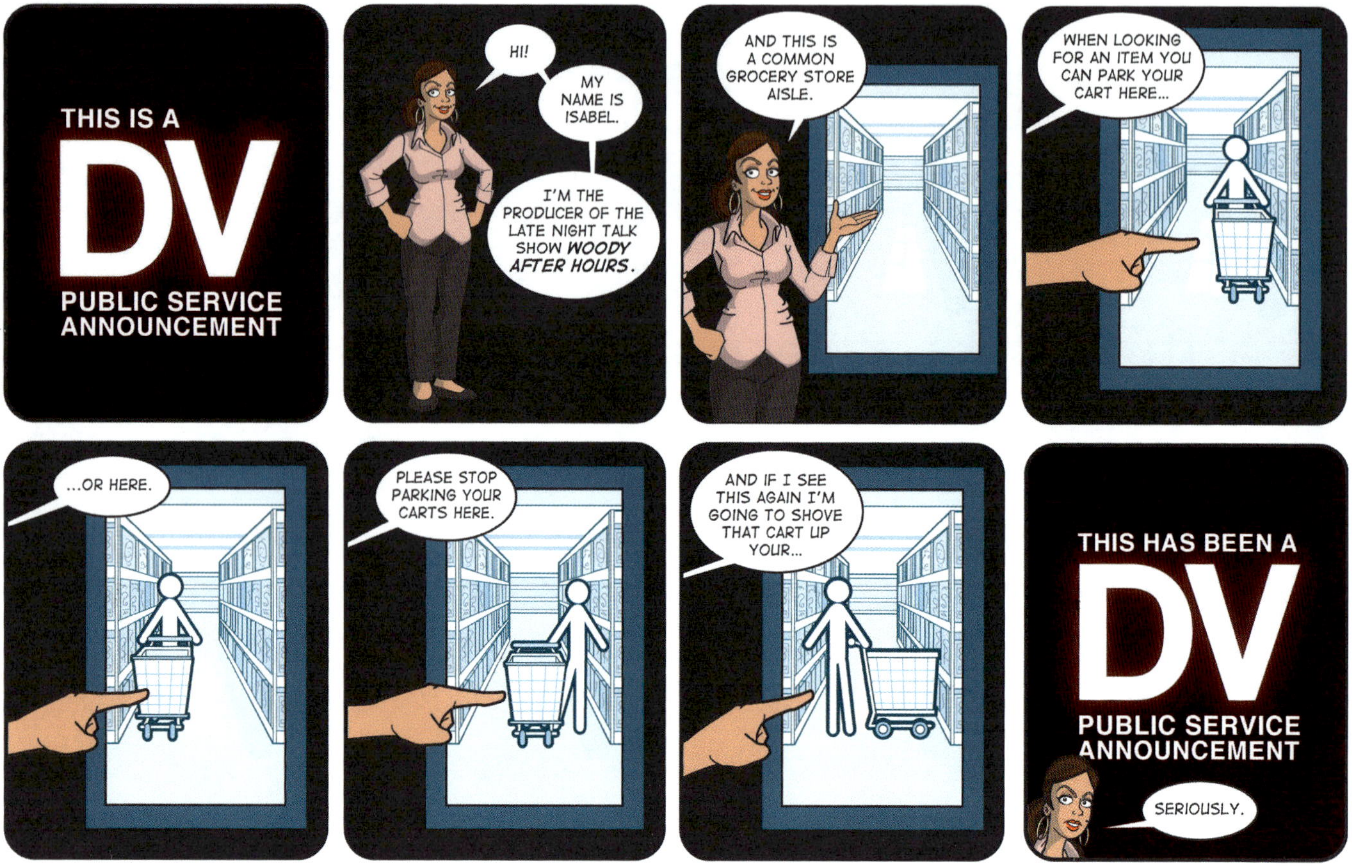
THIS IS A
DV
PUBLIC SERVICE ANNOUNCEMENT
HI!
MY NAME IS ISABEL.
I'M THE PRODUCER OF THE LATE NIGHT TALK SHOW *WOODY AFTER HOURS*.
AND THIS IS A COMMON GROCERY STORE AISLE.
WHEN LOOKING FOR AN ITEM YOU CAN PARK YOUR CART HERE...
...OR HERE.
PLEASE STOP PARKING YOUR CARTS HERE.
AND IF I SEE THIS AGAIN I'M GOING TO SHOVE THAT CART UP YOUR...
THIS HAS BEEN A
DV
PUBLIC SERVICE ANNOUNCEMENT
SERIOUSLY.

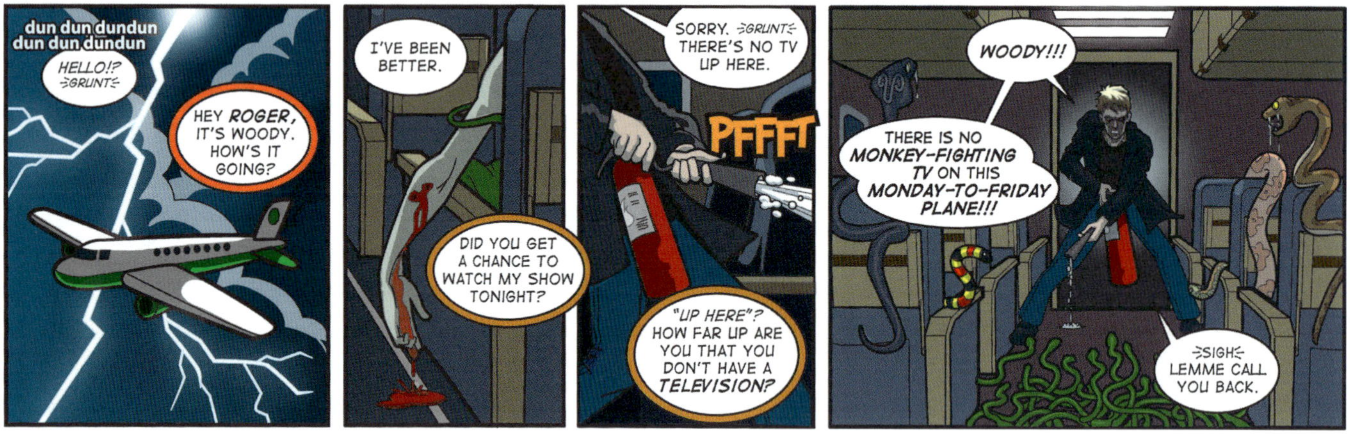
dun dun dundun
dun dun dundun
HELLO!? *GRUNT*
HEY *ROGER*, IT'S WOODY. HOW'S IT GOING?
I'VE BEEN BETTER.
DID YOU GET A CHANCE TO WATCH MY SHOW TONIGHT?
SORRY. *GRUNT* THERE'S NO TV UP HERE.
PFFFT
"UP HERE"? HOW FAR UP ARE YOU THAT YOU DON'T HAVE A *TELEVISION?*
WOODY!!!
THERE IS NO *MONKEY-FIGHTING TV* ON THIS *MONDAY-TO-FRIDAY PLANE!!!*
SIGH LEMME CALL YOU BACK.

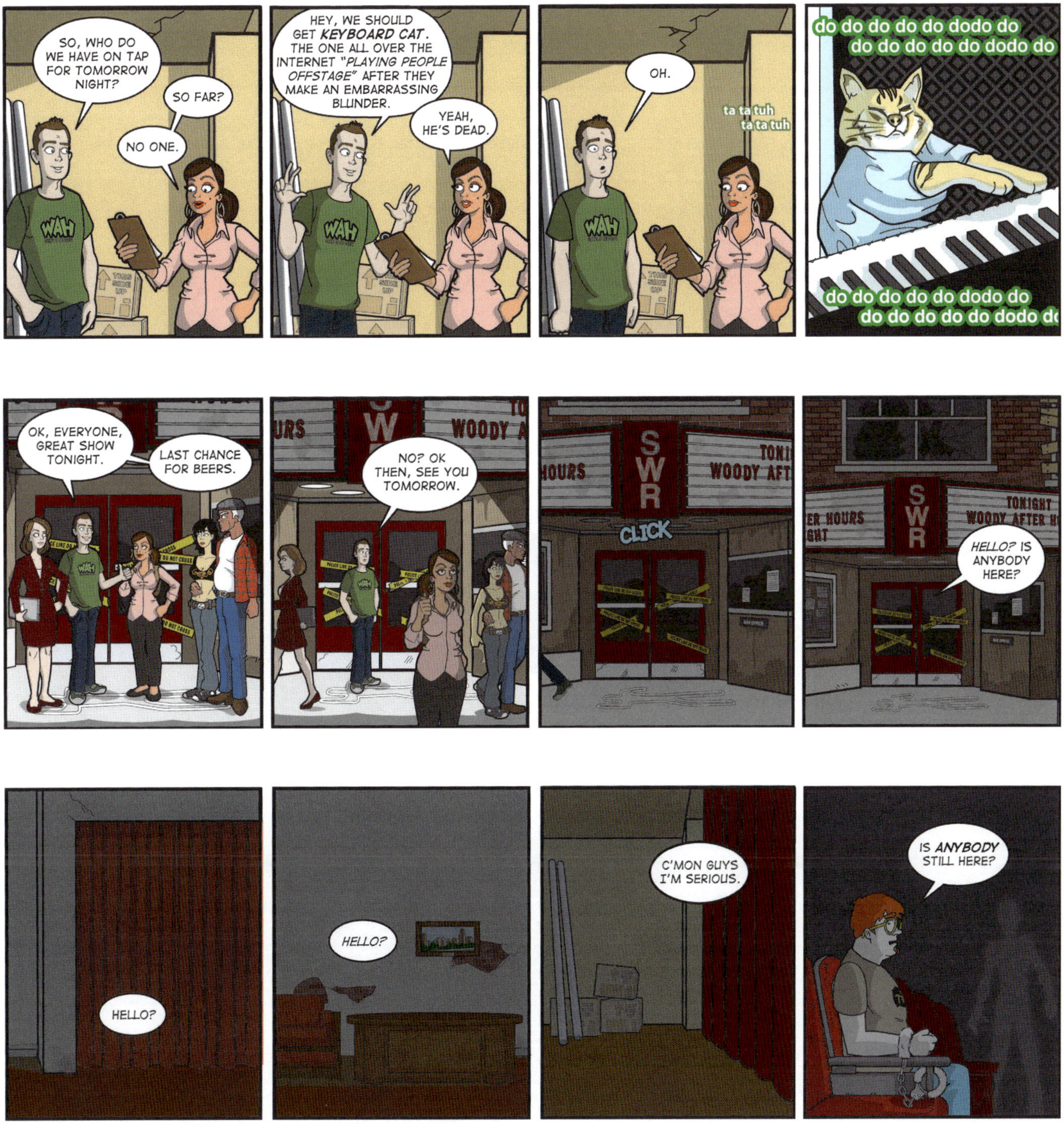
SO, WHO DO WE HAVE ON TAP FOR TOMORROW NIGHT?
SO FAR?
NO ONE.
WAH
THIS SIDE UP
HEY, WE SHOULD GET *KEYBOARD CAT*. THE ONE ALL OVER THE INTERNET *"PLAYING PEOPLE OFFSTAGE"* AFTER THEY MAKE AN EMBARRASSING BLUNDER.
YEAH, HE'S DEAD.
OH.
ta ta tuh
ta ta tuh
do do do do do dodo do
do do do do do dodo do
do do do do do dodo do
do do do do do dodo
OK, EVERYONE, GREAT SHOW TONIGHT.
LAST CHANCE FOR BEERS.
NO? OK THEN, SEE YOU TOMORROW.
SWR
HOURS
WOODY AFT
CLICK
TONIGHT
WOODY AFTER H
HELLO? IS ANYBODY HERE?
HELLO?
HELLO?
C'MON GUYS I'M SERIOUS.
IS *ANYBODY* STILL HERE?

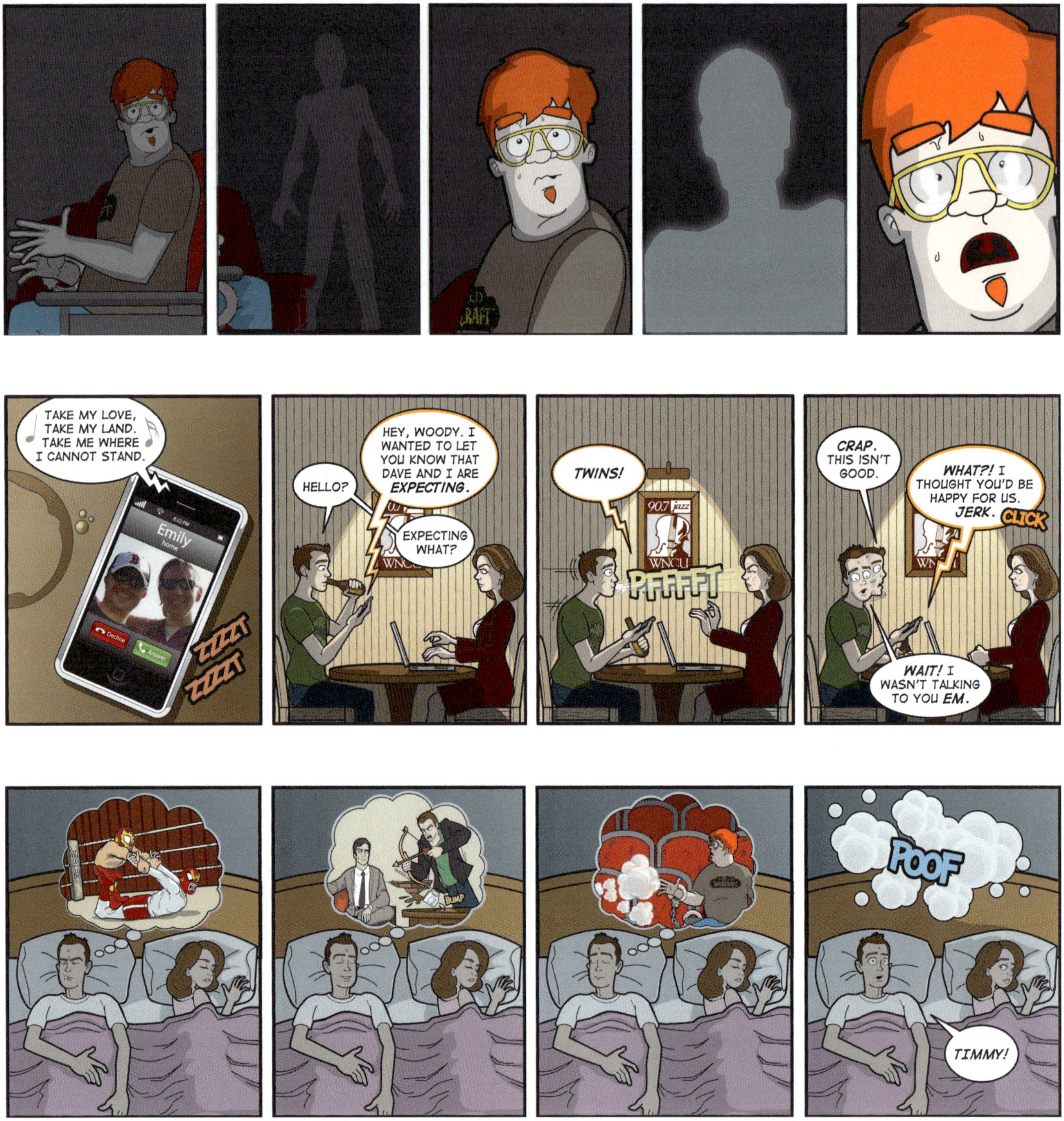
TAKE MY LOVE, TAKE MY LAND. TAKE ME WHERE I CANNOT STAND.
Emily
home
Decline
Answer
ZZZZT
ZZZZT
HELLO?
HEY, WOODY. I WANTED TO LET YOU KNOW THAT DAVE AND I ARE *EXPECTING*.
EXPECTING WHAT?
TWINS!
90.7 jazz
WNCU
PFFFFT
CRAP. THIS ISN'T GOOD.
WHAT?! I THOUGHT YOU'D BE HAPPY FOR US. JERK.
CLICK
WAIT! I WASN'T TALKING TO YOU EM.
BUMP
POOF
TIMMY!

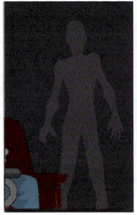

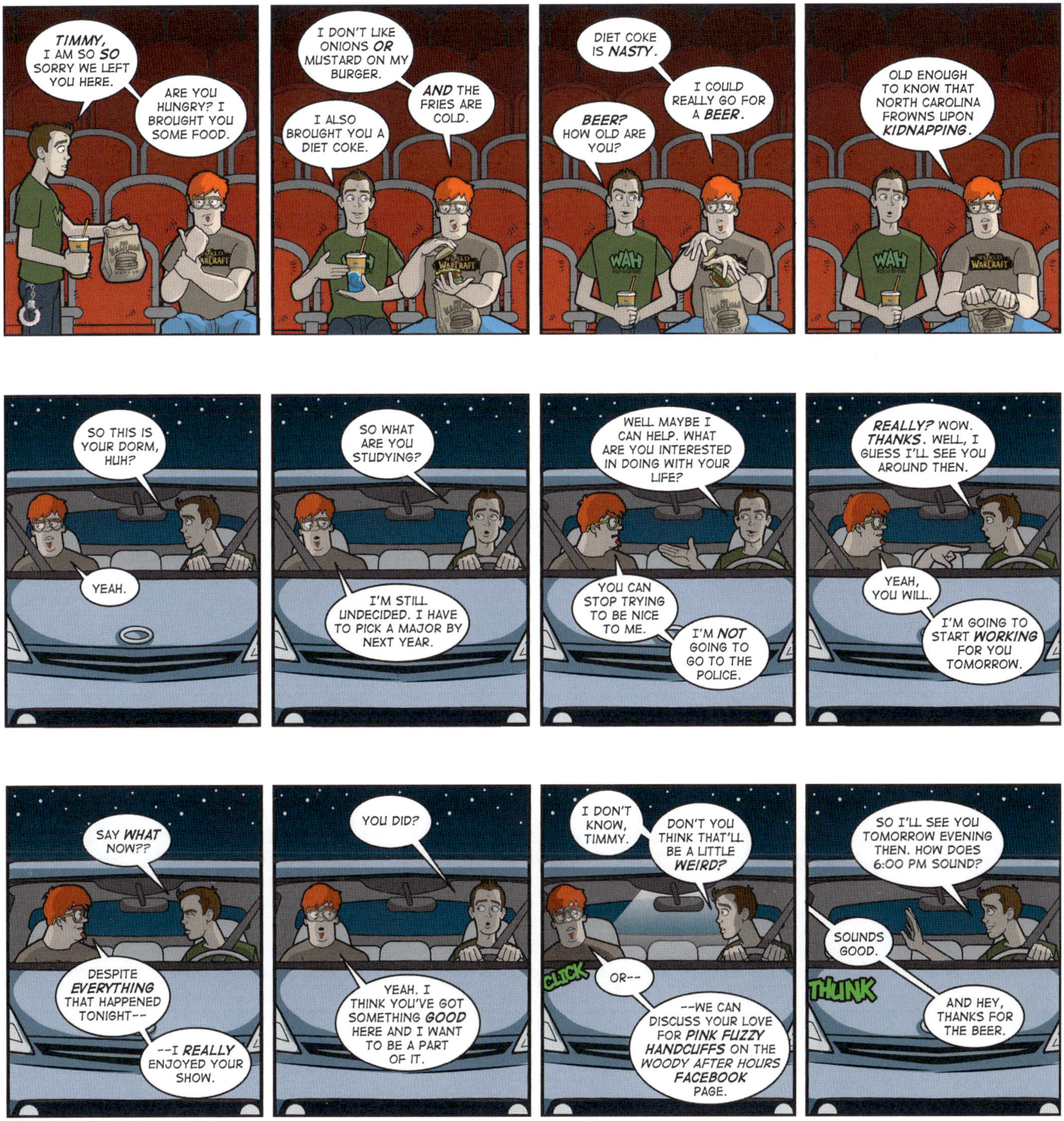
TIMMY, I AM SO SO SORRY WE LEFT YOU HERE.
ARE YOU HUNGRY? I BROUGHT YOU SOME FOOD.
I DON'T LIKE ONIONS OR MUSTARD ON MY BURGER.
AND THE FRIES ARE COLD.
I ALSO BROUGHT YOU A DIET COKE.
DIET COKE IS NASTY.
I COULD REALLY GO FOR A BEER.
BEER? HOW OLD ARE YOU?
OLD ENOUGH TO KNOW THAT NORTH CAROLINA FROWNS UPON KIDNAPPING.
SO THIS IS YOUR DORM, HUH?
YEAH.
SO WHAT ARE YOU STUDYING?
I'M STILL UNDECIDED. I HAVE TO PICK A MAJOR BY NEXT YEAR.
WELL MAYBE I CAN HELP. WHAT ARE YOU INTERESTED IN DOING WITH YOUR LIFE?
YOU CAN STOP TRYING TO BE NICE TO ME.
I'M NOT GOING TO GO TO THE POLICE.
REALLY? WOW. THANKS. WELL, I GUESS I'LL SEE YOU AROUND THEN.
YEAH, YOU WILL.
I'M GOING TO START WORKING FOR YOU TOMORROW.
SAY WHAT NOW??
DESPITE EVERYTHING THAT HAPPENED TONIGHT--
--I REALLY ENJOYED YOUR SHOW.
YOU DID?
YEAH. I THINK YOU'VE GOT SOMETHING GOOD HERE AND I WANT TO BE A PART OF IT.
I DON'T KNOW, TIMMY.
DON'T YOU THINK THAT'LL BE A LITTLE WEIRD?
CLICK
OR--
--WE CAN DISCUSS YOUR LOVE FOR PINK FUZZY HANDCUFFS ON THE WOODY AFTER HOURS FACEBOOK PAGE.
SO I'LL SEE YOU TOMORROW EVENING THEN. HOW DOES 6:00 PM SOUND?
SOUNDS GOOD.
THUNK
AND HEY, THANKS FOR THE BEER.

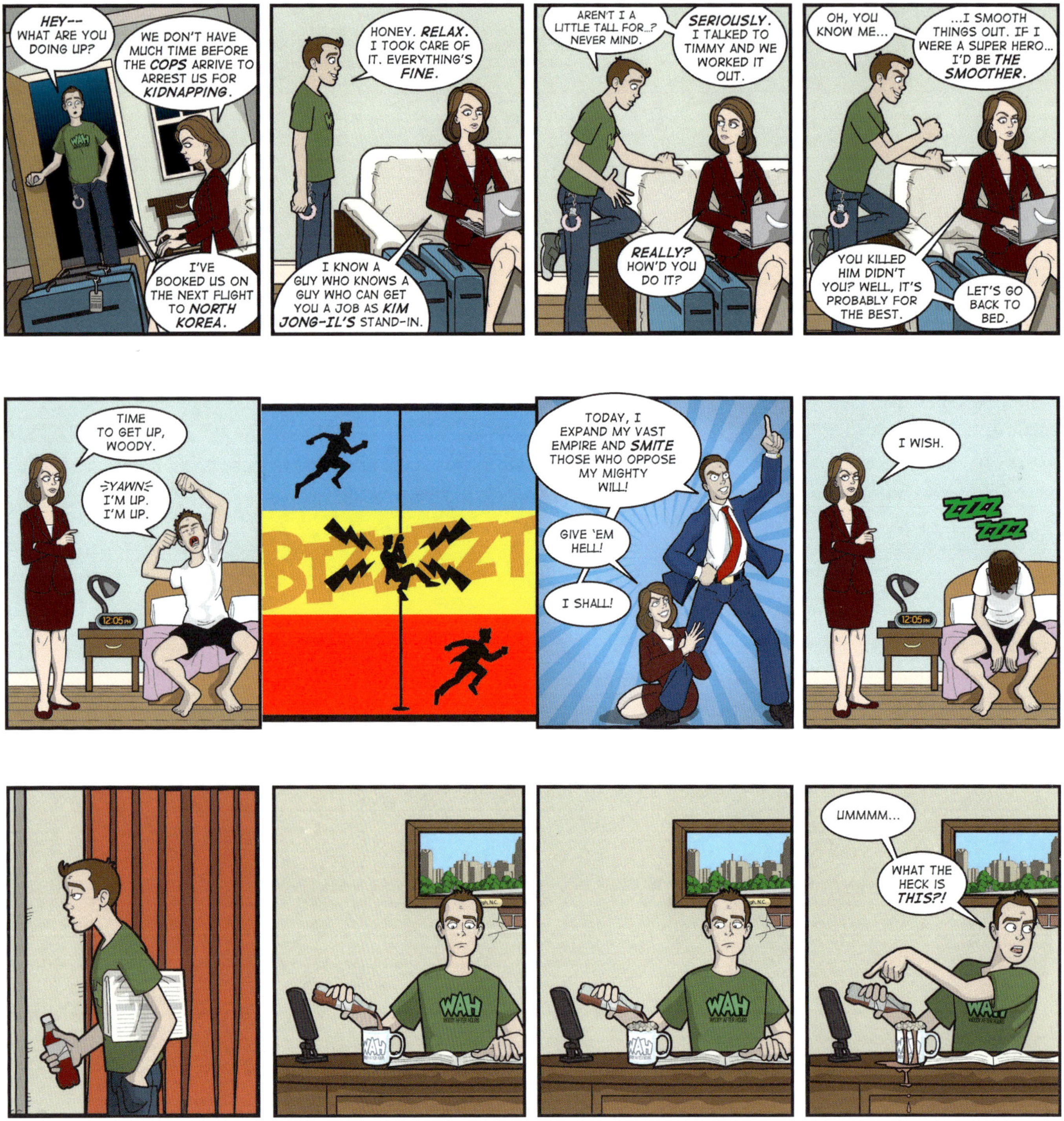
HEY-- WHAT ARE YOU DOING UP?
WE DON'T HAVE MUCH TIME BEFORE THE COPS ARRIVE TO ARREST US FOR KIDNAPPING.
I'VE BOOKED US ON THE NEXT FLIGHT TO NORTH KOREA.
HONEY. RELAX. I TOOK CARE OF IT. EVERYTHING'S FINE.
I KNOW A GUY WHO KNOWS A GUY WHO CAN GET YOU A JOB AS KIM JONG-IL'S STAND-IN.
AREN'T I A LITTLE TALL FOR...? NEVER MIND.
SERIOUSLY. I TALKED TO TIMMY AND WE WORKED IT OUT.
REALLY? HOW'D YOU DO IT?
OH, YOU KNOW ME...
...I SMOOTH THINGS OUT. IF I WERE A SUPER HERO... I'D BE THE SMOOTHER.
YOU KILLED HIM DIDN'T YOU? WELL, IT'S PROBABLY FOR THE BEST.
LET'S GO BACK TO BED.
TIME TO GET UP, WOODY.
YAWN I'M UP. I'M UP.
12:05 PM
BZZZZT
TODAY, I EXPAND MY VAST EMPIRE AND SMITE THOSE WHO OPPOSE MY MIGHTY WILL!
GIVE 'EM HELL!
I SHALL!
I WISH.
ZZZ ZZZ
12:05 PM
WAH
UMMMM...
WHAT THE HECK IS THIS?!

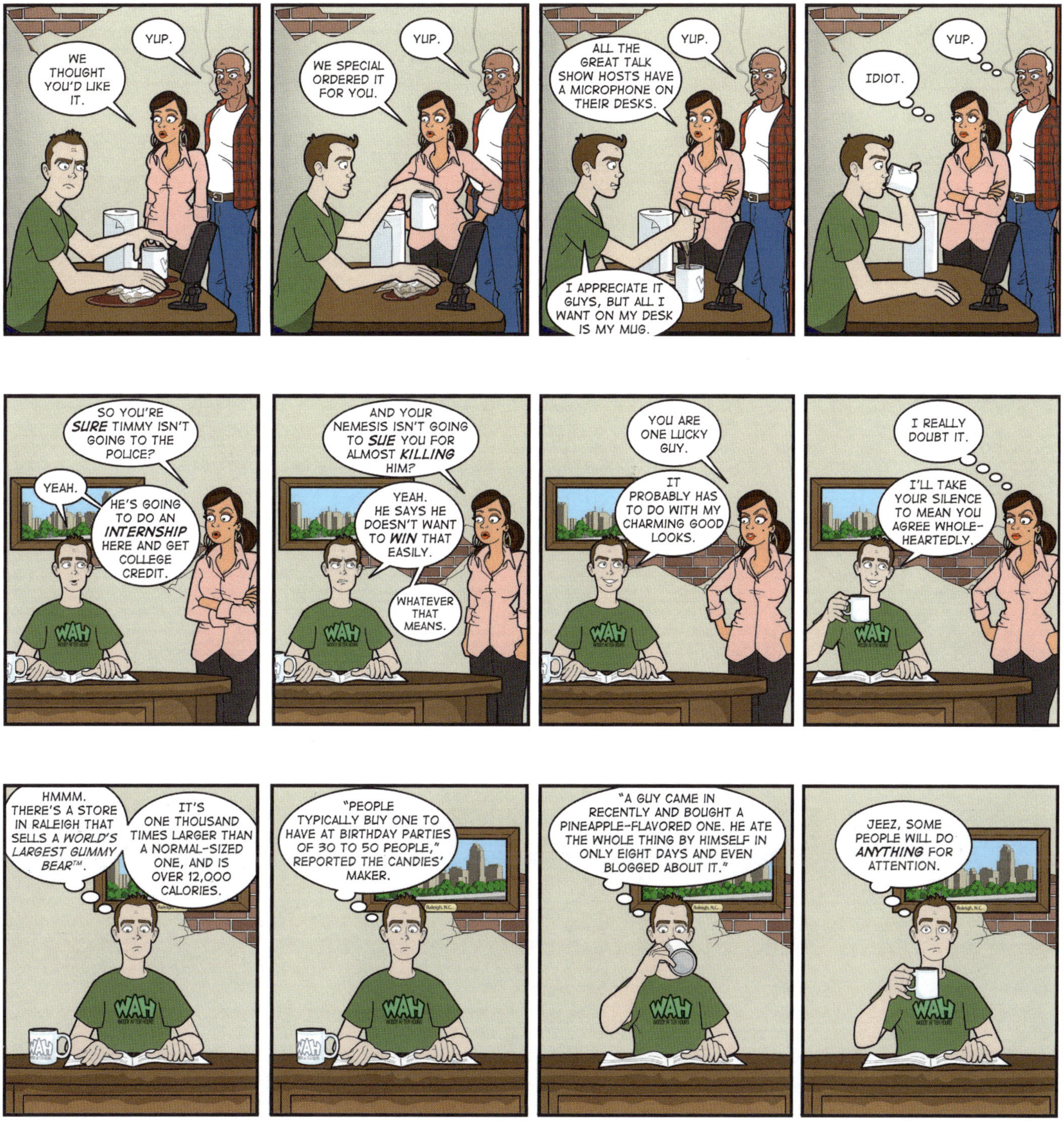

WE THOUGHT YOU'D LIKE IT.
YUP.
WE SPECIAL ORDERED IT FOR YOU.
YUP.
ALL THE GREAT TALK SHOW HOSTS HAVE A MICROPHONE ON THEIR DESKS.
YUP.
I APPRECIATE IT GUYS, BUT ALL I WANT ON MY DESK IS MY MUG.
IDIOT.
YUP.
SO YOU'RE *SURE* TIMMY ISN'T GOING TO THE POLICE?
YEAH.
HE'S GOING TO DO AN *INTERNSHIP* HERE AND GET COLLEGE CREDIT.
AND YOUR NEMESIS ISN'T GOING TO *SUE* YOU FOR ALMOST *KILLING* HIM?
YEAH. HE SAYS HE DOESN'T WANT TO *WIN* THAT EASILY.
WHATEVER THAT MEANS.
YOU ARE ONE LUCKY GUY.
IT PROBABLY HAS TO DO WITH MY CHARMING GOOD LOOKS.
I REALLY DOUBT IT.
I'LL TAKE YOUR SILENCE TO MEAN YOU AGREE WHOLE-HEARTEDLY.
HMMM. THERE'S A STORE IN RALEIGH THAT SELLS A *WORLD'S LARGEST GUMMY BEAR*™.
IT'S ONE THOUSAND TIMES LARGER THAN A NORMAL-SIZED ONE, AND IS OVER 12,000 CALORIES.
"PEOPLE TYPICALLY BUY ONE TO HAVE AT BIRTHDAY PARTIES OF 30 TO 50 PEOPLE," REPORTED THE CANDIES' MAKER.
"A GUY CAME IN RECENTLY AND BOUGHT A PINEAPPLE-FLAVORED ONE. HE ATE THE WHOLE THING BY HIMSELF IN ONLY EIGHT DAYS AND EVEN BLOGGED ABOUT IT."
JEEZ, SOME PEOPLE WILL DO *ANYTHING* FOR ATTENTION.

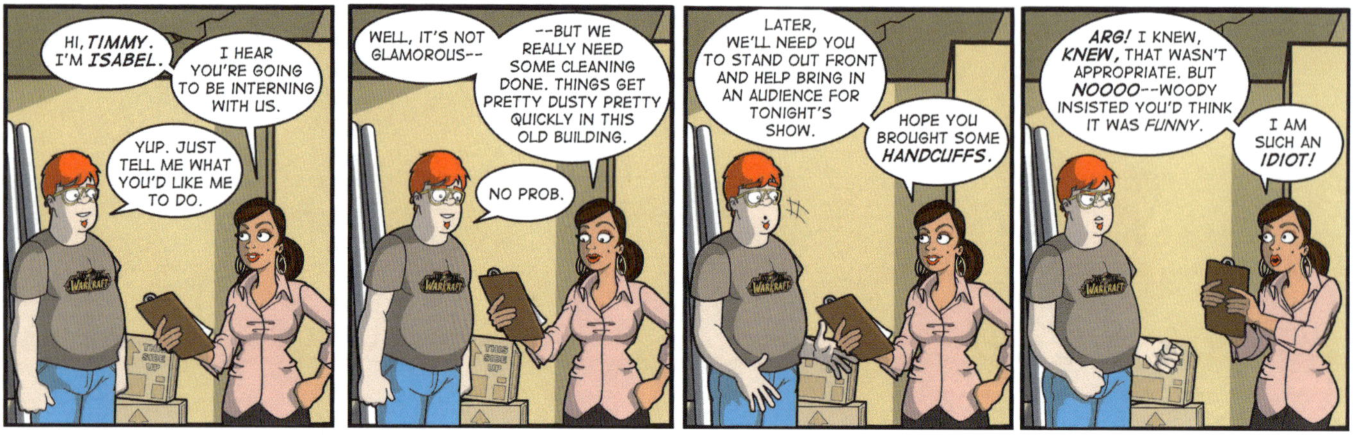
HI, *TIMMY*. I'M *ISABEL*.
I HEAR YOU'RE GOING TO BE INTERNING WITH US.
YUP. JUST TELL ME WHAT YOU'D LIKE ME TO DO.
WELL, IT'S NOT GLAMOROUS--
--BUT WE REALLY NEED SOME CLEANING DONE. THINGS GET PRETTY DUSTY PRETTY QUICKLY IN THIS OLD BUILDING.
NO PROB.
LATER, WE'LL NEED YOU TO STAND OUT FRONT AND HELP BRING IN AN AUDIENCE FOR TONIGHT'S SHOW.
HOPE YOU BROUGHT SOME ***HANDCUFFS***.
ARG! I KNEW, ***KNEW***, THAT WASN'T APPROPRIATE. BUT ***NOOOO***--WOODY INSISTED YOU'D THINK IT WAS *FUNNY*.
I AM SUCH AN ***IDIOT!***

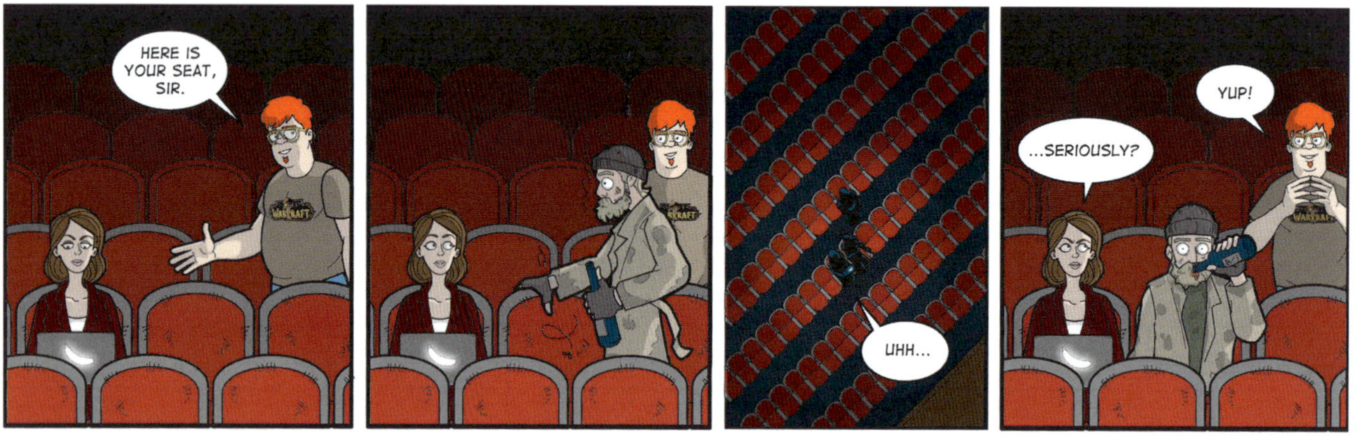
HERE IS YOUR SEAT, SIR.
UHH...
...SERIOUSLY?
YUP!

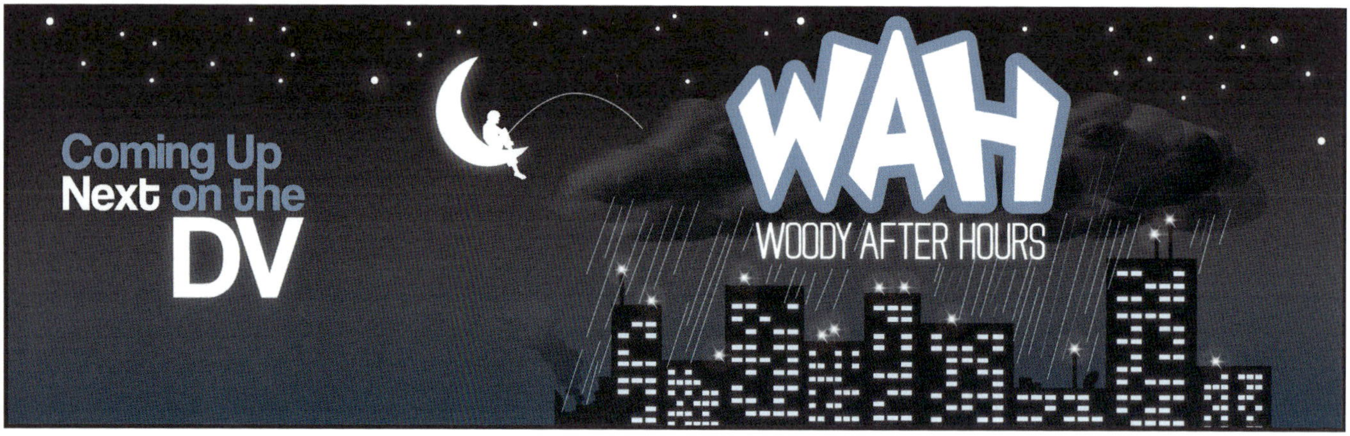
Coming Up Next on the DV
WAH
WOODY AFTER HOURS

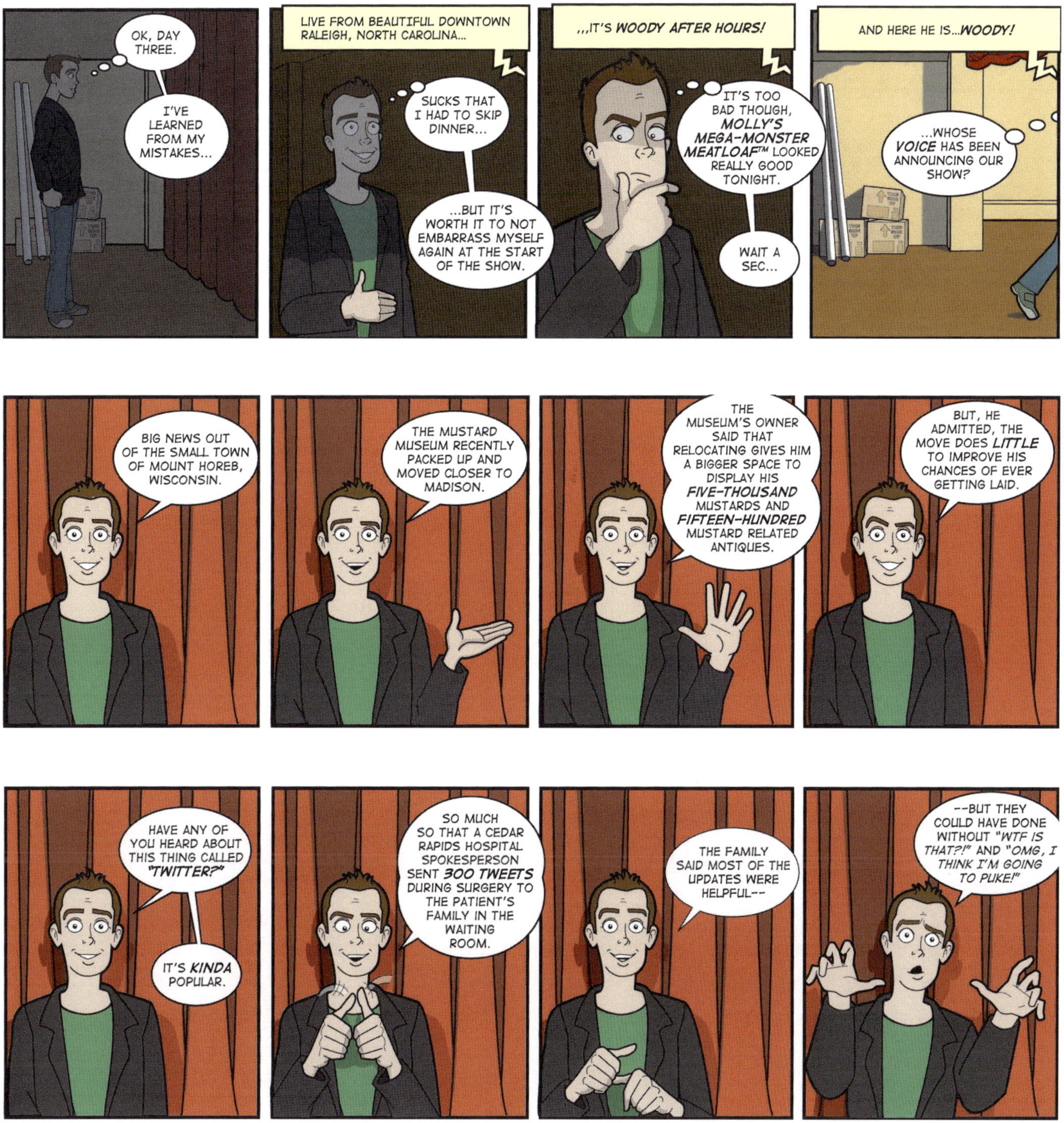
OK, DAY THREE.
I'VE LEARNED FROM MY MISTAKES...
LIVE FROM BEAUTIFUL DOWNTOWN RALEIGH, NORTH CAROLINA...
SUCKS THAT I HAD TO SKIP DINNER...
...BUT IT'S WORTH IT TO NOT EMBARRASS MYSELF AGAIN AT THE START OF THE SHOW.
...IT'S WOODY AFTER HOURS!
IT'S TOO BAD THOUGH, MOLLY'S MEGA-MONSTER MEATLOAF™ LOOKED REALLY GOOD TONIGHT.
WAIT A SEC...
AND HERE HE IS...WOODY!
...WHOSE VOICE HAS BEEN ANNOUNCING OUR SHOW?
BIG NEWS OUT OF THE SMALL TOWN OF MOUNT HOREB, WISCONSIN.
THE MUSTARD MUSEUM RECENTLY PACKED UP AND MOVED CLOSER TO MADISON.
THE MUSEUM'S OWNER SAID THAT RELOCATING GIVES HIM A BIGGER SPACE TO DISPLAY HIS FIVE-THOUSAND MUSTARDS AND FIFTEEN-HUNDRED MUSTARD RELATED ANTIQUES.
BUT, HE ADMITTED, THE MOVE DOES LITTLE TO IMPROVE HIS CHANCES OF EVER GETTING LAID.
HAVE ANY OF YOU HEARD ABOUT THIS THING CALLED "TWITTER?"
IT'S KINDA POPULAR.
SO MUCH SO THAT A CEDAR RAPIDS HOSPITAL SPOKESPERSON SENT 300 TWEETS DURING SURGERY TO THE PATIENT'S FAMILY IN THE WAITING ROOM.
THE FAMILY SAID MOST OF THE UPDATES WERE HELPFUL--
--BUT THEY COULD HAVE DONE WITHOUT "WTF IS THAT?!" AND "OMG, I THINK I'M GOING TO PUKE!"

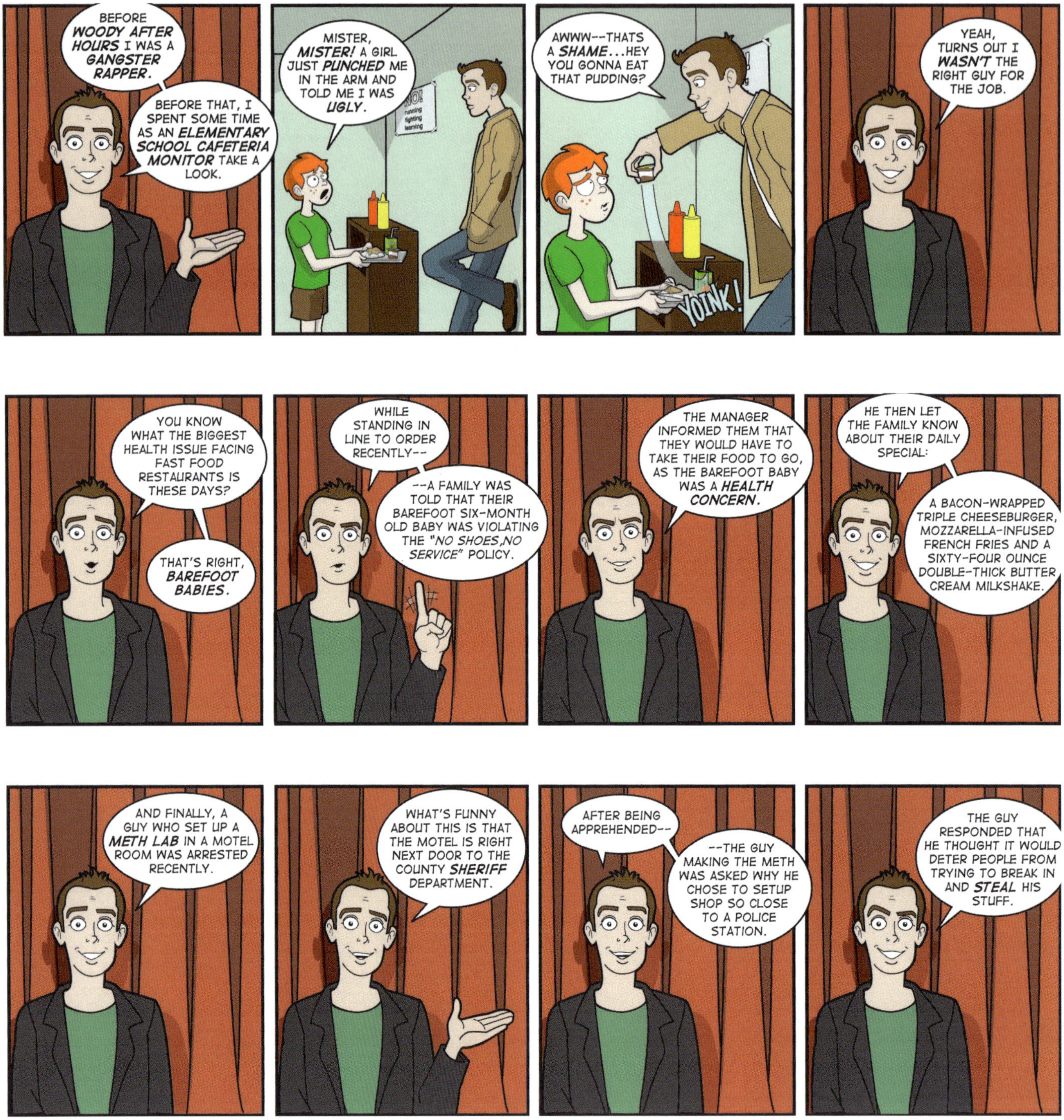
BEFORE WOODY AFTER HOURS I WAS A GANGSTER RAPPER.
BEFORE THAT, I SPENT SOME TIME AS AN ELEMENTARY SCHOOL CAFETERIA MONITOR TAKE A LOOK.
MISTER, MISTER! A GIRL JUST PUNCHED ME IN THE ARM AND TOLD ME I WAS UGLY.
NO! running fighting learning
AWWW--THATS A SHAME...HEY YOU GONNA EAT THAT PUDDING?
YOINK!
YEAH, TURNS OUT I WASN'T THE RIGHT GUY FOR THE JOB.
YOU KNOW WHAT THE BIGGEST HEALTH ISSUE FACING FAST FOOD RESTAURANTS IS THESE DAYS?
THAT'S RIGHT, BAREFOOT BABIES.
WHILE STANDING IN LINE TO ORDER RECENTLY--
--A FAMILY WAS TOLD THAT THEIR BAREFOOT SIX-MONTH OLD BABY WAS VIOLATING THE "NO SHOES,NO SERVICE" POLICY.
THE MANAGER INFORMED THEM THAT THEY WOULD HAVE TO TAKE THEIR FOOD TO GO, AS THE BAREFOOT BABY WAS A HEALTH CONCERN.
HE THEN LET THE FAMILY KNOW ABOUT THEIR DAILY SPECIAL:
A BACON-WRAPPED TRIPLE CHEESEBURGER, MOZZARELLA-INFUSED FRENCH FRIES AND A SIXTY-FOUR OUNCE DOUBLE-THICK BUTTER CREAM MILKSHAKE.
AND FINALLY, A GUY WHO SET UP A METH LAB IN A MOTEL ROOM WAS ARRESTED RECENTLY.
WHAT'S FUNNY ABOUT THIS IS THAT THE MOTEL IS RIGHT NEXT DOOR TO THE COUNTY SHERIFF DEPARTMENT.
AFTER BEING APPREHENDED--
--THE GUY MAKING THE METH WAS ASKED WHY HE CHOSE TO SETUP SHOP SO CLOSE TO A POLICE STATION.
THE GUY RESPONDED THAT HE THOUGHT IT WOULD DETER PEOPLE FROM TRYING TO BREAK IN AND STEAL HIS STUFF.

AND NOW IT'S TIME FOR A SEGMENT I LIKE TO CALL...
WAH
WOODY'S WISE WORDS
YEAH, LADIES--
--I LOOK GOOD!
AND NOW, I SUBMIT TO YOU A FEW OF MY WISE WORDS.
AHEM
CRACK IS WHACK.
I BELIEVE THE CHILDREN ARE OUR FUTURE.
YOU CAN'T SLAP SOMEBODY WHEN YOU'RE ON PROBATION.
GURGLE GURGLE
WHAT? I NEVER SAID THEY WERE GOING TO BE ORIGINAL.
AGAIN, I SUBMIT TO YOU A FEW OF MY WISE WORDS.
THE TWO SECRETS TO HAPPINESS ARE--
--EATING ...AND BUYING THINGS.
DID I JUST BLOW YOUR MIND??

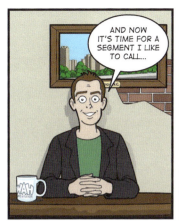

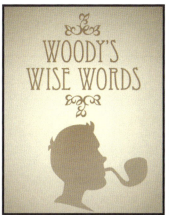

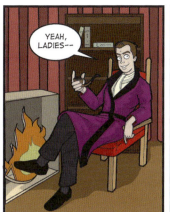

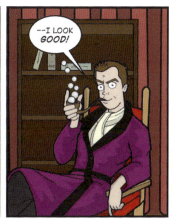

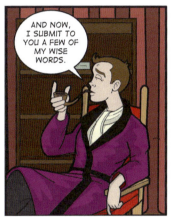

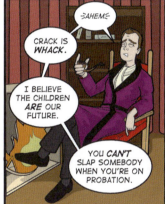

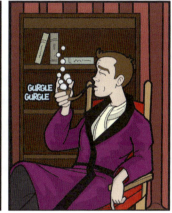

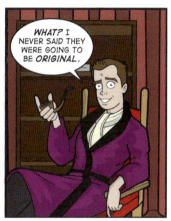

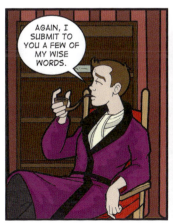

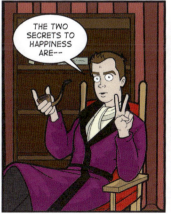

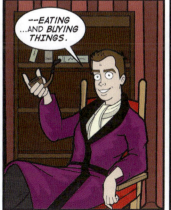

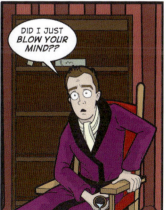

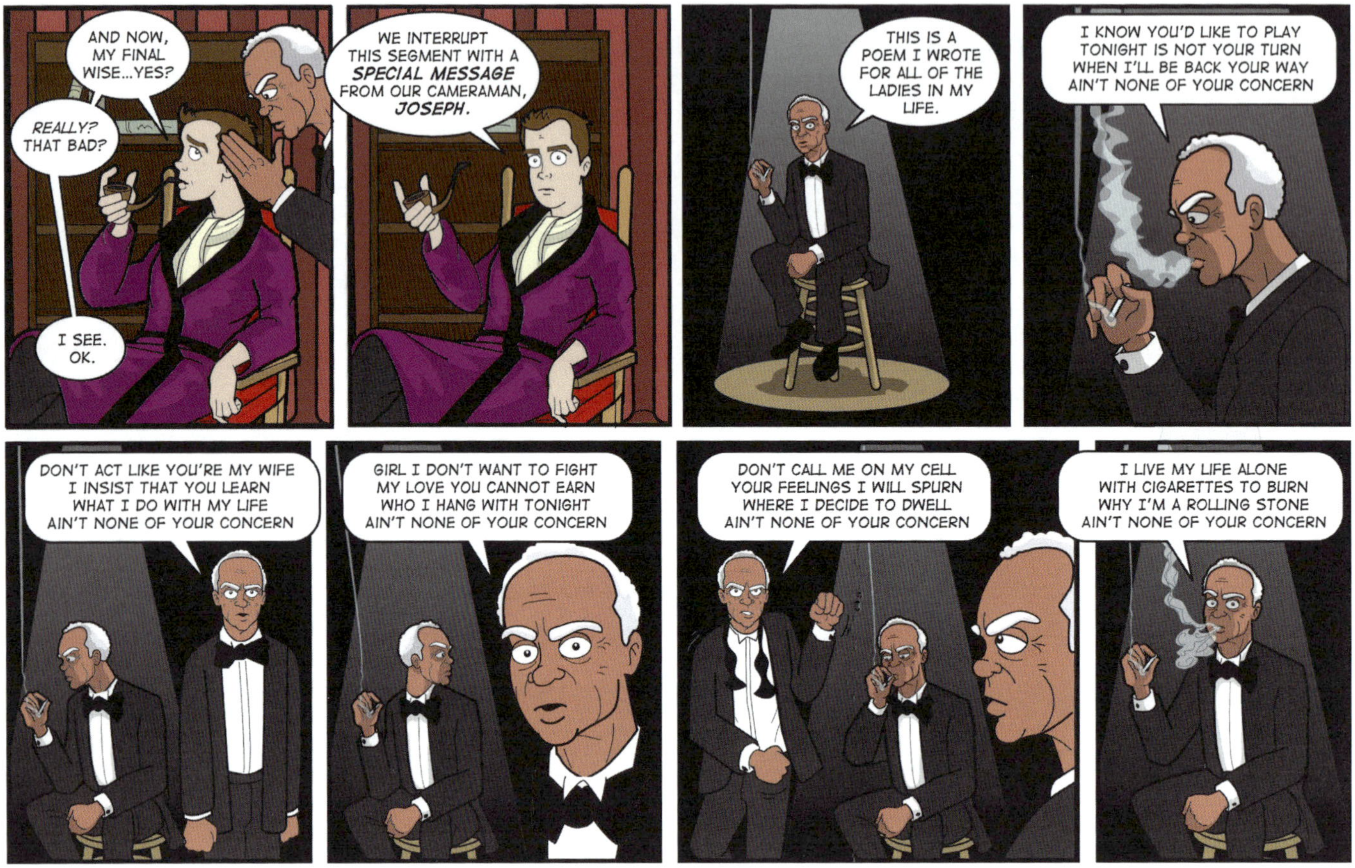
AND NOW, MY FINAL WISE...YES?
REALLY? THAT BAD?
I SEE. OK.
WE INTERRUPT THIS SEGMENT WITH A SPECIAL MESSAGE FROM OUR CAMERAMAN, JOSEPH.
THIS IS A POEM I WROTE FOR ALL OF THE LADIES IN MY LIFE.
I KNOW YOU'D LIKE TO PLAY TONIGHT IS NOT YOUR TURN WHEN I'LL BE BACK YOUR WAY AIN'T NONE OF YOUR CONCERN
DON'T ACT LIKE YOU'RE MY WIFE I INSIST THAT YOU LEARN WHAT I DO WITH MY LIFE AIN'T NONE OF YOUR CONCERN
GIRL I DON'T WANT TO FIGHT MY LOVE YOU CANNOT EARN WHO I HANG WITH TONIGHT AIN'T NONE OF YOUR CONCERN
DON'T CALL ME ON MY CELL YOUR FEELINGS I WILL SPURN WHERE I DECIDE TO DWELL AIN'T NONE OF YOUR CONCERN
I LIVE MY LIFE ALONE WITH CIGARETTES TO BURN WHY I'M A ROLLING STONE AIN'T NONE OF YOUR CONCERN

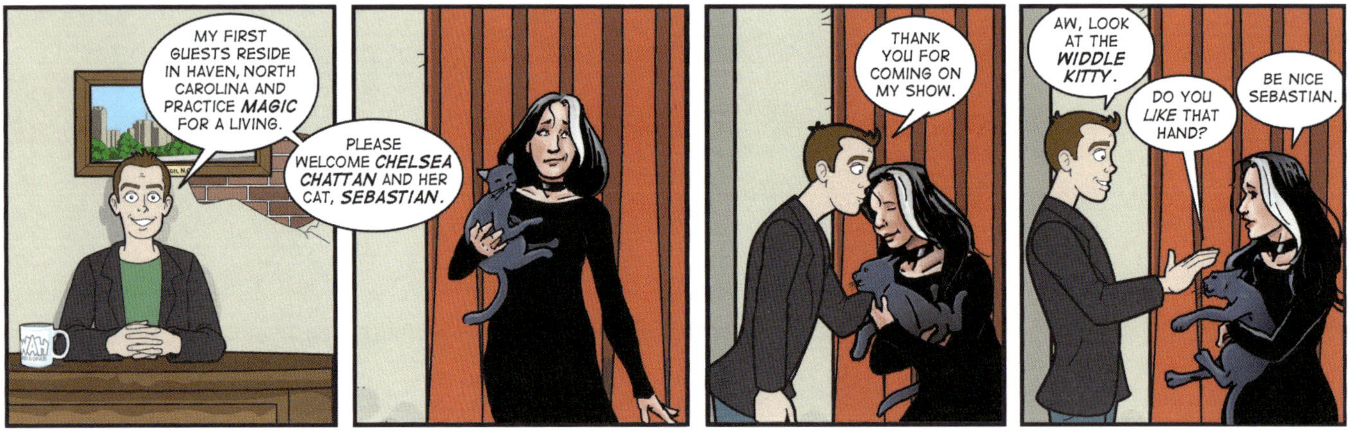
MY FIRST GUESTS RESIDE IN HAVEN, NORTH CAROLINA AND PRACTICE MAGIC FOR A LIVING.
PLEASE WELCOME CHELSEA CHATTAN AND HER CAT, SEBASTIAN.
THANK YOU FOR COMING ON MY SHOW.
AW, LOOK AT THE WIDDLE KITTY.
DO YOU LIKE THAT HAND?
BE NICE SEBASTIAN.

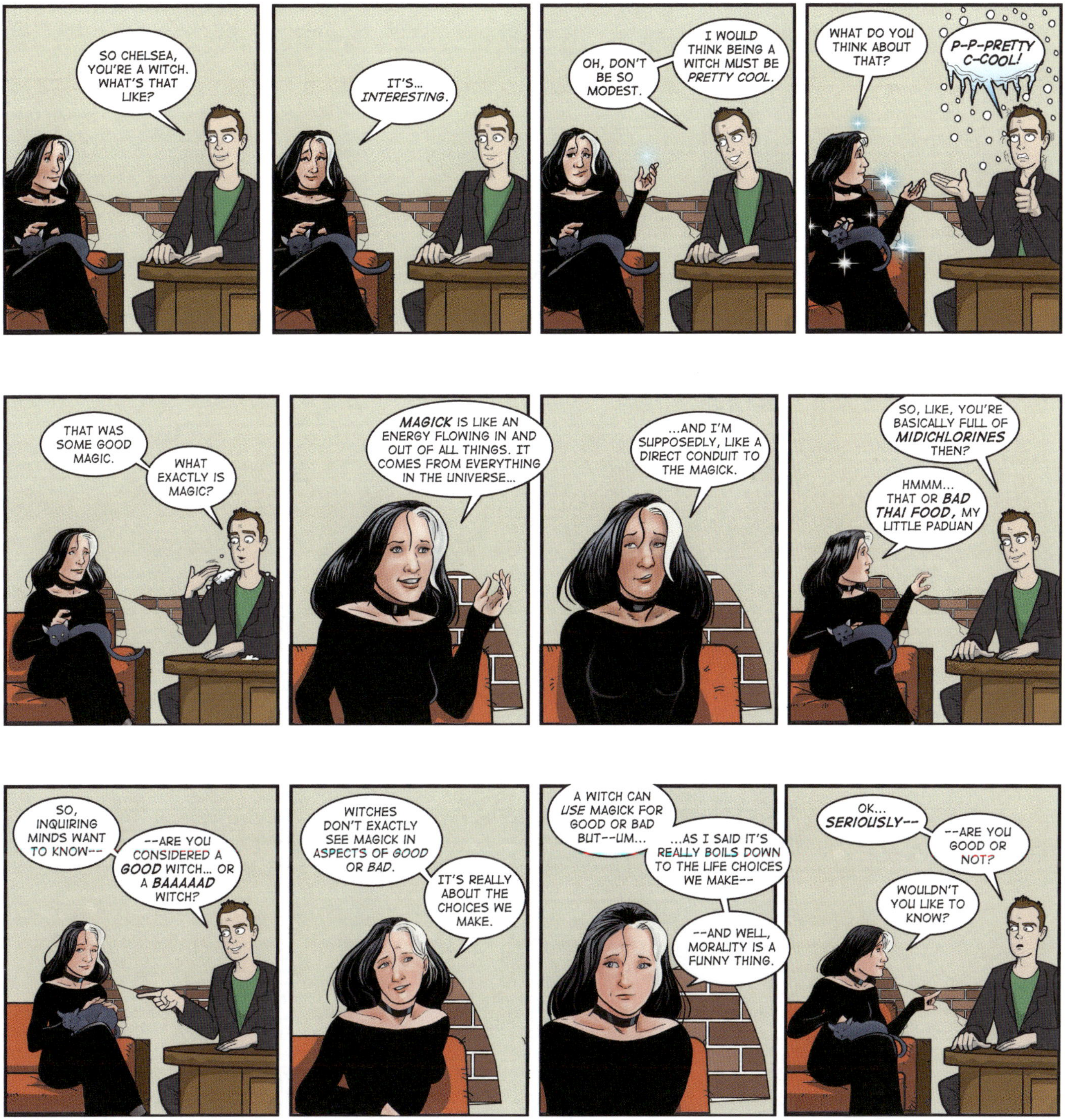

SO CHELSEA, YOU'RE A WITCH. WHAT'S THAT LIKE?
IT'S... INTERESTING.
I WOULD THINK BEING A WITCH MUST BE PRETTY COOL.
OH, DON'T BE SO MODEST.
WHAT DO YOU THINK ABOUT THAT?
P-P-PRETTY C-COOL!
THAT WAS SOME GOOD MAGIC.
WHAT EXACTLY IS MAGIC?
MAGICK IS LIKE AN ENERGY FLOWING IN AND OUT OF ALL THINGS. IT COMES FROM EVERYTHING IN THE UNIVERSE...
...AND I'M SUPPOSEDLY, LIKE A DIRECT CONDUIT TO THE MAGICK.
SO, LIKE, YOU'RE BASICALLY FULL OF MIDICHLORINES THEN?
HMMM... THAT OR BAD THAI FOOD, MY LITTLE PADUAN
SO, INQUIRING MINDS WANT TO KNOW--
--ARE YOU CONSIDERED A GOOD WITCH... OR A BAAAAAD WITCH?
WITCHES DON'T EXACTLY SEE MAGICK IN ASPECTS OF GOOD OR BAD.
IT'S REALLY ABOUT THE CHOICES WE MAKE.
A WITCH CAN USE MAGICK FOR GOOD OR BAD BUT--UM...
...AS I SAID IT'S REALLY BOILS DOWN TO THE LIFE CHOICES WE MAKE--
--AND WELL, MORALITY IS A FUNNY THING.
OK... SERIOUSLY--
--ARE YOU GOOD OR NOT?
WOULDN'T YOU LIKE TO KNOW?

AND SO, *FINALLY*, WE ARRIVED AT CAT'S CRADLE FOR DRINKS AND DANCING--
--BUT I DON'T THINK *RAVEN* WILL WANT TO *PORTAL* ANYWHERE WITH ME AGAIN.
WOW, WHAT A GREAT STORY. REAL QUICK, BEFORE WE GO TO COMMERCIAL--
--TELL ME ABOUT YOUR SISTER, MEL...
LICK
LICK
LICK
SEBASTIAN, YOU'RE A BUTT.
WHEN WE COME BACK, CHELSEA IS GOING TO SHOW US A MAGIC TRICK.
STAY TUNED!
LICK

Coming Up Next on the DV After
WAH
WOODY AFTER HOURS
IN THIS ECONOMY
HOW EASY WAS IT FOR US
TO FIND PEOPLE TO PARTICIPATE IN
A GAME SHOW WHERE CONTESTANTS
BEAT EACH OTHER TO WITHIN AN INCH OF THEIR LIVES
IN ORDER TO WIN A **CHANCE** AT DINNER FOR TWO AT CRACKER BARREL?
EASIER THAN YOU MIGHT THINK!
WITHIN AN INCH
ONLY ON THE DV
Play the home version. Now available at your local liquor store.
WITHIN AN INCH
$$$

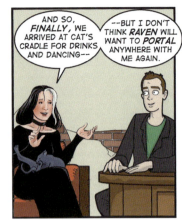

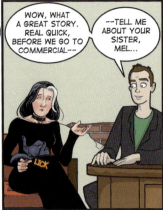

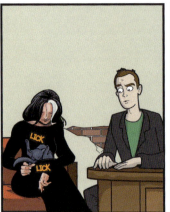

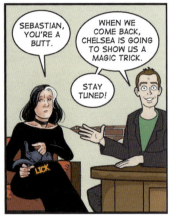

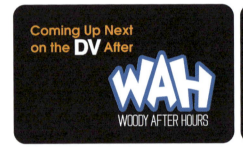

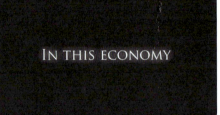

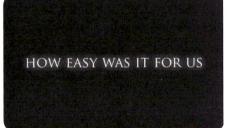

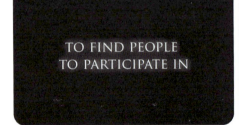

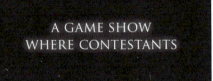

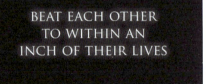

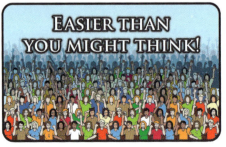

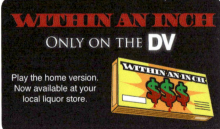

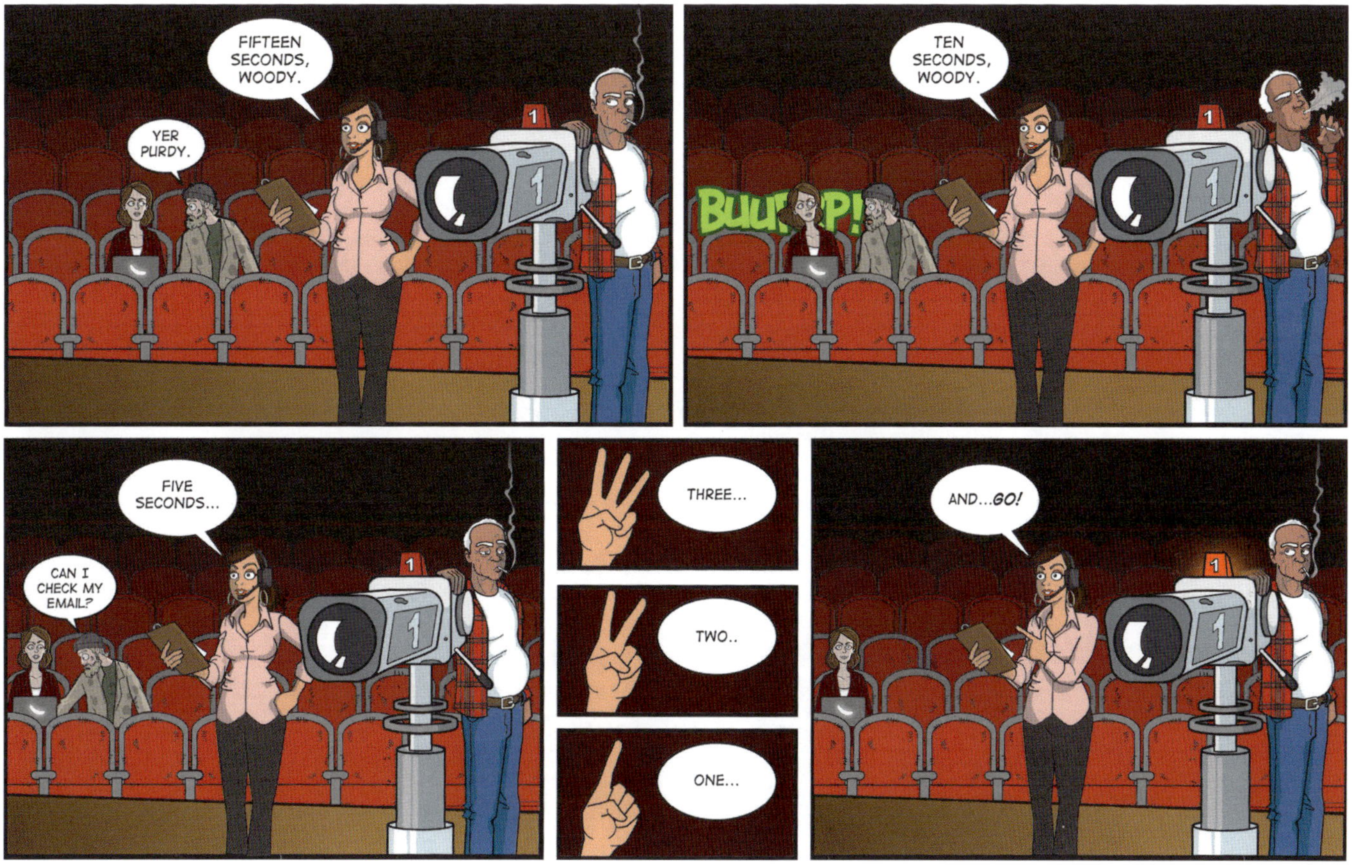
FIFTEEN SECONDS, WOODY.
YER PURDY.
TEN SECONDS, WOODY.
FIVE SECONDS...
CAN I CHECK MY EMAIL?
THREE...
TWO..
ONE...
AND...GO!

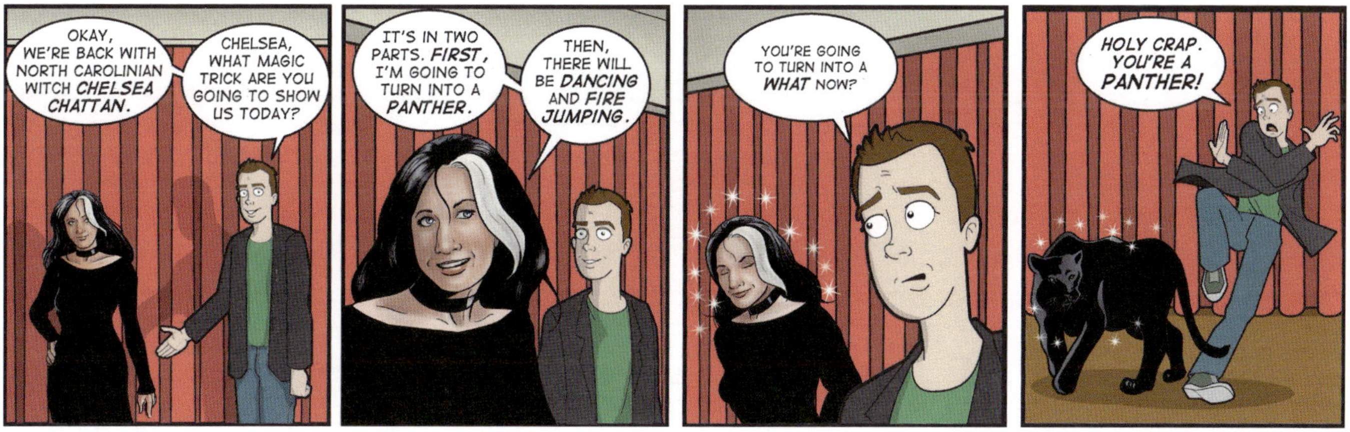
OKAY, WE'RE BACK WITH NORTH CAROLINIAN WITCH CHELSEA CHATTAN.
CHELSEA, WHAT MAGIC TRICK ARE YOU GOING TO SHOW US TODAY?
IT'S IN TWO PARTS. FIRST, I'M GOING TO TURN INTO A PANTHER.
THEN, THERE WILL BE DANCING AND FIRE JUMPING.
YOU'RE GOING TO TURN INTO A WHAT NOW?
HOLY CRAP. YOU'RE A PANTHER!

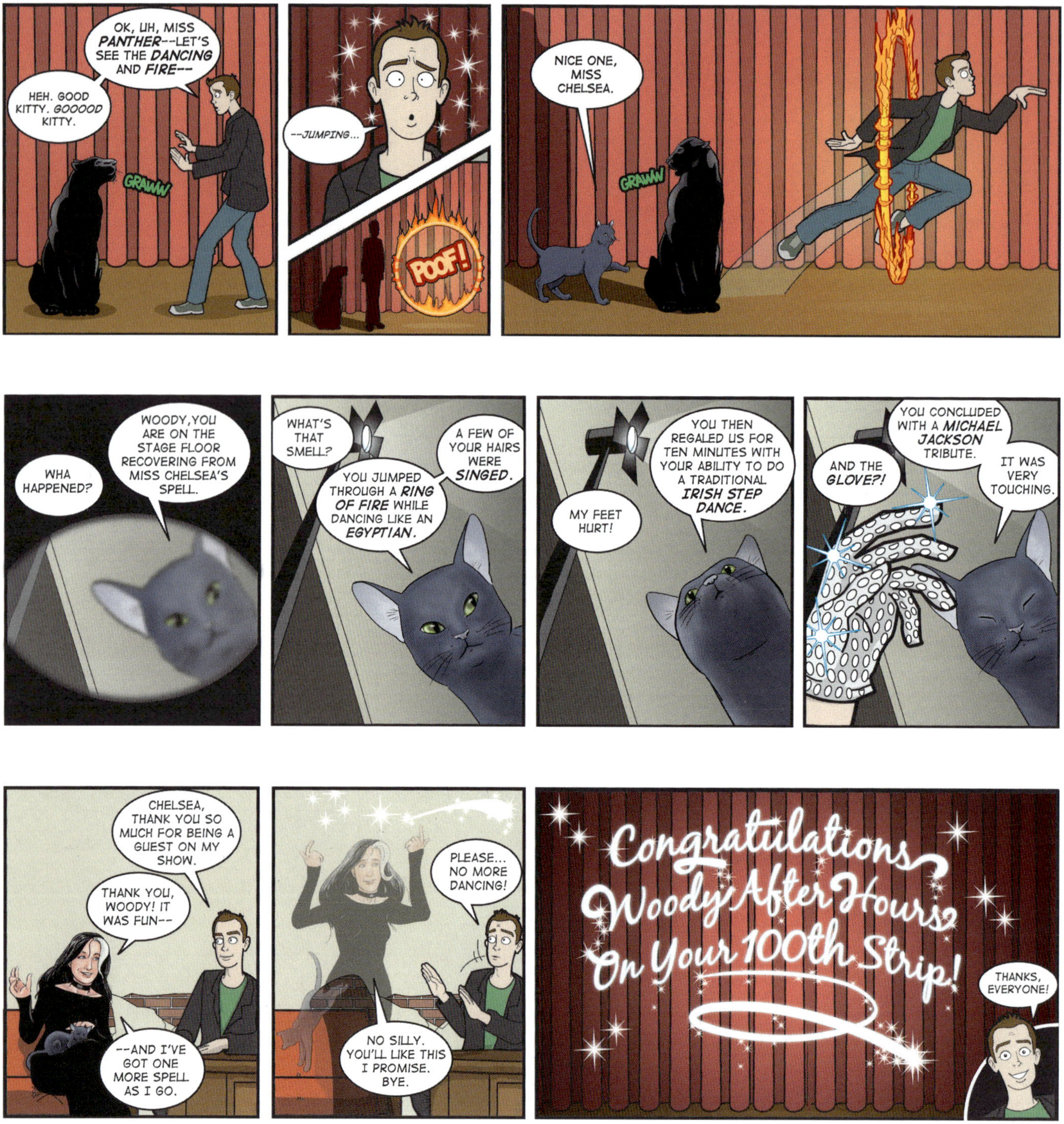
OK, UH, MISS PANTHER--LET'S SEE THE DANCING AND FIRE--
HEH. GOOD KITTY. GOOOOD KITTY.
GRAWW
--JUMPING...
POOF!
NICE ONE, MISS CHELSEA.
GRAWW
WOODY, YOU ARE ON THE STAGE FLOOR RECOVERING FROM MISS CHELSEA'S SPELL.
WHA HAPPENED?
WHAT'S THAT SMELL?
A FEW OF YOUR HAIRS WERE SINGED.
YOU JUMPED THROUGH A RING OF FIRE WHILE DANCING LIKE AN EGYPTIAN.
YOU THEN REGALED US FOR TEN MINUTES WITH YOUR ABILITY TO DO A TRADITIONAL IRISH STEP DANCE.
MY FEET HURT!
YOU CONCLUDED WITH A MICHAEL JACKSON TRIBUTE.
AND THE GLOVE?!
IT WAS VERY TOUCHING.
CHELSEA, THANK YOU SO MUCH FOR BEING A GUEST ON MY SHOW.
THANK YOU, WOODY! IT WAS FUN--
--AND I'VE GOT ONE MORE SPELL AS I GO.
PLEASE... NO MORE DANCING!
NO SILLY. YOU'LL LIKE THIS I PROMISE. BYE.
Congratulations Woody After Hours On Your 100th Strip!
THANKS, EVERYONE!

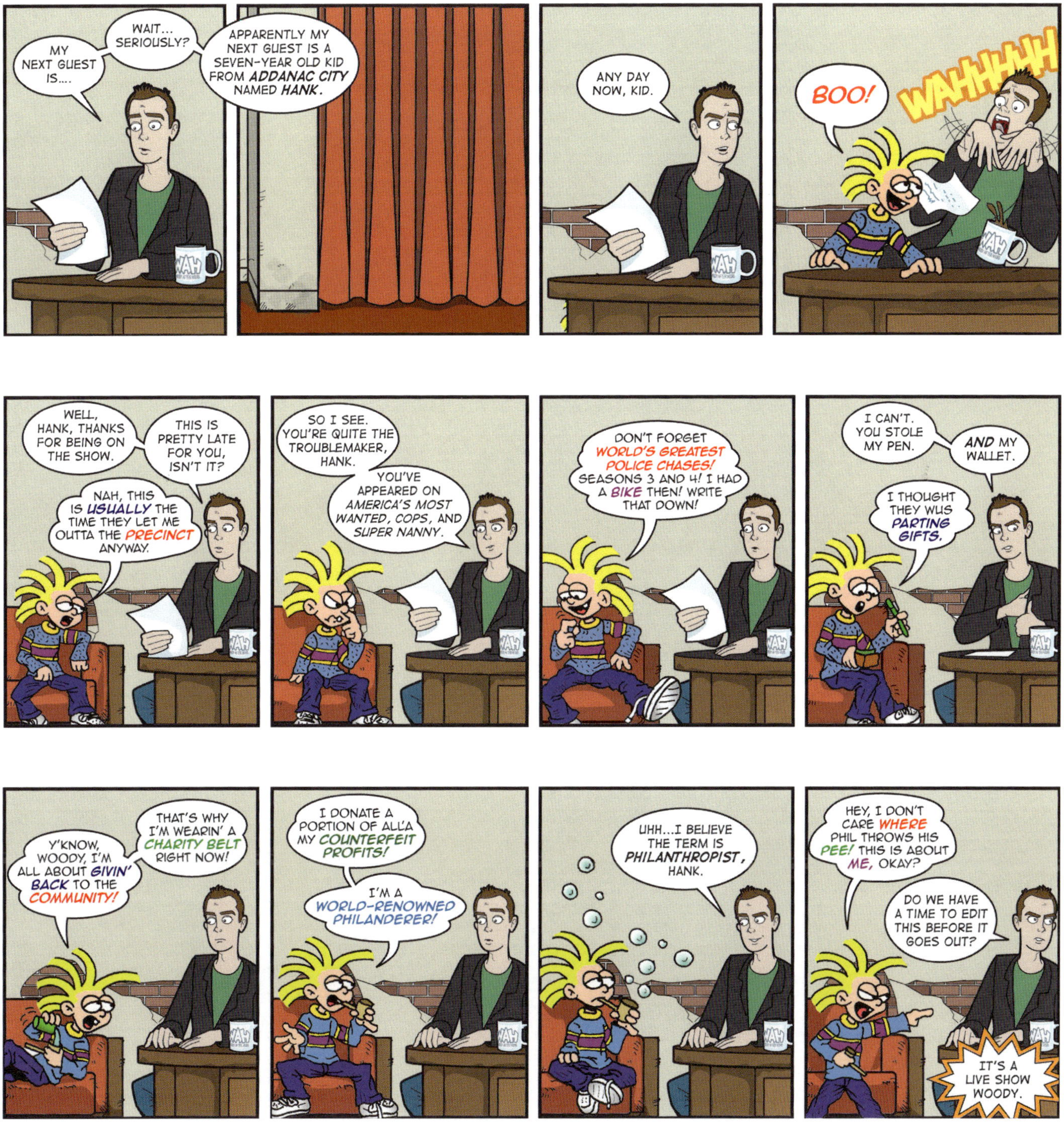

MY NEXT GUEST IS....
WAIT... SERIOUSLY?
APPARENTLY MY NEXT GUEST IS A SEVEN-YEAR OLD KID FROM ADDANAC CITY NAMED HANK.
ANY DAY NOW, KID.
BOO!
WAHHHHH
WELL, HANK, THANKS FOR BEING ON THE SHOW.
THIS IS PRETTY LATE FOR YOU, ISN'T IT?
NAH, THIS IS USUALLY THE TIME THEY LET ME OUTTA THE PRECINCT ANYWAY.
SO I SEE. YOU'RE QUITE THE TROUBLEMAKER, HANK.
YOU'VE APPEARED ON AMERICA'S MOST WANTED, COPS, AND SUPER NANNY.
DON'T FORGET WORLD'S GREATEST POLICE CHASES! SEASONS 3 AND 4! I HAD A BIKE THEN! WRITE THAT DOWN!
I CAN'T. YOU STOLE MY PEN.
AND MY WALLET.
I THOUGHT THEY WUS PARTING GIFTS.
Y'KNOW, WOODY, I'M ALL ABOUT GIVIN' BACK TO THE COMMUNITY!
THAT'S WHY I'M WEARIN' A CHARITY BELT RIGHT NOW!
I DONATE A PORTION OF ALL'A MY COUNTERFEIT PROFITS!
I'M A WORLD-RENOWNED PHILANDERER!
UHH...I BELIEVE THE TERM IS PHILANTHROPIST, HANK.
HEY, I DON'T CARE WHERE PHIL THROWS HIS PEE! THIS IS ABOUT ME, OKAY?
DO WE HAVE A TIME TO EDIT THIS BEFORE IT GOES OUT?
IT'S A LIVE SHOW WOODY.

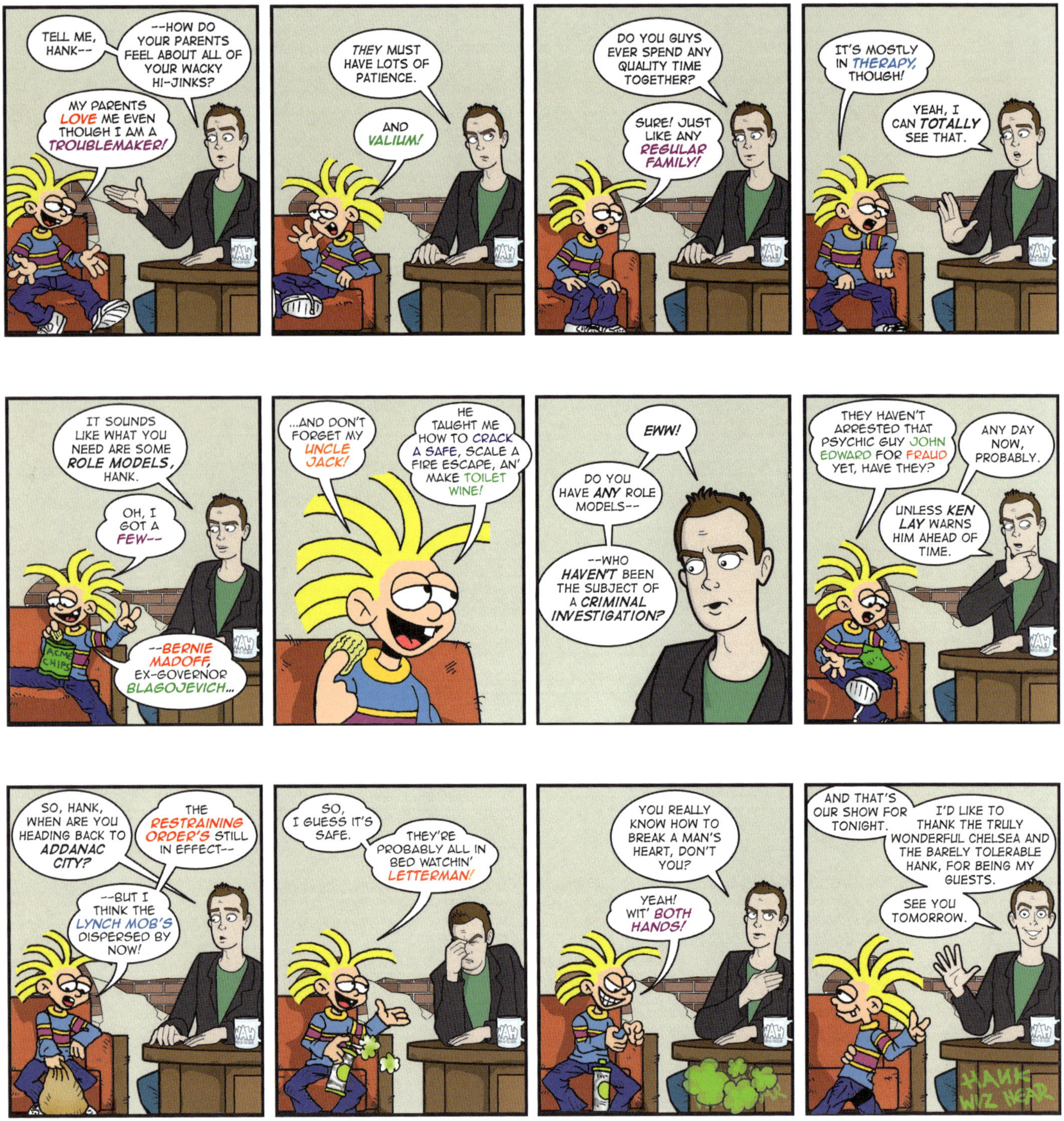
TELL ME, HANK--
--HOW DO YOUR PARENTS FEEL ABOUT ALL OF YOUR WACKY HI-JINKS?
MY PARENTS LOVE ME EVEN THOUGH I AM A TROUBLEMAKER!
THEY MUST HAVE LOTS OF PATIENCE.
AND VALIUM!
DO YOU GUYS EVER SPEND ANY QUALITY TIME TOGETHER?
SURE! JUST LIKE ANY REGULAR FAMILY!
IT'S MOSTLY IN THERAPY, THOUGH!
YEAH, I CAN TOTALLY SEE THAT.
IT SOUNDS LIKE WHAT YOU NEED ARE SOME ROLE MODELS, HANK.
OH, I GOT A FEW--
--BERNIE MADOFF, EX-GOVERNOR BLAGOJEVICH...
ACME CHIPS
...AND DON'T FORGET MY UNCLE JACK!
HE TAUGHT ME HOW TO CRACK A SAFE, SCALE A FIRE ESCAPE, AN' MAKE TOILET WINE!
EWW!
DO YOU HAVE ANY ROLE MODELS--
--WHO HAVEN'T BEEN THE SUBJECT OF A CRIMINAL INVESTIGATION?
THEY HAVEN'T ARRESTED THAT PSYCHIC GUY JOHN EDWARD FOR FRAUD YET, HAVE THEY?
ANY DAY NOW, PROBABLY.
UNLESS KEN LAY WARNS HIM AHEAD OF TIME.
SO, HANK, WHEN ARE YOU HEADING BACK TO ADDANAC CITY?
THE RESTRAINING ORDER'S STILL IN EFFECT--
--BUT I THINK THE LYNCH MOB'S DISPERSED BY NOW!
SO, I GUESS IT'S SAFE.
THEY'RE PROBABLY ALL IN BED WATCHIN' LETTERMAN!
YOU REALLY KNOW HOW TO BREAK A MAN'S HEART, DON'T YOU?
YEAH! WIT' BOTH HANDS!
AND THAT'S OUR SHOW FOR TONIGHT.
I'D LIKE TO THANK THE TRULY WONDERFUL CHELSEA AND THE BARELY TOLERABLE HANK, FOR BEING MY GUESTS.
SEE YOU TOMORROW.
HANK WUZ HEAR

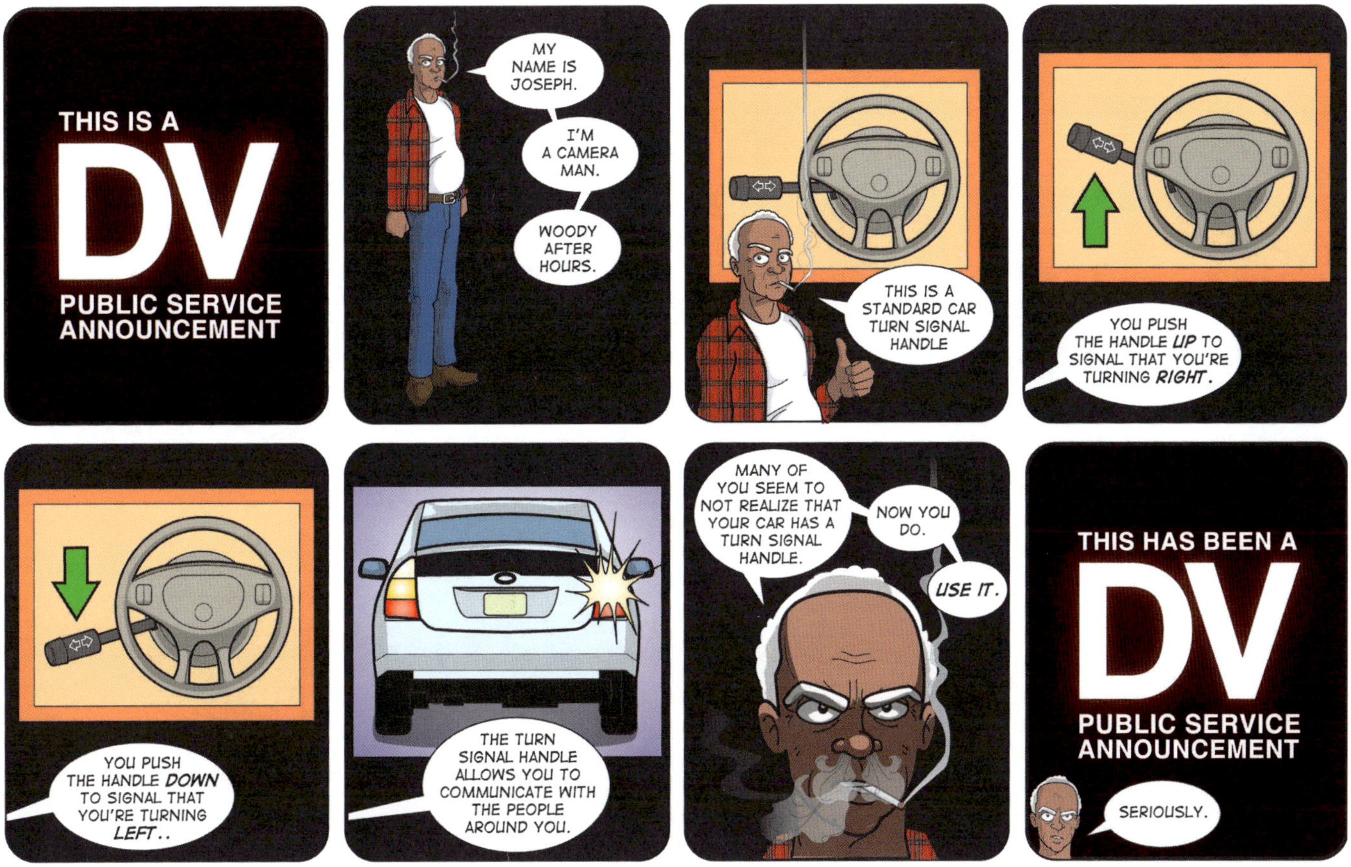
THIS IS A
DV
PUBLIC SERVICE ANNOUNCEMENT
MY NAME IS JOSEPH.
I'M A CAMERA MAN.
WOODY AFTER HOURS.
THIS IS A STANDARD CAR TURN SIGNAL HANDLE
YOU PUSH THE HANDLE *UP* TO SIGNAL THAT YOU'RE TURNING *RIGHT*.
YOU PUSH THE HANDLE *DOWN* TO SIGNAL THAT YOU'RE TURNING *LEFT*..
THE TURN SIGNAL HANDLE ALLOWS YOU TO COMMUNICATE WITH THE PEOPLE AROUND YOU.
MANY OF YOU SEEM TO NOT REALIZE THAT YOUR CAR HAS A TURN SIGNAL HANDLE.
NOW YOU DO.
USE IT.
THIS HAS BEEN A
DV
PUBLIC SERVICE ANNOUNCEMENT
SERIOUSLY.

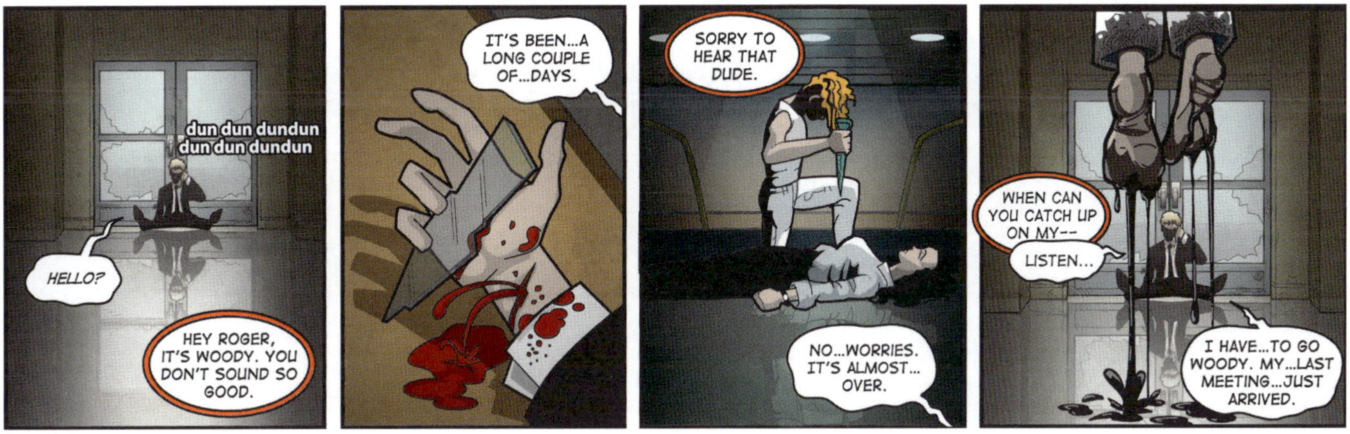
dun dun dundun
dun dun dundun
HELLO?
HEY ROGER, IT'S WOODY. YOU DON'T SOUND SO GOOD.
IT'S BEEN...A LONG COUPLE OF...DAYS.
SORRY TO HEAR THAT DUDE.
NO...WORRIES. IT'S ALMOST... OVER.
WHEN CAN YOU CATCH UP ON MY--
LISTEN...
I HAVE...TO GO WOODY. MY...LAST MEETING...JUST ARRIVED.

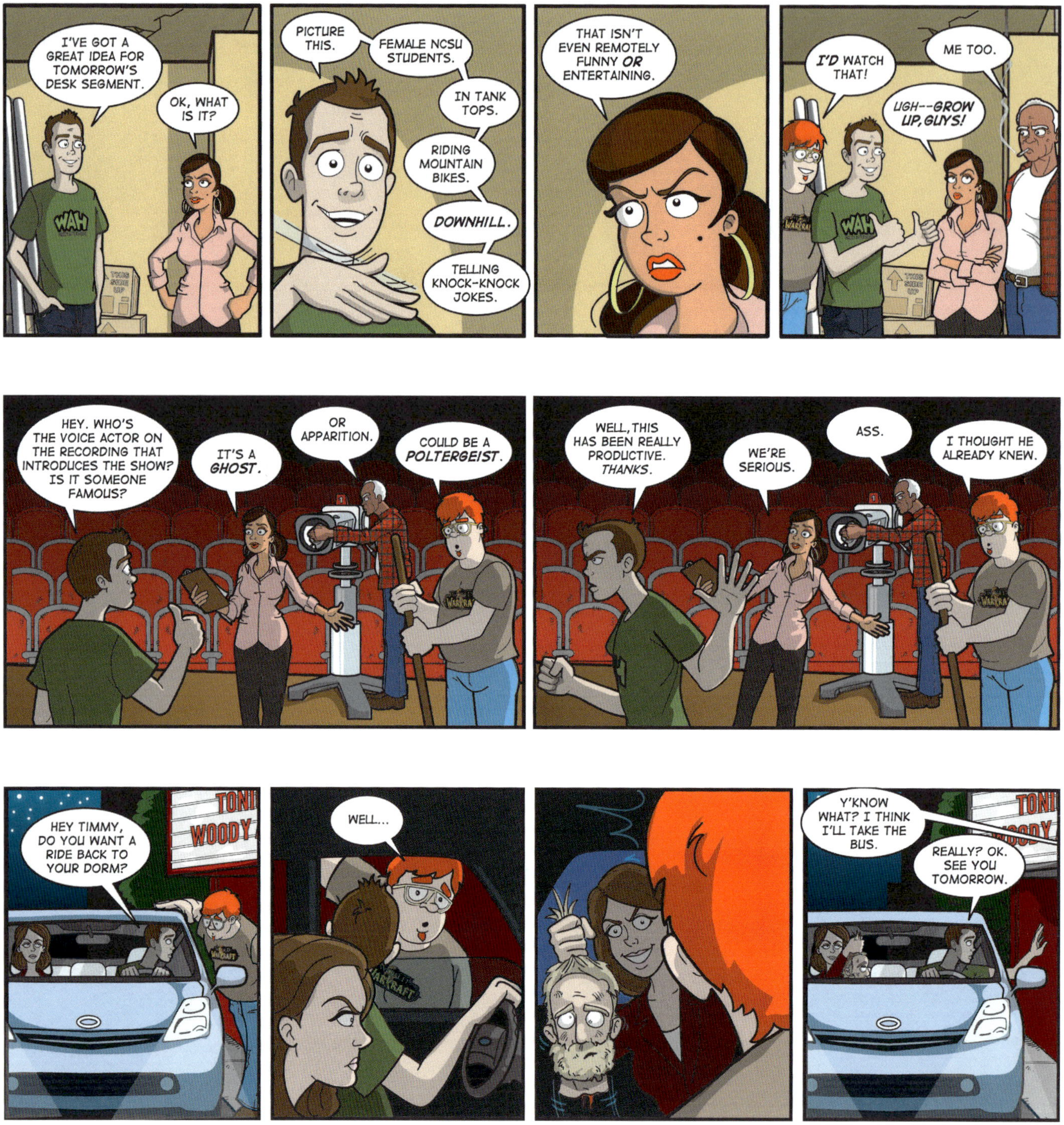

I'VE GOT A GREAT IDEA FOR TOMORROW'S DESK SEGMENT.
OK, WHAT IS IT?
PICTURE THIS.
FEMALE NCSU STUDENTS.
IN TANK TOPS.
RIDING MOUNTAIN BIKES.
DOWNHILL.
TELLING KNOCK-KNOCK JOKES.
THAT ISN'T EVEN REMOTELY FUNNY OR ENTERTAINING.
I'D WATCH THAT!
ME TOO.
UGH--GROW UP, GUYS!
WAH
HEY. WHO'S THE VOICE ACTOR ON THE RECORDING THAT INTRODUCES THE SHOW? IS IT SOMEONE FAMOUS?
IT'S A GHOST.
OR APPARITION.
COULD BE A POLTERGEIST.
WELL, THIS HAS BEEN REALLY PRODUCTIVE. THANKS.
WE'RE SERIOUS.
ASS.
I THOUGHT HE ALREADY KNEW.
HEY TIMMY, DO YOU WANT A RIDE BACK TO YOUR DORM?
WELL...
Y'KNOW WHAT? I THINK I'LL TAKE THE BUS.
REALLY? OK. SEE YOU TOMORROW.

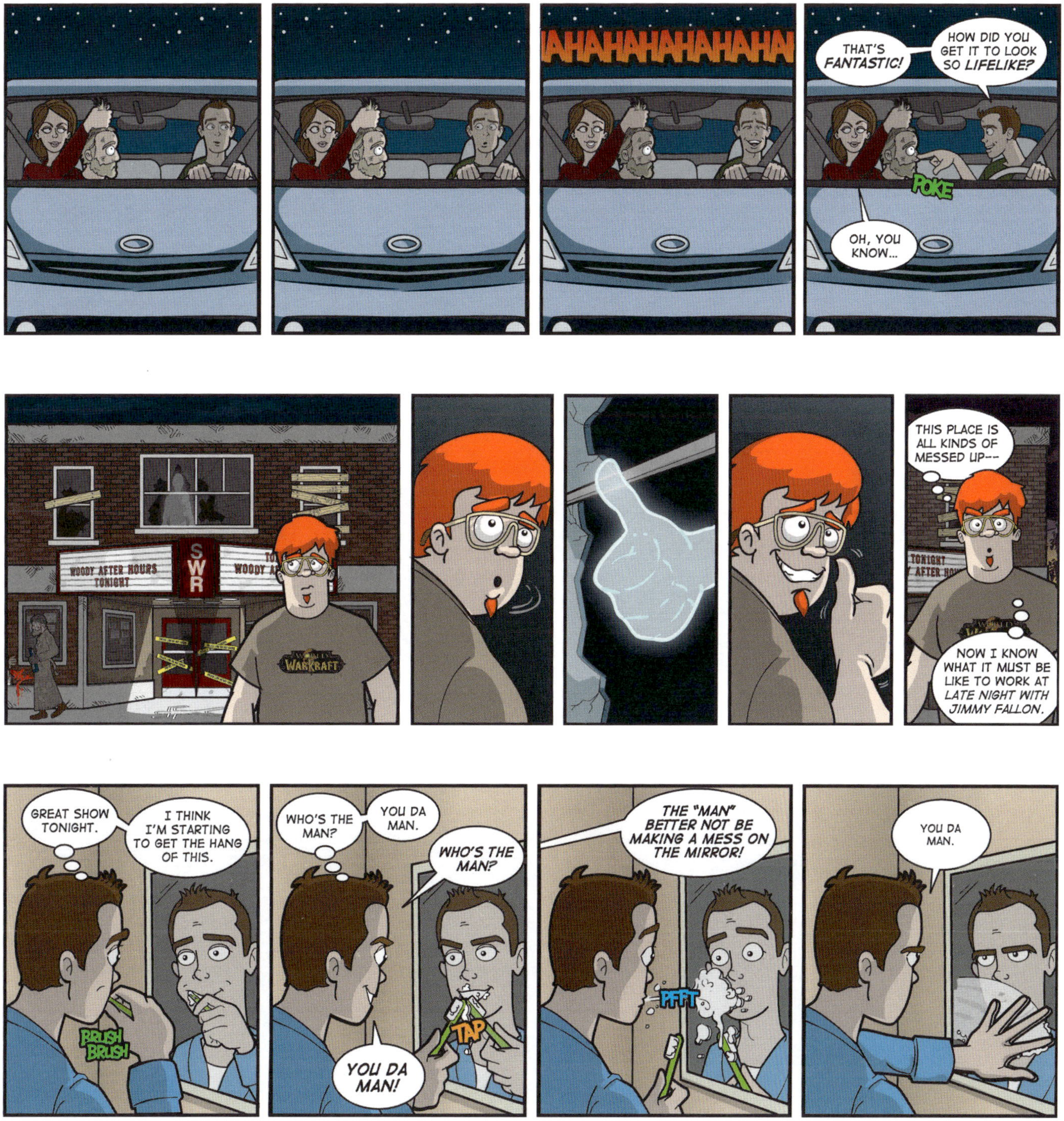
AHAHAHAHAHAHAHAH
THAT'S *FANTASTIC!*
HOW DID YOU GET IT TO LOOK SO *LIFELIKE?*
POKE
OH, YOU KNOW...
WOODY AFTER HOURS TONIGHT
SWR
WORLD OF WARCRAFT
THIS PLACE IS ALL KINDS OF MESSED UP--
NOW I KNOW WHAT IT MUST BE LIKE TO WORK AT *LATE NIGHT WITH JIMMY FALLON.*
GREAT SHOW TONIGHT.
I THINK I'M STARTING TO GET THE HANG OF THIS.
BRUSH BRUSH
WHO'S THE MAN?
YOU DA MAN.
WHO'S THE MAN?
YOU DA MAN!
TAP
THE "MAN" BETTER NOT BE MAKING A MESS ON THE MIRROR!
PFFT
YOU DA MAN.

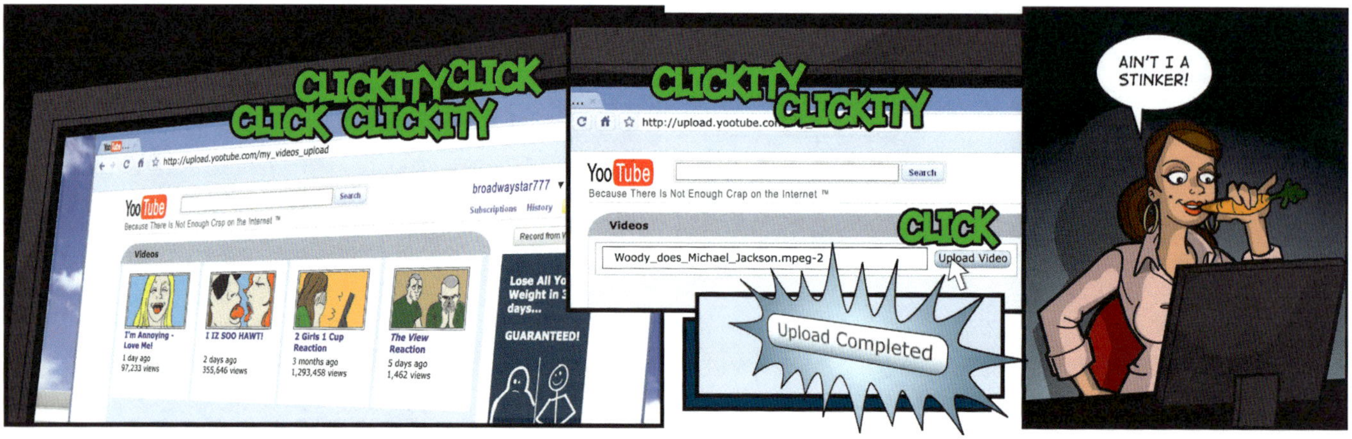
CLICKITY CLICK
CLICK CLICKITY
http://upload.yootube.com/my_videos_upload
broadwaystar777
YooTube
Because There Is Not Enough Crap on the Internet ™
Videos
I'm Annoying - Love Me!
I IZ SOO HAWT!
2 Girls 1 Cup Reaction
The View Reaction
GUARANTEED!
CLICKITY CLICKITY
YooTube
Because There Is Not Enough Crap on the Internet ™
Videos
CLICK
Woody_does_Michael_Jackson.mpeg-2
Upload Video
Upload Completed
AIN'T I A STINKER!

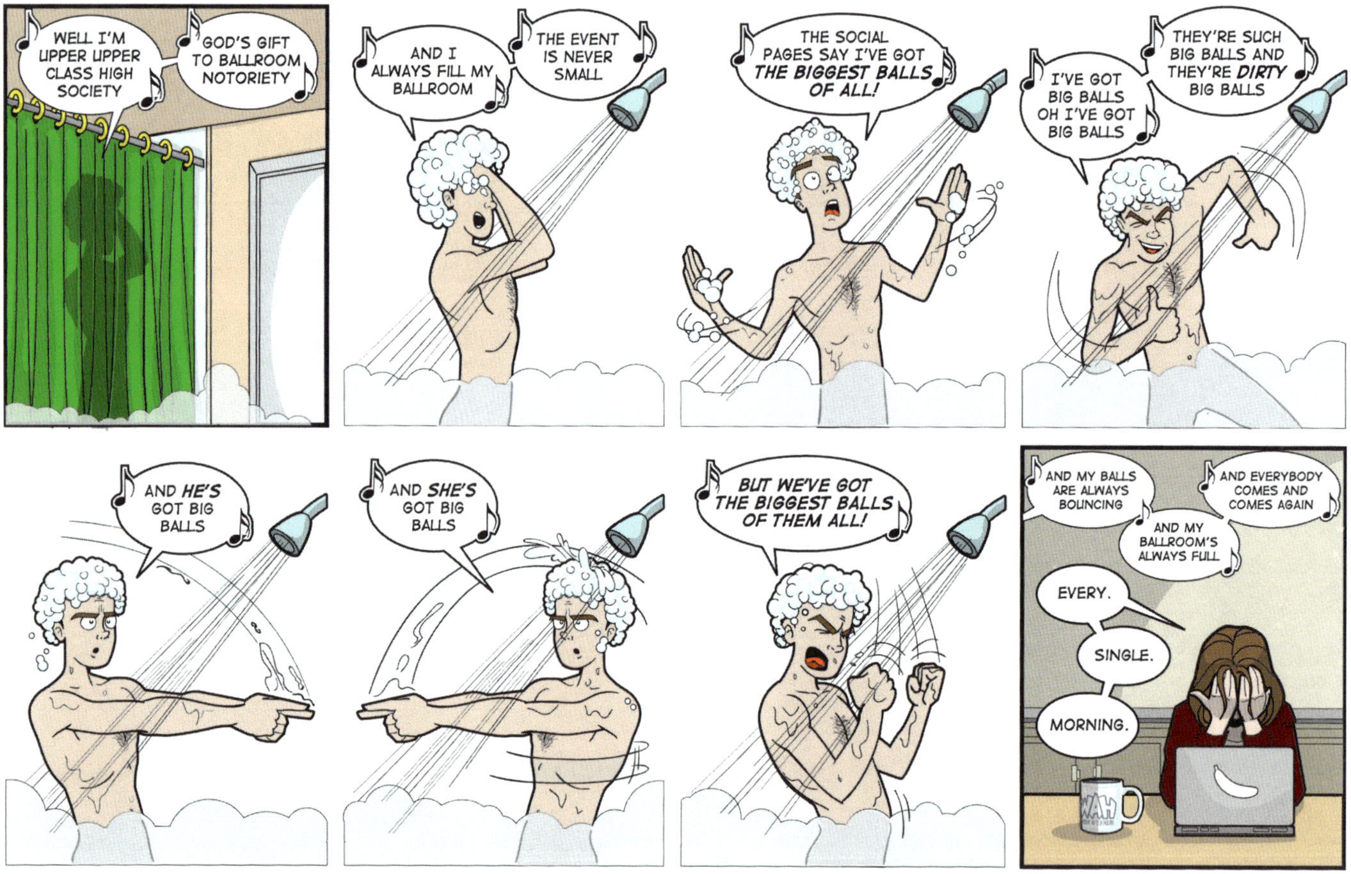
WELL I'M UPPER UPPER CLASS HIGH SOCIETY
GOD'S GIFT TO BALLROOM NOTORIETY
AND I ALWAYS FILL MY BALLROOM
THE EVENT IS NEVER SMALL
THE SOCIAL PAGES SAY I'VE GOT THE BIGGEST BALLS OF ALL!
I'VE GOT BIG BALLS OH I'VE GOT BIG BALLS
THEY'RE SUCH BIG BALLS AND THEY'RE DIRTY BIG BALLS
AND HE'S GOT BIG BALLS
AND SHE'S GOT BIG BALLS
BUT WE'VE GOT THE BIGGEST BALLS OF THEM ALL!
AND MY BALLS ARE ALWAYS BOUNCING
AND EVERYBODY COMES AND COMES AGAIN
AND MY BALLROOM'S ALWAYS FULL
EVERY.
SINGLE.
MORNING.
WAH

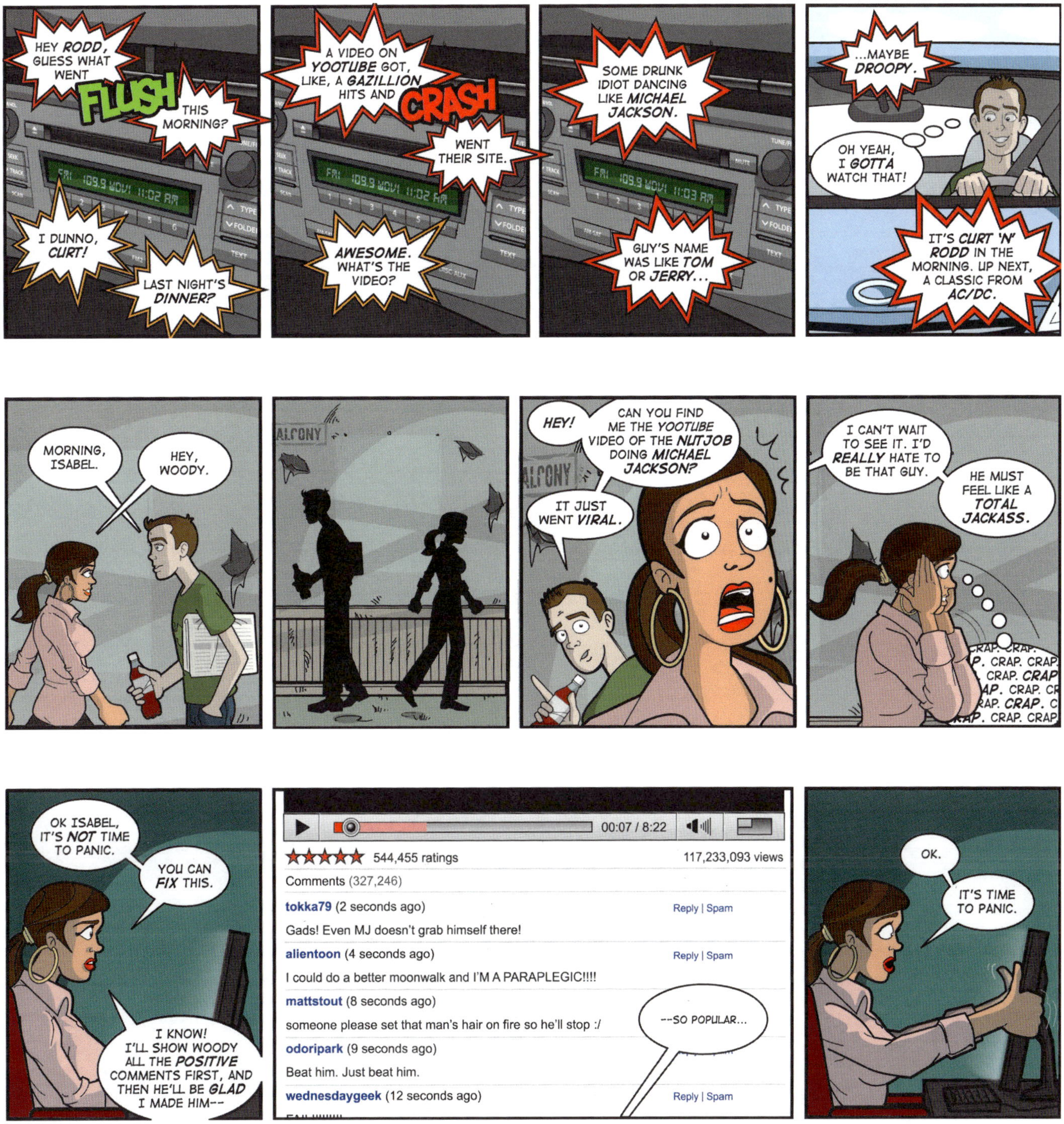
HEY RODD, GUESS WHAT WENT
FLUSH
THIS MORNING?
I DUNNO, CURT!
LAST NIGHT'S DINNER?
FM1 109.9 WDVI 11:02 AM
A VIDEO ON YOOTUBE GOT, LIKE, A GAZILLION HITS AND
CRASH
WENT THEIR SITE.
AWESOME. WHAT'S THE VIDEO?
SOME DRUNK IDIOT DANCING LIKE MICHAEL JACKSON.
FM1 109.9 WDVI 11:03 AM
GUY'S NAME WAS LIKE TOM OR JERRY...
...MAYBE DROOPY.
OH YEAH, I GOTTA WATCH THAT!
IT'S CURT 'N' RODD IN THE MORNING. UP NEXT, A CLASSIC FROM AC/DC.
MORNING, ISABEL.
HEY, WOODY.
HEY!
CAN YOU FIND ME THE YOOTUBE VIDEO OF THE NUTJOB DOING MICHAEL JACKSON?
IT JUST WENT VIRAL.
I CAN'T WAIT TO SEE IT. I'D REALLY HATE TO BE THAT GUY.
HE MUST FEEL LIKE A TOTAL JACKASS.
CRAP. CRAP. CRAP. CRAP.
OK ISABEL, IT'S NOT TIME TO PANIC.
YOU CAN FIX THIS.
I KNOW! I'LL SHOW WOODY ALL THE POSITIVE COMMENTS FIRST, AND THEN HE'LL BE GLAD I MADE HIM--
00:07 / 8:22
544,455 ratings
117,233,093 views
Comments (327,246)
tokka79 (2 seconds ago)
Reply | Spam
Gads! Even MJ doesn't grab himself there!
alientoon (4 seconds ago)
Reply | Spam
I could do a better moonwalk and I'M A PARAPLEGIC!!!!
mattstout (8 seconds ago)
someone please set that man's hair on fire so he'll stop :/
--SO POPULAR...
odoripark (9 seconds ago)
Beat him. Just beat him.
wednesdaygeek (12 seconds ago)
Reply | Spam
OK.
IT'S TIME TO PANIC.

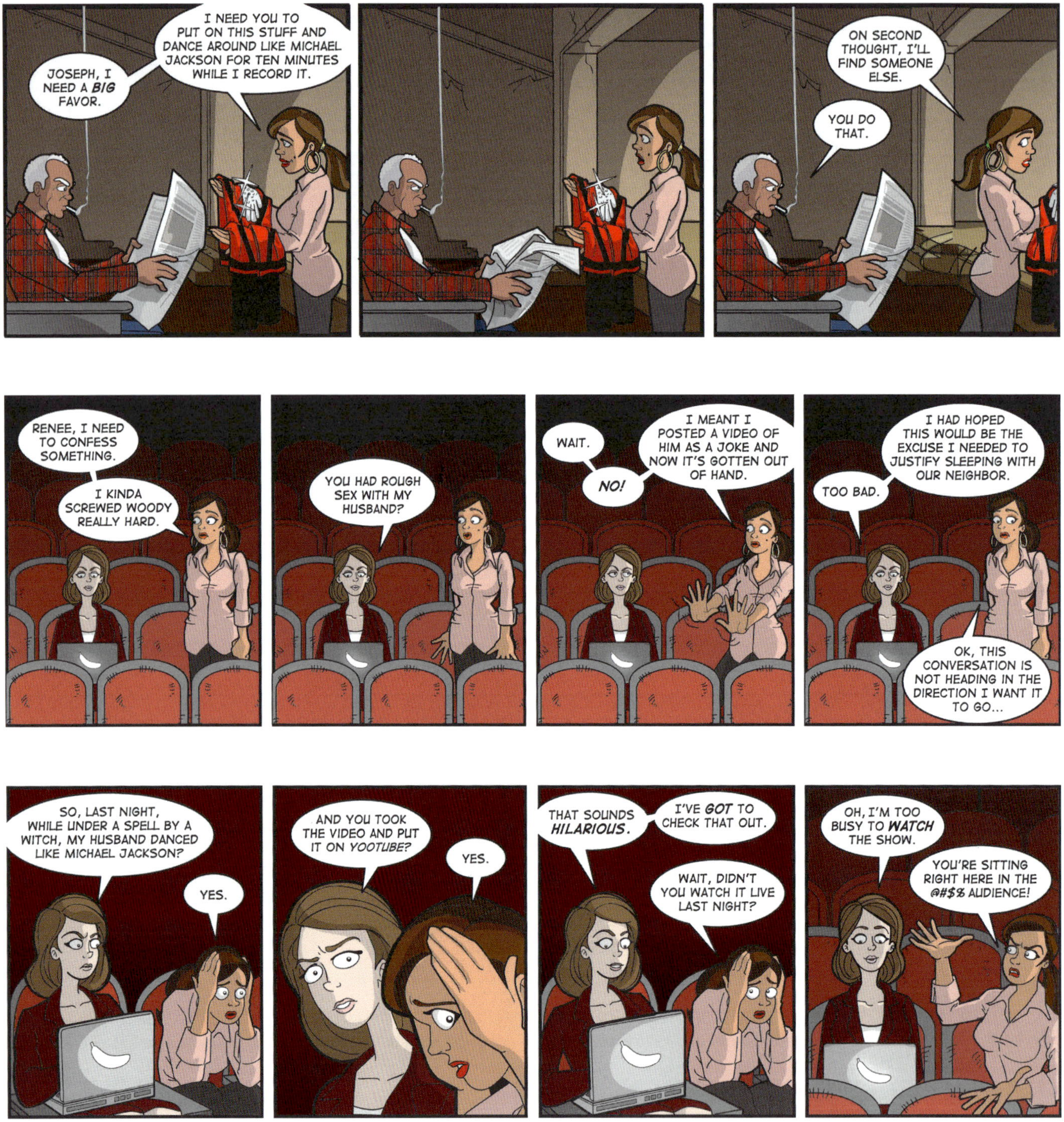
JOSEPH, I NEED A **BIG** FAVOR.
I NEED YOU TO PUT ON THIS STUFF AND DANCE AROUND LIKE MICHAEL JACKSON FOR TEN MINUTES WHILE I RECORD IT.
ON SECOND THOUGHT, I'LL FIND SOMEONE ELSE.
YOU DO THAT.
RENEE, I NEED TO CONFESS SOMETHING.
I KINDA SCREWED WOODY REALLY HARD.
YOU HAD ROUGH SEX WITH MY HUSBAND?
WAIT.
NO!
I MEANT I POSTED A VIDEO OF HIM AS A JOKE AND NOW IT'S GOTTEN OUT OF HAND.
I HAD HOPED THIS WOULD BE THE EXCUSE I NEEDED TO JUSTIFY SLEEPING WITH OUR NEIGHBOR.
TOO BAD.
OK, THIS CONVERSATION IS NOT HEADING IN THE DIRECTION I WANT IT TO GO...
SO, LAST NIGHT, WHILE UNDER A SPELL BY A WITCH, MY HUSBAND DANCED LIKE MICHAEL JACKSON?
YES.
AND YOU TOOK THE VIDEO AND PUT IT ON *YOUTUBE?*
YES.
THAT SOUNDS ***HILARIOUS.***
I'VE ***GOT*** TO CHECK THAT OUT.
WAIT, DIDN'T YOU WATCH IT LIVE LAST NIGHT?
OH, I'M TOO BUSY TO ***WATCH*** THE SHOW.
YOU'RE SITTING RIGHT HERE IN THE ***@#$%*** AUDIENCE!

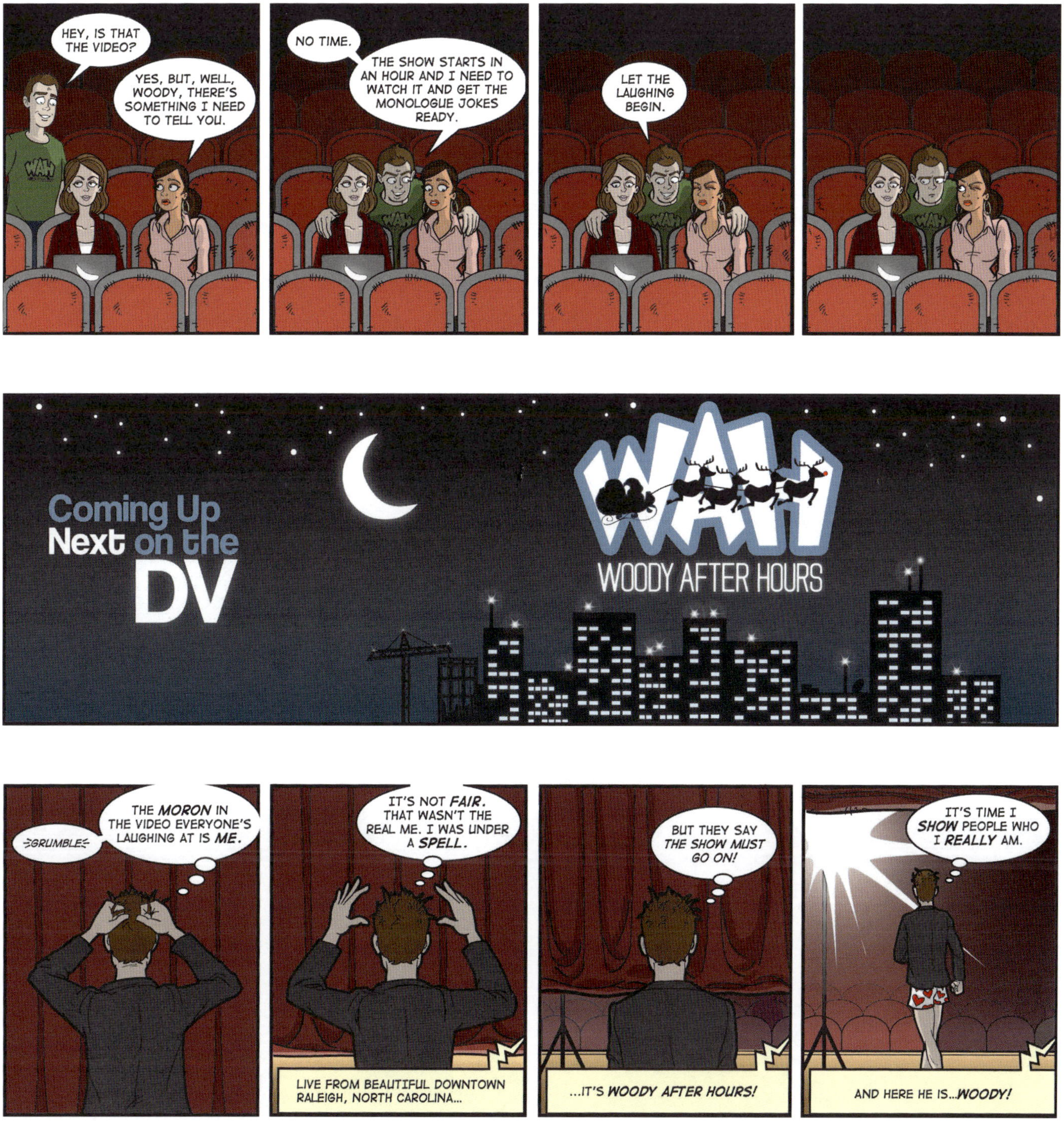
HEY, IS THAT THE VIDEO?
YES, BUT, WELL, WOODY, THERE'S SOMETHING I NEED TO TELL YOU.
NO TIME.
THE SHOW STARTS IN AN HOUR AND I NEED TO WATCH IT AND GET THE MONOLOGUE JOKES READY.
LET THE LAUGHING BEGIN.
Coming Up Next on the DV
WAH
WOODY AFTER HOURS
GRUMBLE
THE MORON IN THE VIDEO EVERYONE'S LAUGHING AT IS ME.
IT'S NOT FAIR. THAT WASN'T THE REAL ME. I WAS UNDER A SPELL.
LIVE FROM BEAUTIFUL DOWNTOWN RALEIGH, NORTH CAROLINA...
BUT THEY SAY THE SHOW MUST GO ON!
...IT'S WOODY AFTER HOURS!
IT'S TIME I SHOW PEOPLE WHO I REALLY AM.
AND HERE HE IS...WOODY!

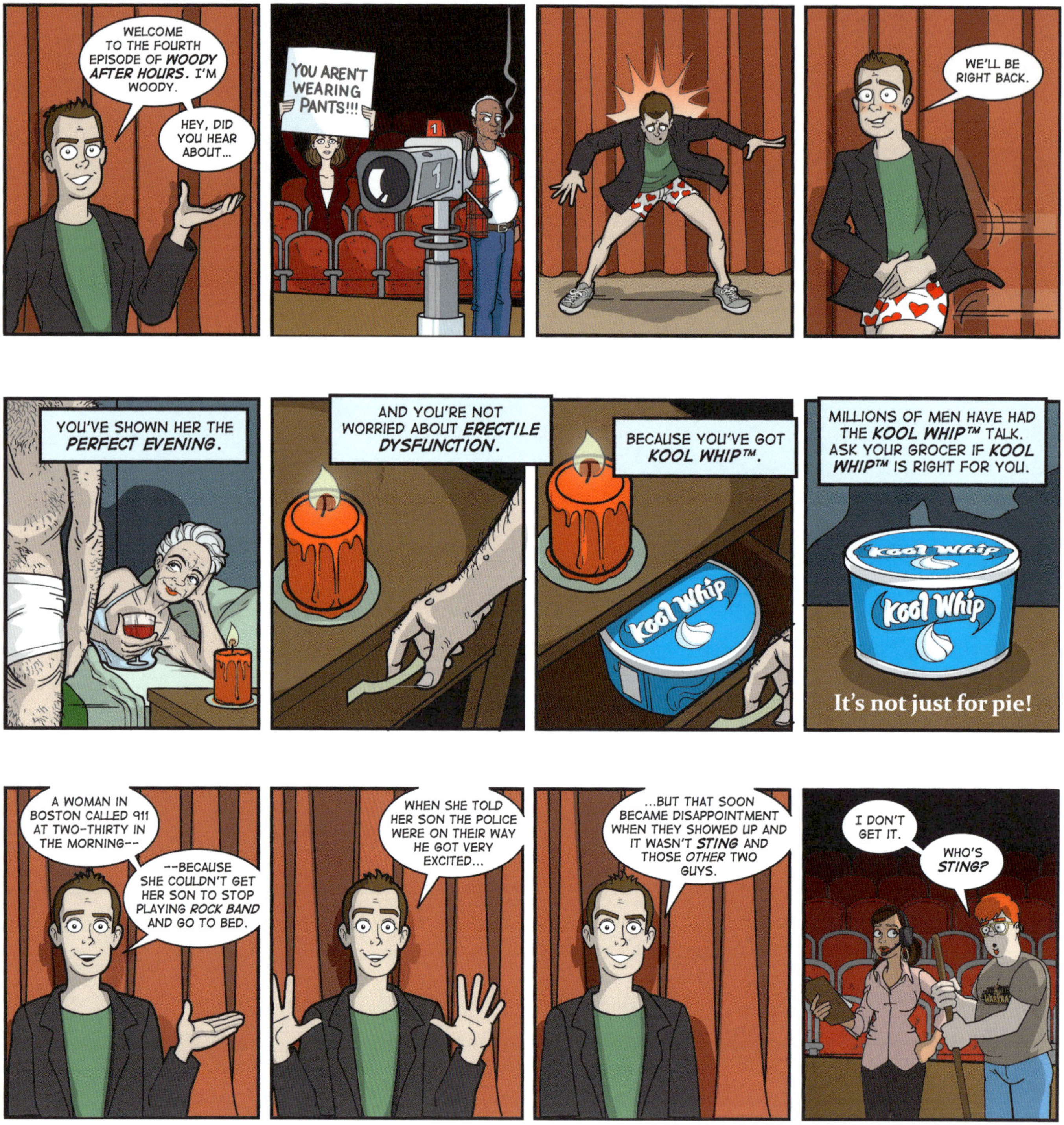

WELCOME TO THE FOURTH EPISODE OF *WOODY AFTER HOURS*. I'M WOODY.
HEY, DID YOU HEAR ABOUT...
YOU AREN'T WEARING PANTS!!!
1
WE'LL BE RIGHT BACK.
YOU'VE SHOWN HER THE *PERFECT EVENING*.
AND YOU'RE NOT WORRIED ABOUT *ERECTILE DYSFUNCTION*.
BECAUSE YOU'VE GOT *KOOL WHIP™*.
Kool Whip
MILLIONS OF MEN HAVE HAD THE *KOOL WHIP™* TALK. ASK YOUR GROCER IF *KOOL WHIP™* IS RIGHT FOR YOU.
Kool Whip
It's not just for pie!
A WOMAN IN BOSTON CALLED 911 AT TWO-THIRTY IN THE MORNING--
--BECAUSE SHE COULDN'T GET HER SON TO STOP PLAYING *ROCK BAND* AND GO TO BED.
WHEN SHE TOLD HER SON THE POLICE WERE ON THEIR WAY HE GOT VERY EXCITED...
...BUT THAT SOON BECAME DISAPPOINTMENT WHEN THEY SHOWED UP AND IT WASN'T *STING* AND THOSE *OTHER* TWO GUYS.
I DON'T GET IT.
WHO'S *STING?*

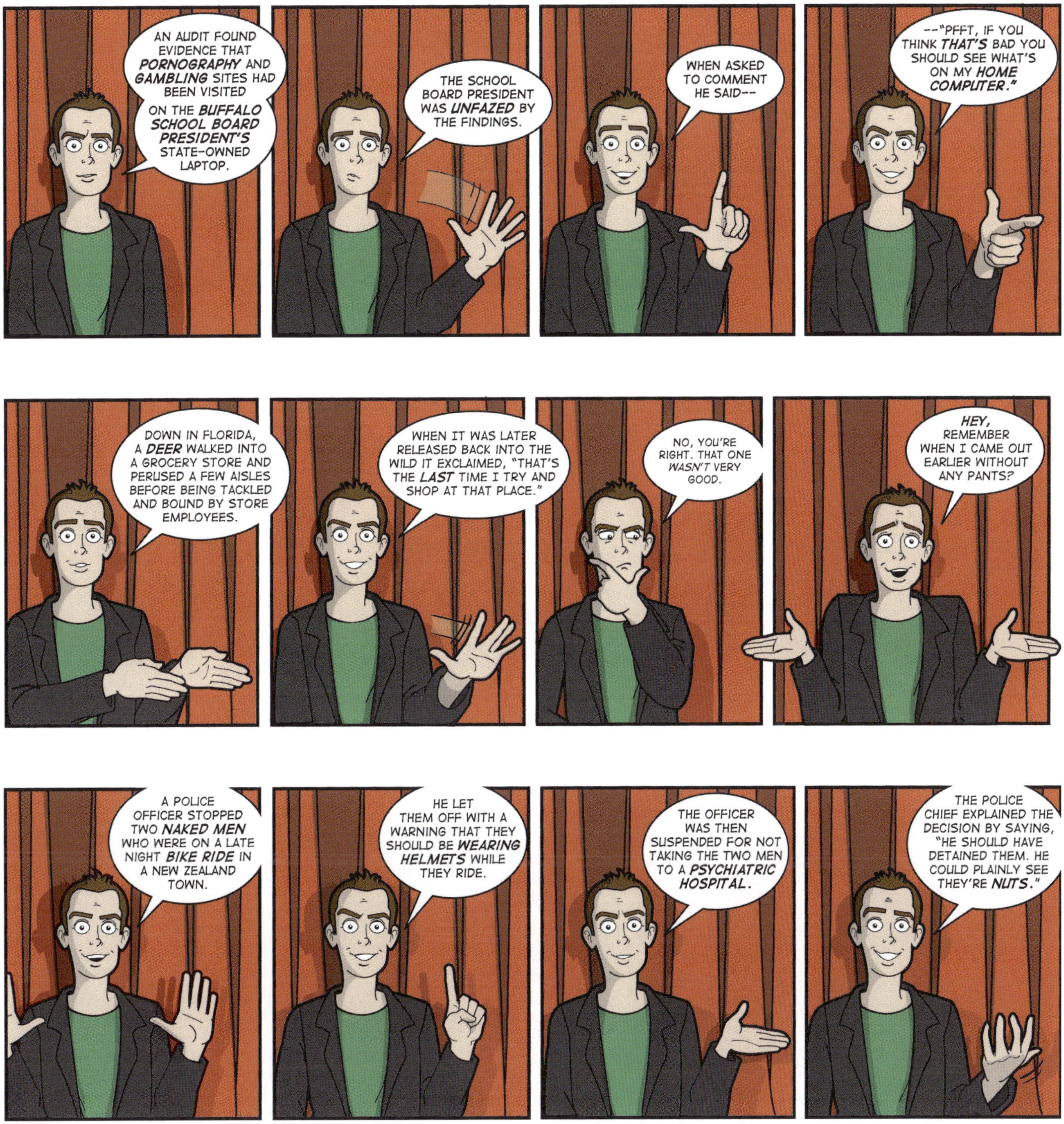
AN AUDIT FOUND EVIDENCE THAT PORNOGRAPHY AND GAMBLING SITES HAD BEEN VISITED
ON THE BUFFALO SCHOOL BOARD PRESIDENT'S STATE-OWNED LAPTOP.
THE SCHOOL BOARD PRESIDENT WAS UNFAZED BY THE FINDINGS.
WHEN ASKED TO COMMENT HE SAID--
--"PFFT, IF YOU THINK THAT'S BAD YOU SHOULD SEE WHAT'S ON MY HOME COMPUTER."
DOWN IN FLORIDA, A DEER WALKED INTO A GROCERY STORE AND PERUSED A FEW AISLES BEFORE BEING TACKLED AND BOUND BY STORE EMPLOYEES.
WHEN IT WAS LATER RELEASED BACK INTO THE WILD IT EXCLAIMED, "THAT'S THE LAST TIME I TRY AND SHOP AT THAT PLACE."
NO, YOU'RE RIGHT. THAT ONE WASN'T VERY GOOD.
HEY, REMEMBER WHEN I CAME OUT EARLIER WITHOUT ANY PANTS?
A POLICE OFFICER STOPPED TWO NAKED MEN WHO WERE ON A LATE NIGHT BIKE RIDE IN A NEW ZEALAND TOWN.
HE LET THEM OFF WITH A WARNING THAT THEY SHOULD BE WEARING HELMETS WHILE THEY RIDE.
THE OFFICER WAS THEN SUSPENDED FOR NOT TAKING THE TWO MEN TO A PSYCHIATRIC HOSPITAL.
THE POLICE CHIEF EXPLAINED THE DECISION BY SAYING, "HE SHOULD HAVE DETAINED THEM. HE COULD PLAINLY SEE THEY'RE NUTS."

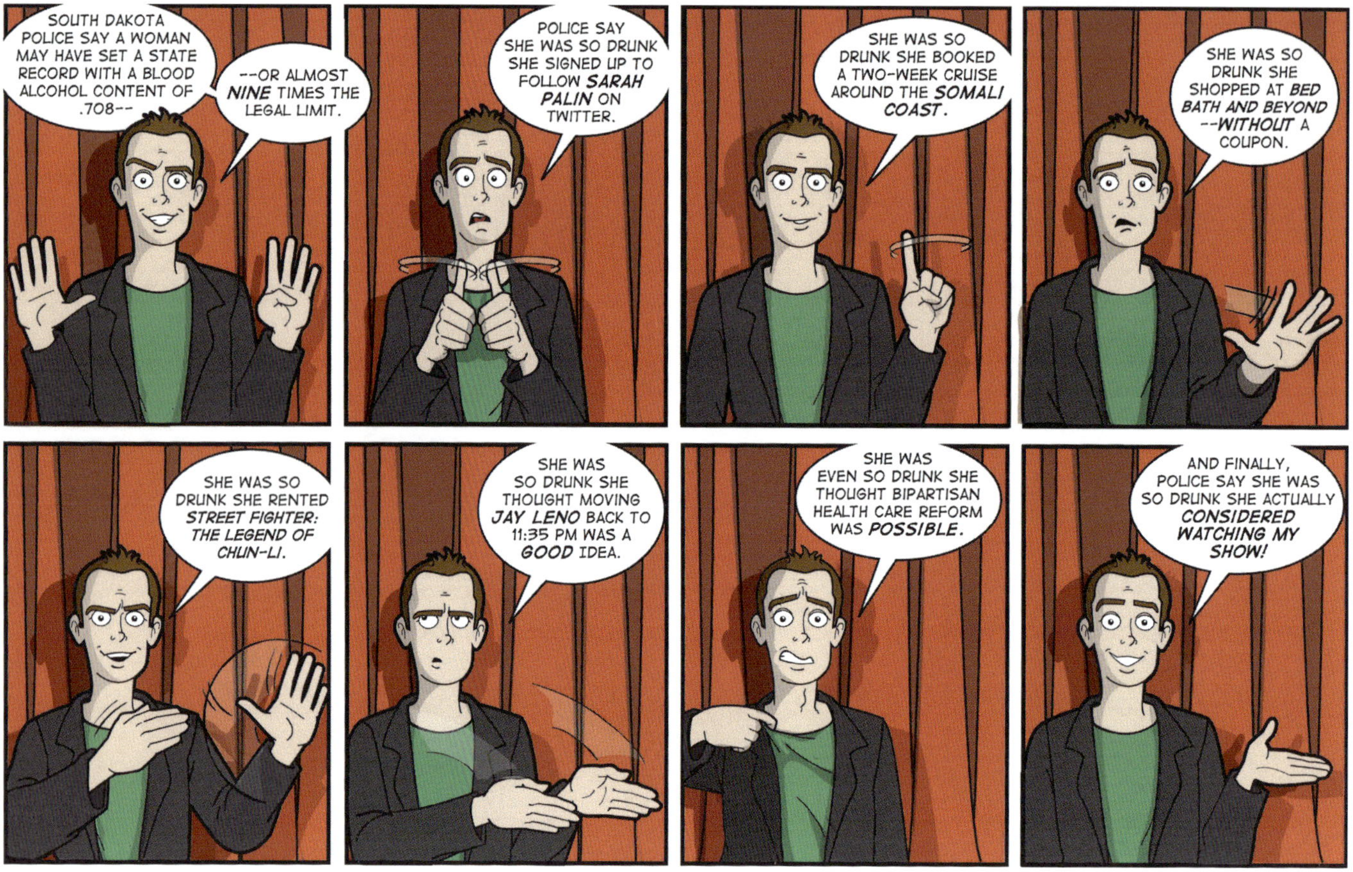
SOUTH DAKOTA POLICE SAY A WOMAN MAY HAVE SET A STATE RECORD WITH A BLOOD ALCOHOL CONTENT OF .708--
--OR ALMOST *NINE* TIMES THE LEGAL LIMIT.
POLICE SAY SHE WAS SO DRUNK SHE SIGNED UP TO FOLLOW ***SARAH PALIN*** ON TWITTER.
SHE WAS SO DRUNK SHE BOOKED A TWO-WEEK CRUISE AROUND THE ***SOMALI COAST***.
SHE WAS SO DRUNK SHE SHOPPED AT *BED BATH AND BEYOND* --*WITHOUT* A COUPON.
SHE WAS SO DRUNK SHE RENTED *STREET FIGHTER: THE LEGEND OF CHUN-LI*.
SHE WAS SO DRUNK SHE THOUGHT MOVING *JAY LENO* BACK TO 11:35 PM WAS A *GOOD* IDEA.
SHE WAS EVEN SO DRUNK SHE THOUGHT BIPARTISAN HEALTH CARE REFORM WAS *POSSIBLE*.
AND FINALLY, POLICE SAY SHE WAS SO DRUNK SHE ACTUALLY ***CONSIDERED WATCHING MY SHOW!***

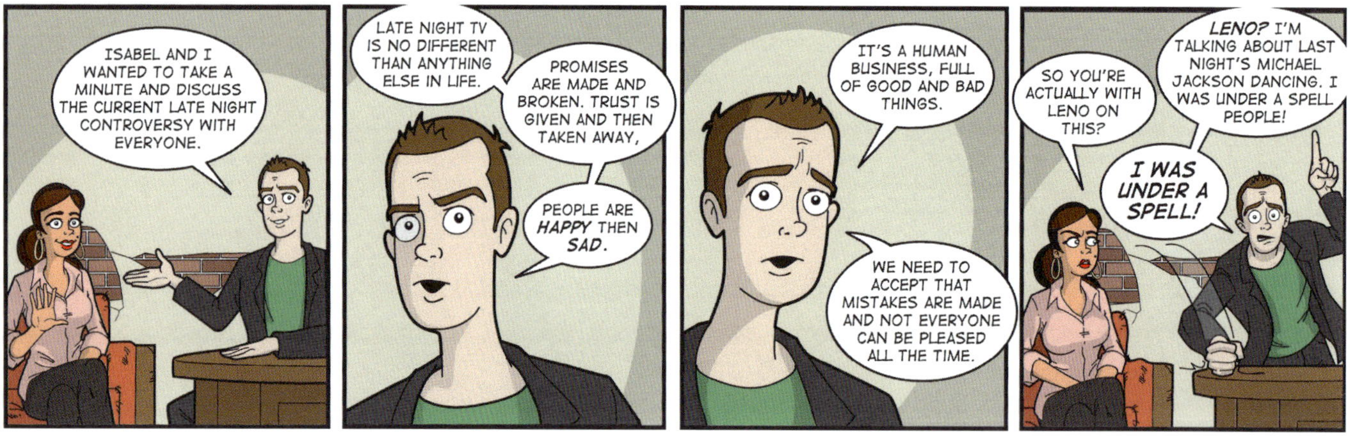
ISABEL AND I WANTED TO TAKE A MINUTE AND DISCUSS THE CURRENT LATE NIGHT CONTROVERSY WITH EVERYONE.
LATE NIGHT TV IS NO DIFFERENT THAN ANYTHING ELSE IN LIFE.
PROMISES ARE MADE AND BROKEN. TRUST IS GIVEN AND THEN TAKEN AWAY,
PEOPLE ARE *HAPPY* THEN *SAD*.
IT'S A HUMAN BUSINESS, FULL OF GOOD AND BAD THINGS.
WE NEED TO ACCEPT THAT MISTAKES ARE MADE AND NOT EVERYONE CAN BE PLEASED ALL THE TIME.
SO YOU'RE ACTUALLY WITH LENO ON THIS?
LENO? I'M TALKING ABOUT LAST NIGHT'S MICHAEL JACKSON DANCING. I WAS UNDER A SPELL PEOPLE!
I WAS UNDER A SPELL!

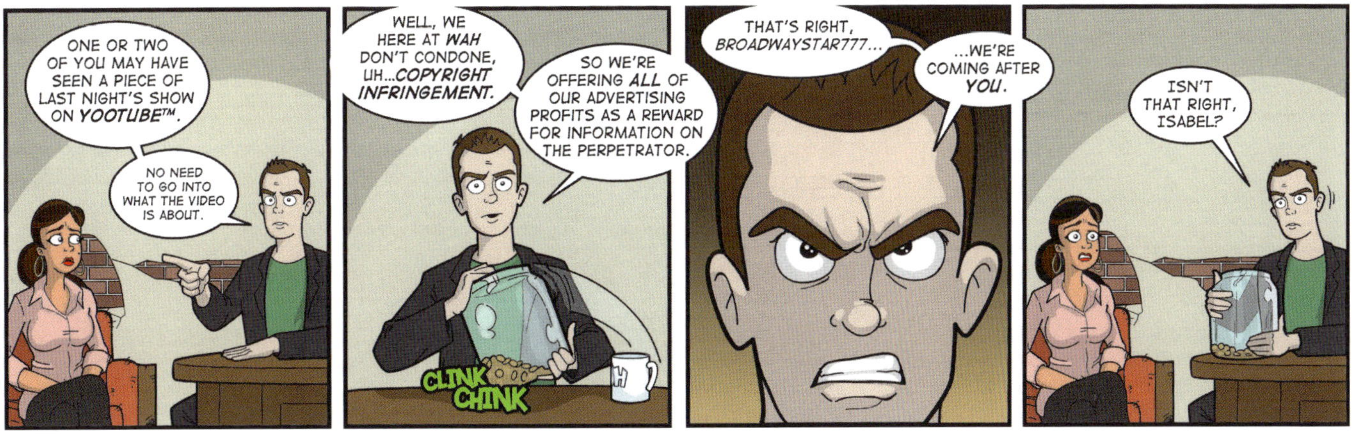
ONE OR TWO OF YOU MAY HAVE SEEN A PIECE OF LAST NIGHT'S SHOW ON YOOTUBE™.
NO NEED TO GO INTO WHAT THE VIDEO IS ABOUT.
WELL, WE HERE AT WAH DON'T CONDONE, UH...COPYRIGHT INFRINGEMENT.
SO WE'RE OFFERING ALL OF OUR ADVERTISING PROFITS AS A REWARD FOR INFORMATION ON THE PERPETRATOR.
CLINK
CHINK
THAT'S RIGHT, BROADWAYSTAR777...
...WE'RE COMING AFTER YOU.
ISN'T THAT RIGHT, ISABEL?

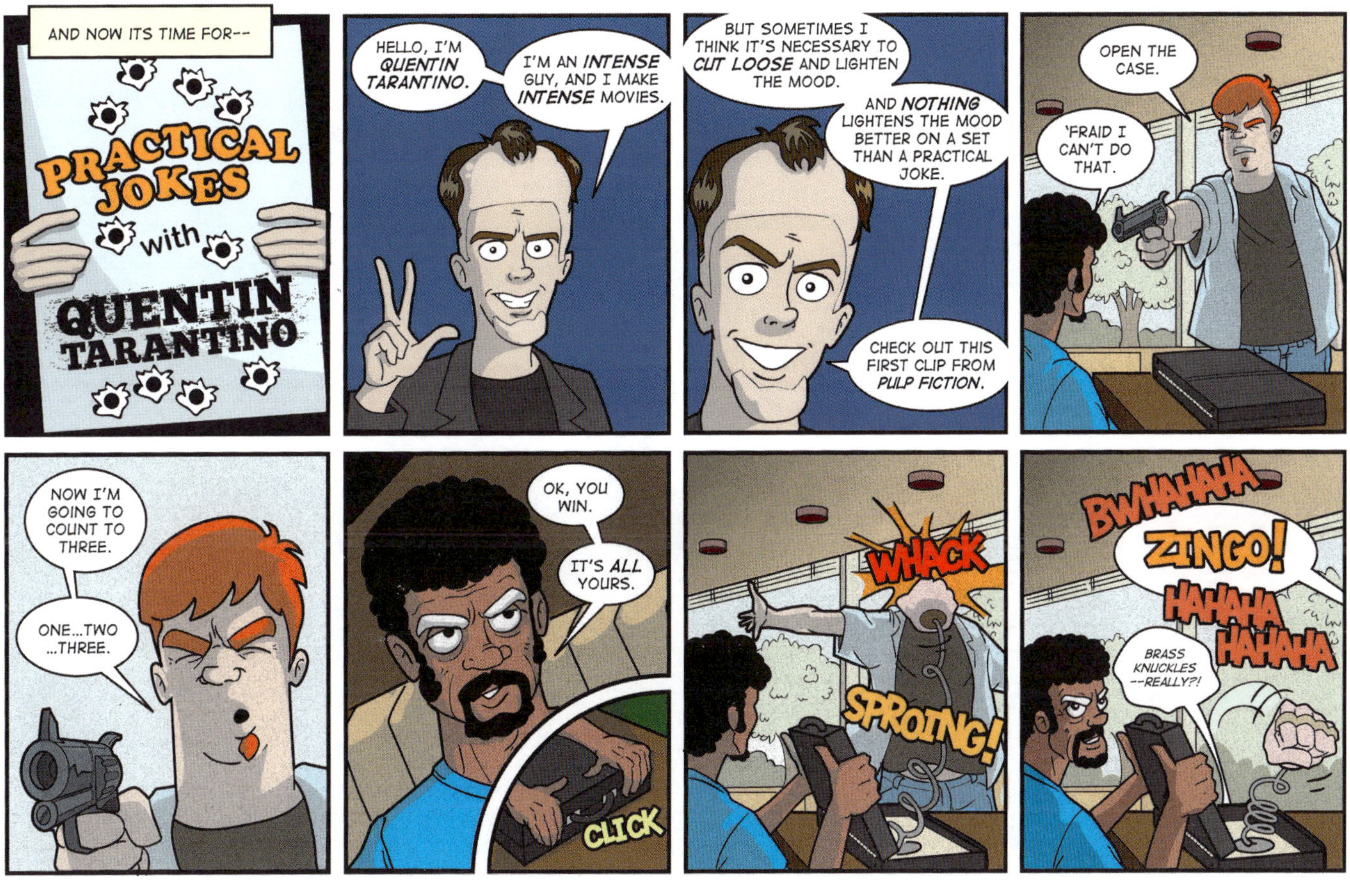
AND NOW ITS TIME FOR--
PRACTICAL JOKES
with
QUENTIN TARANTINO
HELLO, I'M QUENTIN TARANTINO.
I'M AN INTENSE GUY, AND I MAKE INTENSE MOVIES.
BUT SOMETIMES I THINK IT'S NECESSARY TO CUT LOOSE AND LIGHTEN THE MOOD.
AND NOTHING LIGHTENS THE MOOD BETTER ON A SET THAN A PRACTICAL JOKE.
CHECK OUT THIS FIRST CLIP FROM PULP FICTION.
OPEN THE CASE.
'FRAID I CAN'T DO THAT.
NOW I'M GOING TO COUNT TO THREE.
ONE...TWO ...THREE.
OK, YOU WIN.
IT'S ALL YOURS.
CLICK
WHACK
SPROING!
BWHAHAHA
ZINGO!
HAHAHA
HAHAHA
BRASS KNUCKLES --REALLY?!

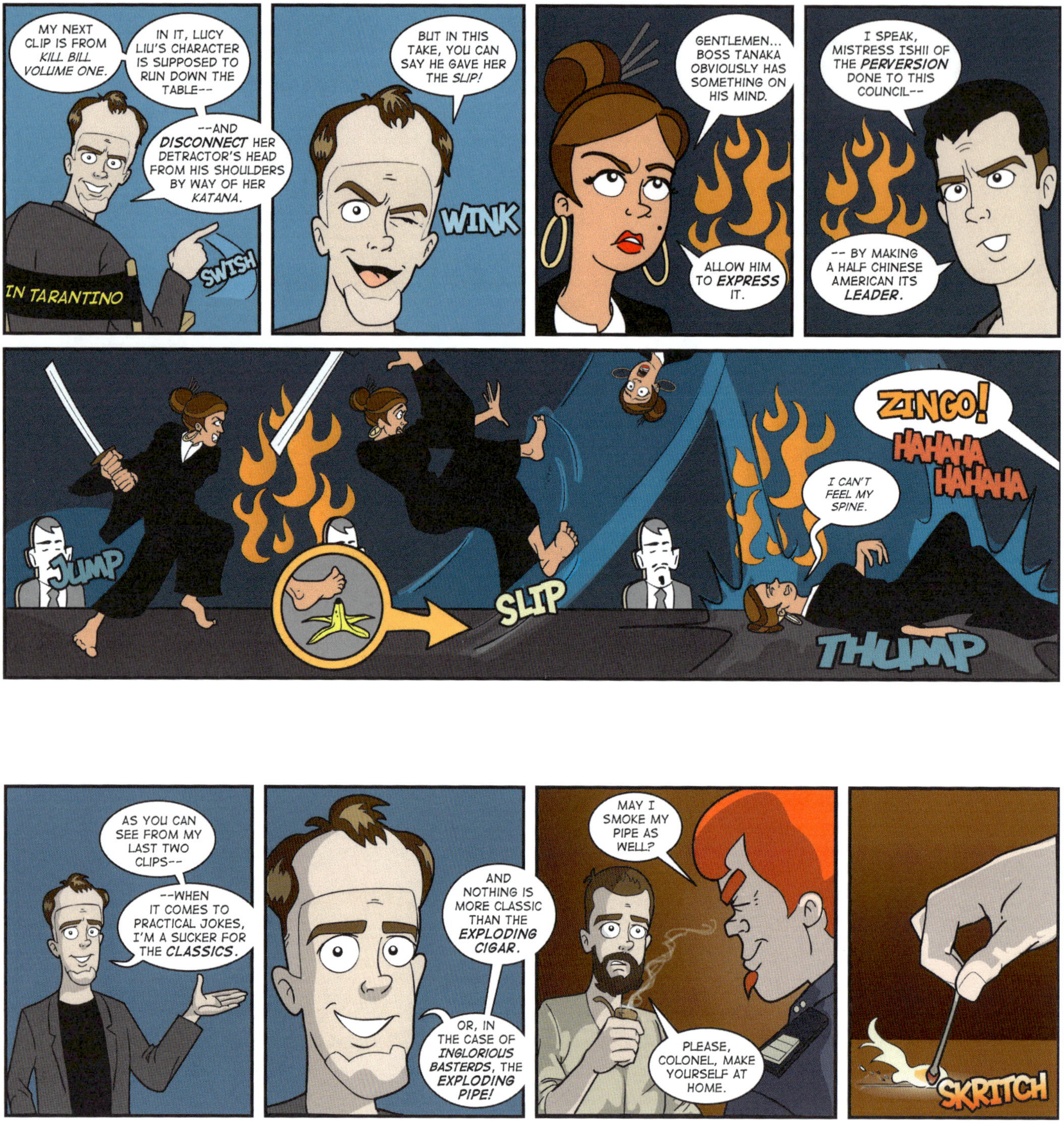

MY NEXT CLIP IS FROM KILL BILL VOLUME ONE.
IN IT, LUCY LIU'S CHARACTER IS SUPPOSED TO RUN DOWN THE TABLE--
--AND DISCONNECT HER DETRACTOR'S HEAD FROM HIS SHOULDERS BY WAY OF HER KATANA.
IN TARANTINO
SWISH
BUT IN THIS TAKE, YOU CAN SAY HE GAVE HER THE SLIP!
WINK
GENTLEMEN... BOSS TANAKA OBVIOUSLY HAS SOMETHING ON HIS MIND.
ALLOW HIM TO EXPRESS IT.
I SPEAK, MISTRESS ISHII OF THE PERVERSION DONE TO THIS COUNCIL--
-- BY MAKING A HALF CHINESE AMERICAN ITS LEADER.
JUMP
SLIP
ZINGO!
HAHAHA HAHAHA
I CAN'T FEEL MY SPINE.
THUMP
AS YOU CAN SEE FROM MY LAST TWO CLIPS--
--WHEN IT COMES TO PRACTICAL JOKES, I'M A SUCKER FOR THE CLASSICS.
AND NOTHING IS MORE CLASSIC THAN THE EXPLODING CIGAR.
OR, IN THE CASE OF INGLORIOUS BASTERDS, THE EXPLODING PIPE!
MAY I SMOKE MY PIPE AS WELL?
PLEASE, COLONEL, MAKE YOURSELF AT HOME.
SKRITCH

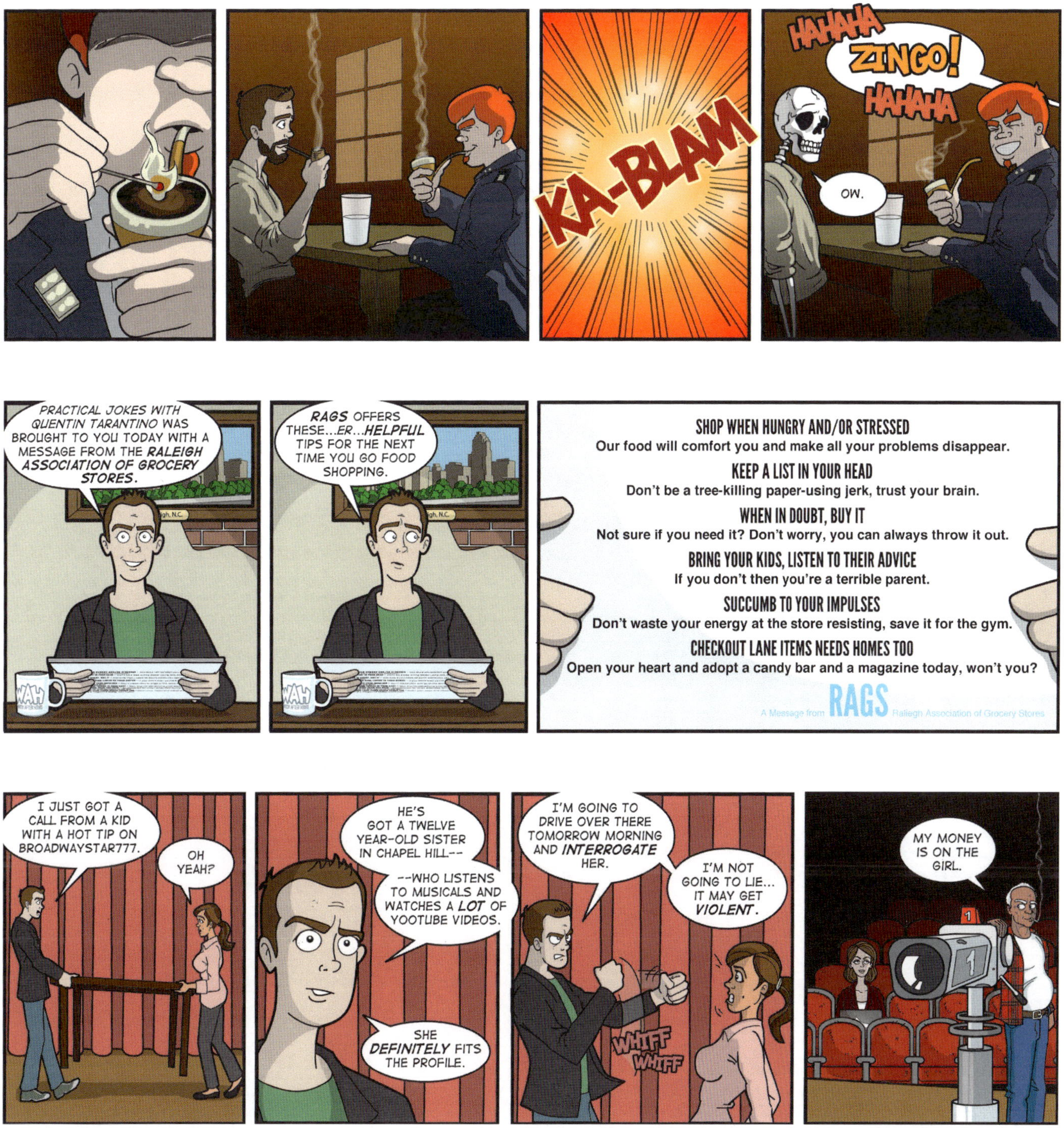

KA-BLAM
HAHAHA
ZINGO!
HAHAHA
OW.
PRACTICAL JOKES WITH QUENTIN TARANTINO WAS BROUGHT TO YOU TODAY WITH A MESSAGE FROM THE RALEIGH ASSOCIATION OF GROCERY STORES.
RAGS OFFERS THESE...ER...HELPFUL TIPS FOR THE NEXT TIME YOU GO FOOD SHOPPING.
SHOP WHEN HUNGRY AND/OR STRESSED
Our food will comfort you and make all your problems disappear.
KEEP A LIST IN YOUR HEAD
Don't be a tree-killing paper-using jerk, trust your brain.
WHEN IN DOUBT, BUY IT
Not sure if you need it? Don't worry, you can always throw it out.
BRING YOUR KIDS, LISTEN TO THEIR ADVICE
If you don't then you're a terrible parent.
SUCCUMB TO YOUR IMPULSES
Don't waste your energy at the store resisting, save it for the gym.
CHECKOUT LANE ITEMS NEEDS HOMES TOO
Open your heart and adopt a candy bar and a magazine today, won't you?
A Message from RAGS Raliegh Association of Grocery Stores
I JUST GOT A CALL FROM A KID WITH A HOT TIP ON BROADWAYSTAR777.
OH YEAH?
HE'S GOT A TWELVE YEAR-OLD SISTER IN CHAPEL HILL--
--WHO LISTENS TO MUSICALS AND WATCHES A LOT OF YOUTUBE VIDEOS.
SHE DEFINITELY FITS THE PROFILE.
I'M GOING TO DRIVE OVER THERE TOMORROW MORNING AND INTERROGATE HER.
I'M NOT GOING TO LIE... IT MAY GET VIOLENT.
WHIFF
WHIFF
MY MONEY IS ON THE GIRL.

THE FOLLOWING PREVIEW IS SUITABLE FOR
ALL AUDIENCES
THE CONSPIRACIES ARE INEXPLICABLE
TOP SECRET
FOR YOUR EYES ONLY
THE CORRUPTION IS INEXCUSABLE
THE STAKES ARE INCOMPREHENSIBLE
THE REPERCUSSIONS ARE INCALCULABLE
WANTED
THE GUILTY ARE INSCRUTABLE
BUT FORMER COAST GUARD RESERVIST RAM TOUGHATON WILL SHOW THEM EVERY ACTION HAS CONSEQUENCES
OH, YES--
--THERE WILL BE CONSEQUENCES!
CLIVE OWEN IS
THE RAMIFICATIONATOR
UMA THURMAN · PHILIP SEYMOUR HOFFMAN · BEYONCE
NOT COMING SOON TO A THEATRE NEAR YOU
©MMX

WHERE ARE YOU?
YOU'RE ON WITH WOODY IN THIRTY SECONDS.
YOU ASKED IF I'D BE A GUEST TOMORROW NIGHT.
NO, YOUR APPEARANCE IS TONIGHT.
RIGHT NOW.
OH...
...WELL I'M GOING TO BE LATE.
HOW LATE?
PRETTY LATE.

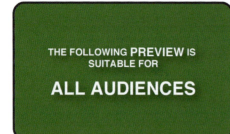

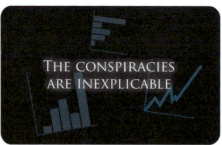

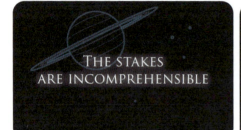

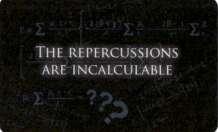

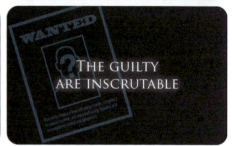

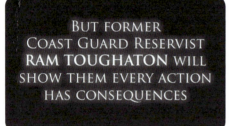

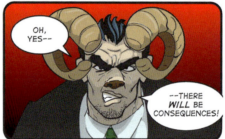

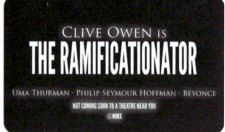

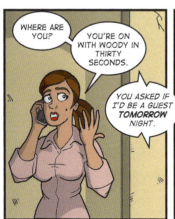

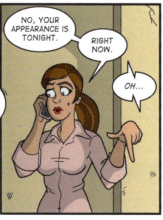

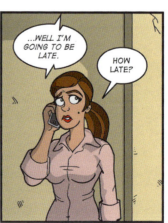

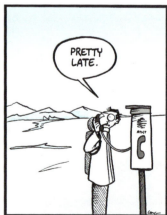

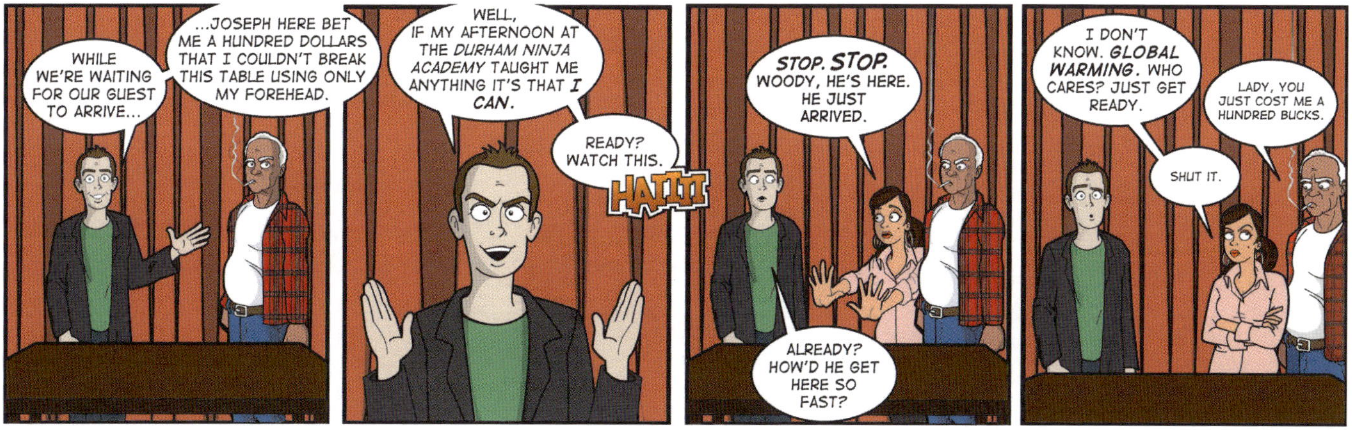
WHILE WE'RE WAITING FOR OUR GUEST TO ARRIVE...
...JOSEPH HERE BET ME A HUNDRED DOLLARS THAT I COULDN'T BREAK THIS TABLE USING ONLY MY FOREHEAD.
WELL, IF MY AFTERNOON AT THE *DURHAM NINJA ACADEMY* TAUGHT ME ANYTHING IT'S THAT ***I CAN.***
READY? WATCH THIS.
HAIIII
STOP. STOP. WOODY, HE'S HERE. HE JUST ARRIVED.
ALREADY? HOW'D HE GET HERE SO FAST?
I DON'T KNOW. ***GLOBAL WARMING.*** WHO CARES? JUST GET READY.
LADY, YOU JUST COST ME A HUNDRED BUCKS.
SHUT IT.

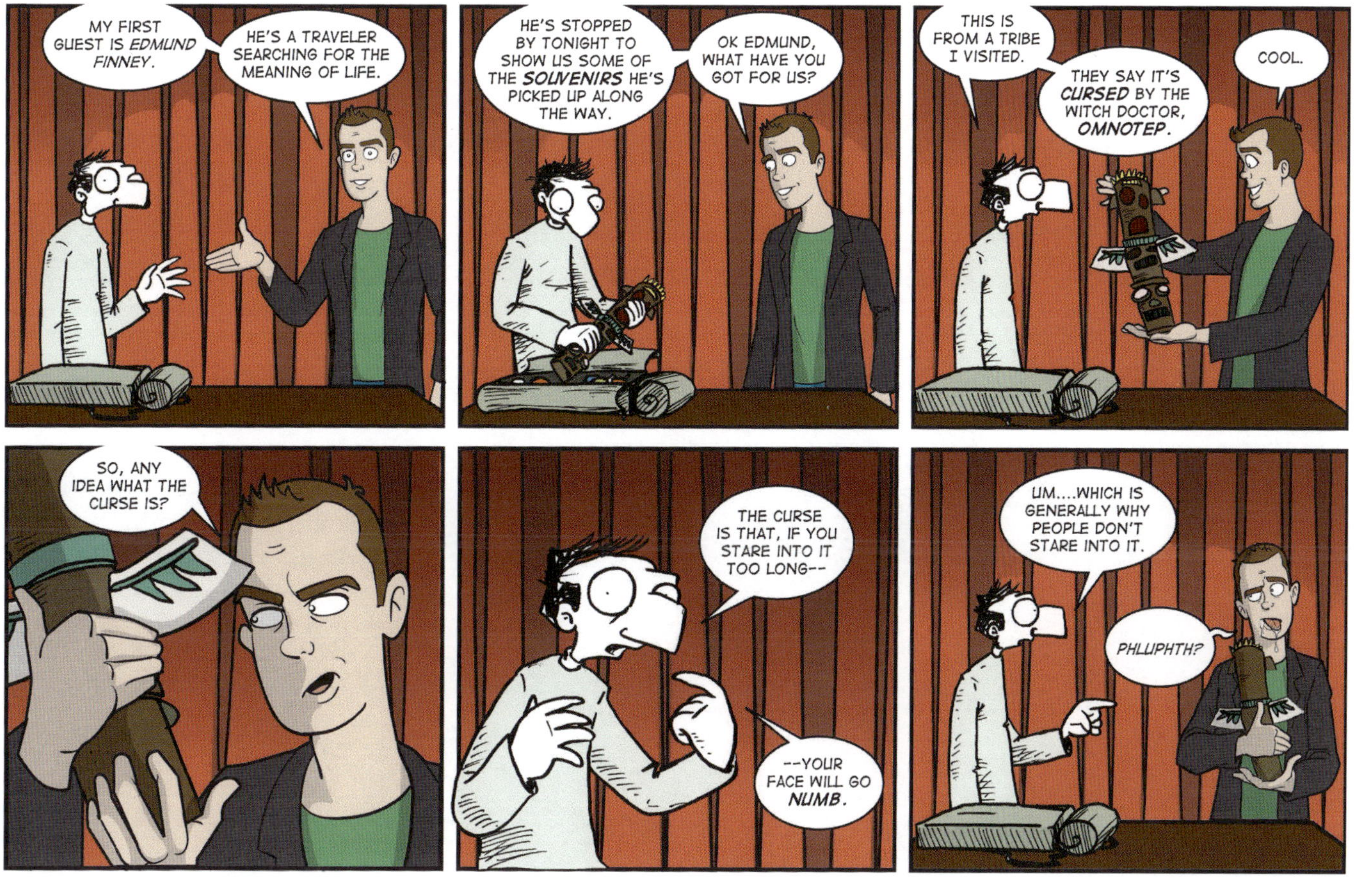
MY FIRST GUEST IS *EDMUND FINNEY.*
HE'S A TRAVELER SEARCHING FOR THE MEANING OF LIFE.
HE'S STOPPED BY TONIGHT TO SHOW US SOME OF THE ***SOUVENIRS*** HE'S PICKED UP ALONG THE WAY.
OK EDMUND, WHAT HAVE YOU GOT FOR US?
THIS IS FROM A TRIBE I VISITED.
THEY SAY IT'S ***CURSED*** BY THE WITCH DOCTOR, ***OMNOTEP.***
COOL.
SO, ANY IDEA WHAT THE CURSE IS?
THE CURSE IS THAT, IF YOU STARE INTO IT TOO LONG--
--YOUR FACE WILL GO ***NUMB.***
UM....WHICH IS GENERALLY WHY PEOPLE DON'T STARE INTO IT.
PHLUPHTH?

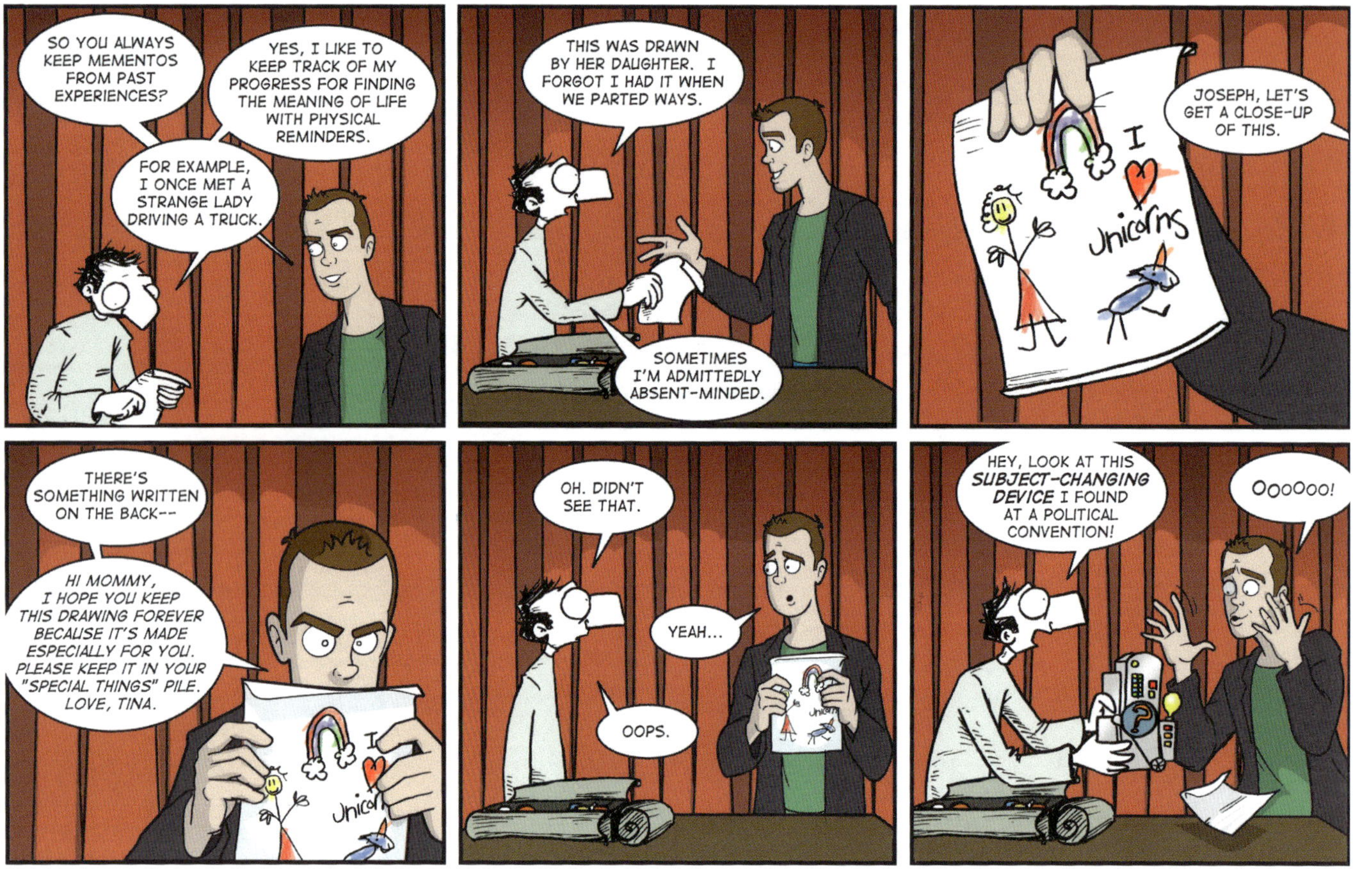
SO YOU ALWAYS KEEP MEMENTOS FROM PAST EXPERIENCES?
YES, I LIKE TO KEEP TRACK OF MY PROGRESS FOR FINDING THE MEANING OF LIFE WITH PHYSICAL REMINDERS.
FOR EXAMPLE, I ONCE MET A STRANGE LADY DRIVING A TRUCK.
THIS WAS DRAWN BY HER DAUGHTER. I FORGOT I HAD IT WHEN WE PARTED WAYS.
SOMETIMES I'M ADMITTEDLY ABSENT-MINDED.
JOSEPH, LET'S GET A CLOSE-UP OF THIS.
THERE'S SOMETHING WRITTEN ON THE BACK--
HI MOMMY, I HOPE YOU KEEP THIS DRAWING FOREVER BECAUSE IT'S MADE ESPECIALLY FOR YOU. PLEASE KEEP IT IN YOUR "SPECIAL THINGS" PILE. LOVE, TINA.
OH. DIDN'T SEE THAT.
YEAH...
OOPS.
HEY, LOOK AT THIS SUBJECT-CHANGING DEVICE I FOUND AT A POLITICAL CONVENTION!
OOoOoo!

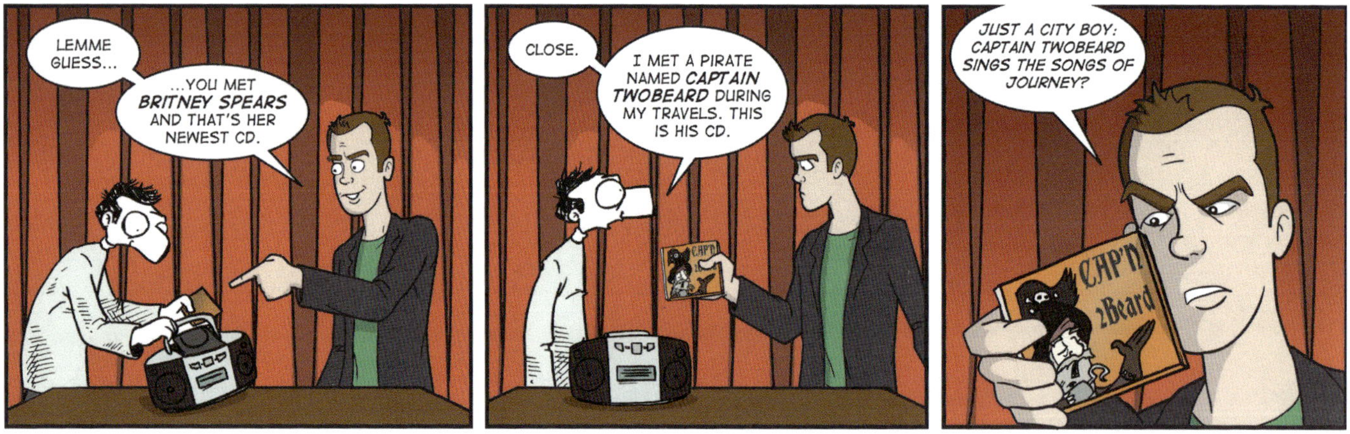
LEMME GUESS...
...YOU MET BRITNEY SPEARS AND THAT'S HER NEWEST CD.
CLOSE.
I MET A PIRATE NAMED CAPTAIN TWOBEARD DURING MY TRAVELS. THIS IS HIS CD.
JUST A CITY BOY: CAPTAIN TWOBEARD SINGS THE SONGS OF JOURNEY?

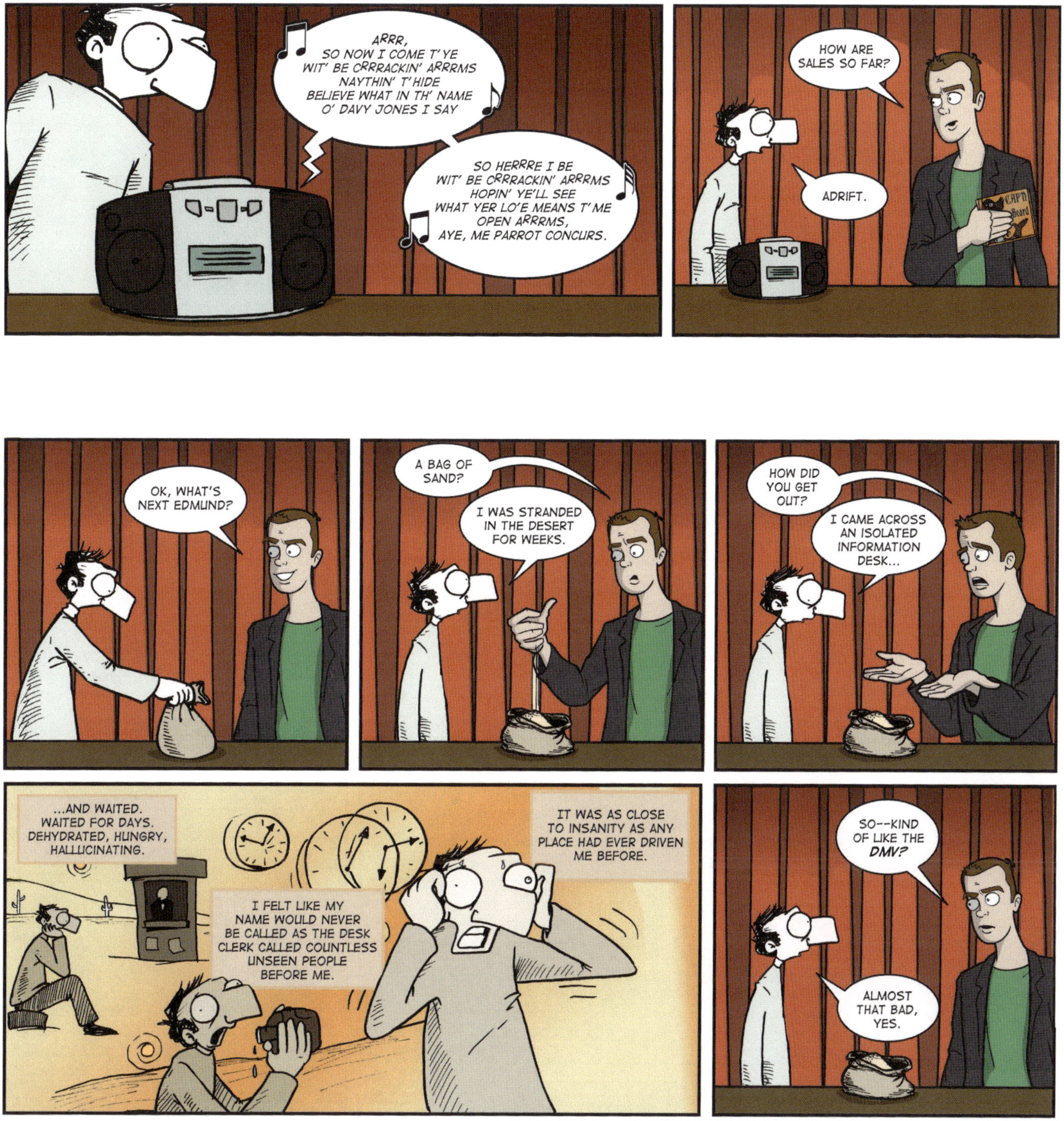
ARRR,
SO NOW I COME T'YE
WIT' BE CRRRACKIN' ARRRMS
NAYTHIN' T'HIDE
BELIEVE WHAT IN TH' NAME
O' DAVY JONES I SAY
SO HERRRE I BE
WIT' BE CRRRACKIN' ARRRMS
HOPIN' YE'LL SEE
WHAT YER LO'E MEANS T'ME
OPEN ARRRMS,
AYE, ME PARROT CONCURS.
HOW ARE SALES SO FAR?
ADRIFT.
OK, WHAT'S NEXT EDMUND?
A BAG OF SAND?
I WAS STRANDED IN THE DESERT FOR WEEKS.
HOW DID YOU GET OUT?
I CAME ACROSS AN ISOLATED INFORMATION DESK...
...AND WAITED. WAITED FOR DAYS. DEHYDRATED, HUNGRY, HALLUCINATING.
I FELT LIKE MY NAME WOULD NEVER BE CALLED AS THE DESK CLERK CALLED COUNTLESS UNSEEN PEOPLE BEFORE ME.
IT WAS AS CLOSE TO INSANITY AS ANY PLACE HAD EVER DRIVEN ME BEFORE.
SO--KIND OF LIKE THE ***DMV?***
ALMOST THAT BAD, YES.

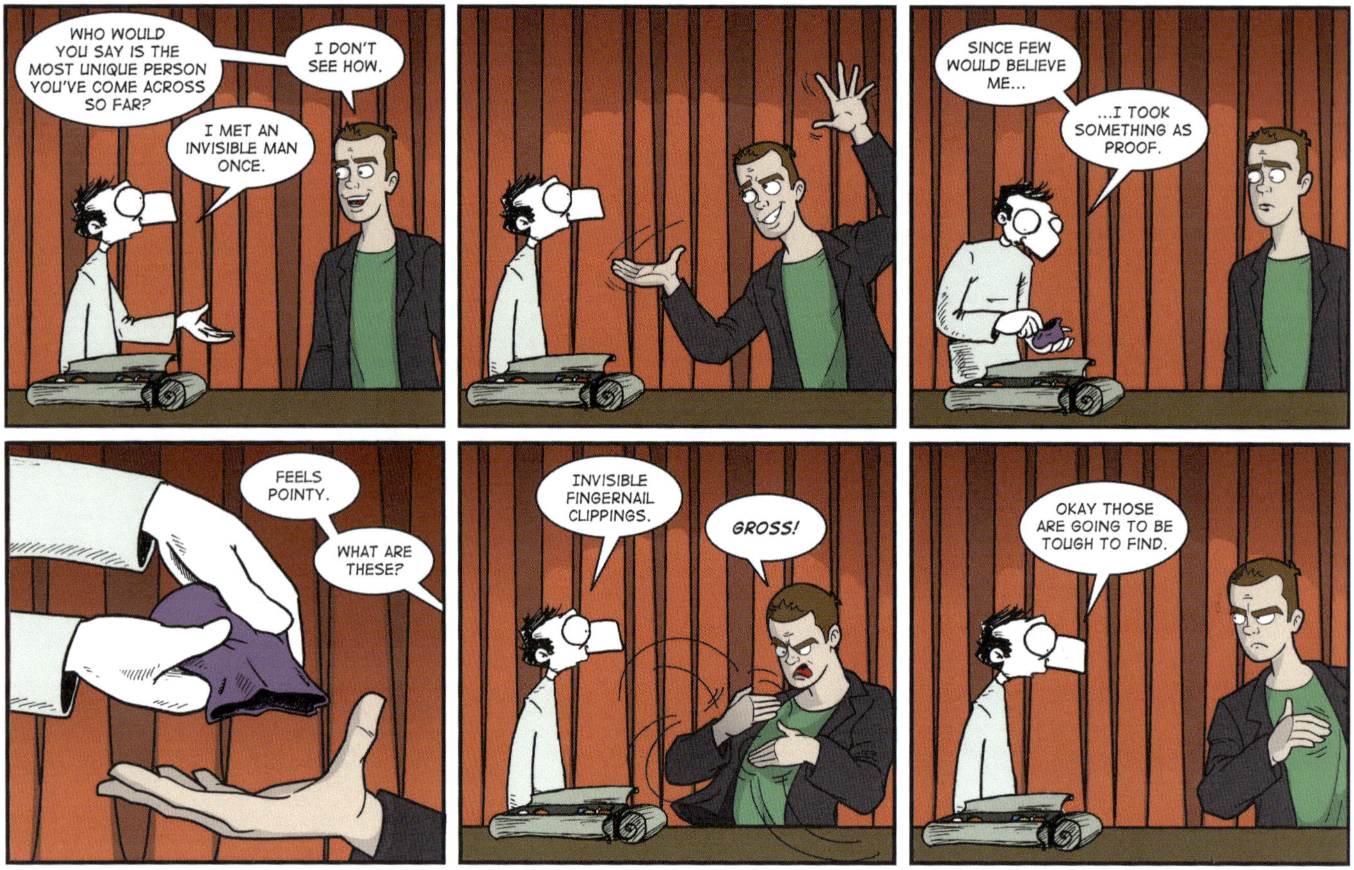
WHO WOULD YOU SAY IS THE MOST UNIQUE PERSON YOU'VE COME ACROSS SO FAR?
I DON'T SEE HOW.
I MET AN INVISIBLE MAN ONCE.
SINCE FEW WOULD BELIEVE ME...
...I TOOK SOMETHING AS PROOF.
FEELS POINTY.
WHAT ARE THESE?
INVISIBLE FINGERNAIL CLIPPINGS.
GROSS!
OKAY THOSE ARE GOING TO BE TOUGH TO FIND.

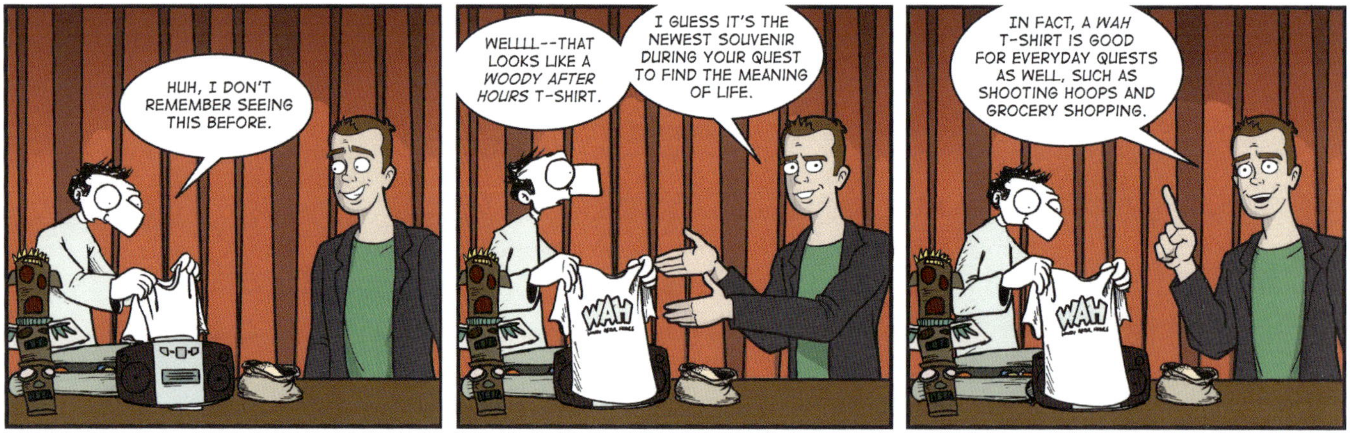
HUH, I DON'T REMEMBER SEEING THIS BEFORE.
WELLLL--THAT LOOKS LIKE A *WOODY AFTER HOURS* T-SHIRT.
I GUESS IT'S THE NEWEST SOUVENIR DURING YOUR QUEST TO FIND THE MEANING OF LIFE.
WAH
IN FACT, A *WAH* T-SHIRT IS GOOD FOR EVERYDAY QUESTS AS WELL, SUCH AS SHOOTING HOOPS AND GROCERY SHOPPING.

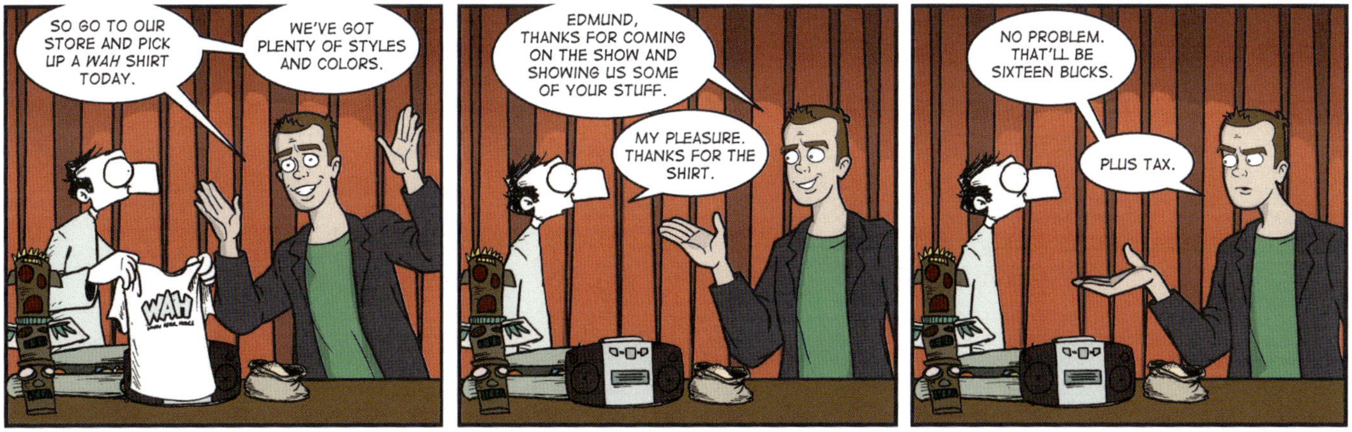
SO GO TO OUR STORE AND PICK UP A *WAH* SHIRT TODAY.
WE'VE GOT PLENTY OF STYLES AND COLORS.
WAH
EDMUND, THANKS FOR COMING ON THE SHOW AND SHOWING US SOME OF YOUR STUFF.
MY PLEASURE. THANKS FOR THE SHIRT.
NO PROBLEM. THAT'LL BE SIXTEEN BUCKS.
PLUS TAX.

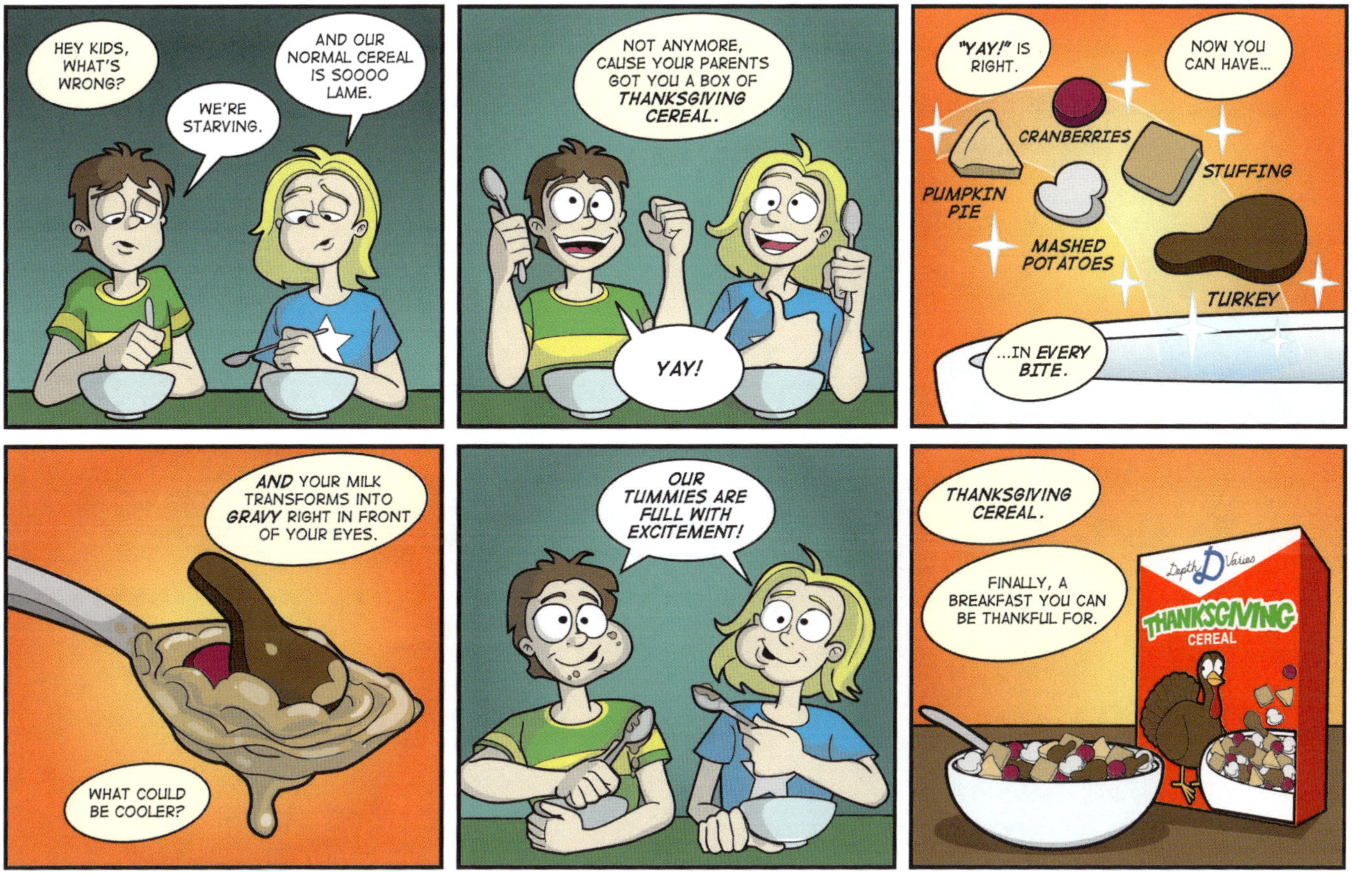
HEY KIDS, WHAT'S WRONG?
WE'RE STARVING.
AND OUR NORMAL CEREAL IS SOOOO LAME.
NOT ANYMORE, CAUSE YOUR PARENTS GOT YOU A BOX OF ***THANKSGIVING CEREAL.***
YAY!
"YAY!" IS RIGHT.
NOW YOU CAN HAVE...
CRANBERRIES
STUFFING
PUMPKIN PIE
MASHED POTATOES
TURKEY
...IN *EVERY BITE.*
AND YOUR MILK TRANSFORMS INTO ***GRAVY*** RIGHT IN FRONT OF YOUR EYES.
WHAT COULD BE COOLER?
OUR TUMMIES ARE FULL WITH EXCITEMENT!
THANKSGIVING CEREAL.
FINALLY, A BREAKFAST YOU CAN BE THANKFUL FOR.
THANKSGIVING CEREAL

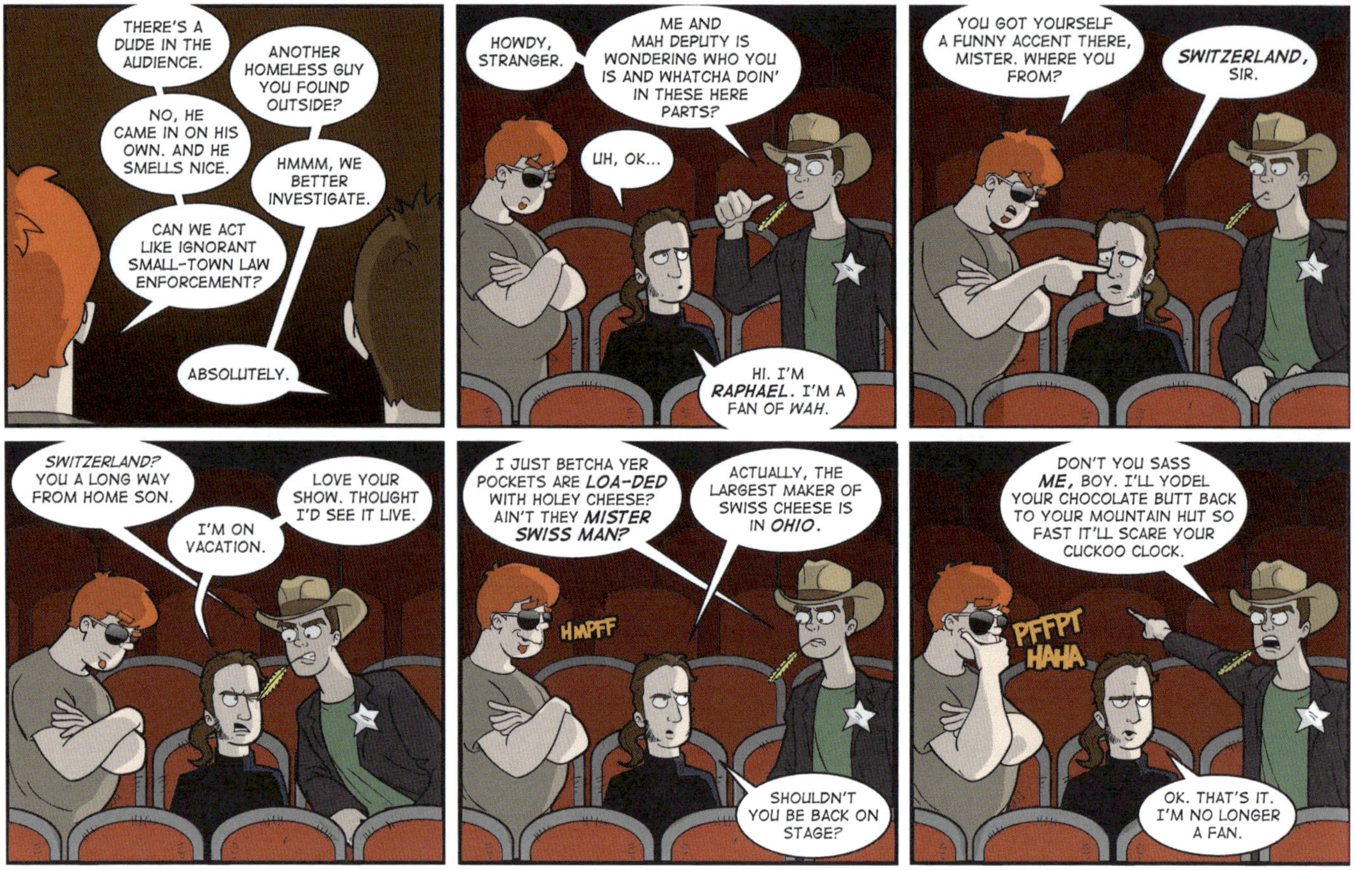
THERE'S A DUDE IN THE AUDIENCE.
ANOTHER HOMELESS GUY YOU FOUND OUTSIDE?
NO, HE CAME IN ON HIS OWN. AND HE SMELLS NICE.
HMMM, WE BETTER INVESTIGATE.
CAN WE ACT LIKE IGNORANT SMALL-TOWN LAW ENFORCEMENT?
ABSOLUTELY.
HOWDY, STRANGER.
ME AND MAH DEPUTY IS WONDERING WHO YOU IS AND WHATCHA DOIN' IN THESE HERE PARTS?
UH, OK...
HI. I'M *RAPHAEL*. I'M A FAN OF *WAH*.
YOU GOT YOURSELF A FUNNY ACCENT THERE, MISTER. WHERE YOU FROM?
SWITZERLAND, SIR.
SWITZERLAND? YOU A LONG WAY FROM HOME SON.
I'M ON VACATION.
LOVE YOUR SHOW. THOUGHT I'D SEE IT LIVE.
I JUST BETCHA YER POCKETS ARE *LOA-DED* WITH HOLEY CHEESE? AIN'T THEY *MISTER SWISS MAN?*
ACTUALLY, THE LARGEST MAKER OF SWISS CHEESE IS IN *OHIO*.
HMPFF
SHOULDN'T YOU BE BACK ON STAGE?
DON'T YOU SASS *ME*, BOY. I'LL YODEL YOUR CHOCOLATE BUTT BACK TO YOUR MOUNTAIN HUT SO FAST IT'LL SCARE YOUR CUCKOO CLOCK.
PFFPT HAHA
OK. THAT'S IT. I'M NO LONGER A FAN.

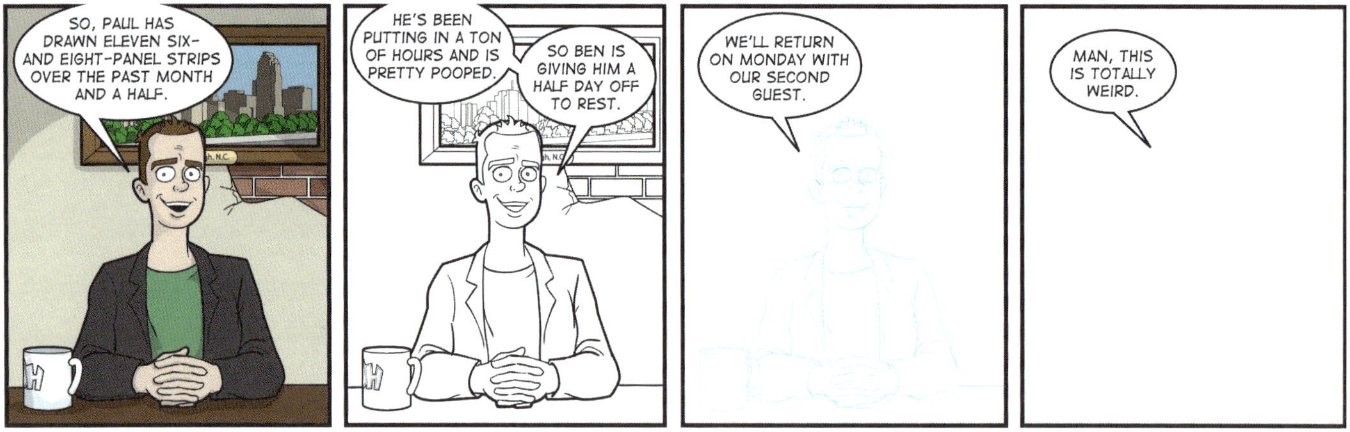
SO, PAUL HAS DRAWN ELEVEN SIX- AND EIGHT-PANEL STRIPS OVER THE PAST MONTH AND A HALF.
HE'S BEEN PUTTING IN A TON OF HOURS AND IS PRETTY POOPED.
SO BEN IS GIVING HIM A HALF DAY OFF TO REST.
WE'LL RETURN ON MONDAY WITH OUR SECOND GUEST.
MAN, THIS IS TOTALLY WEIRD.

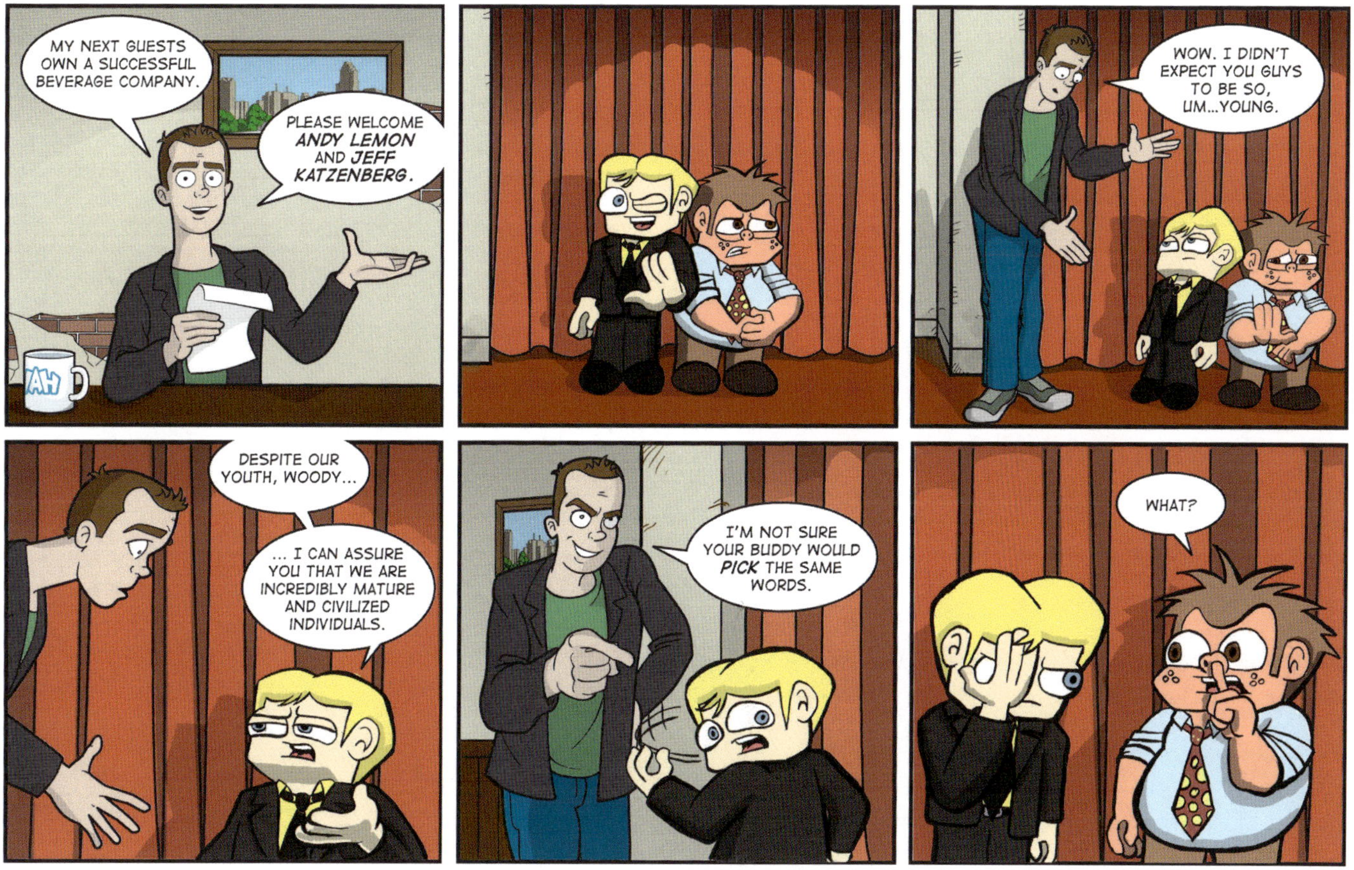
MY NEXT GUESTS OWN A SUCCESSFUL BEVERAGE COMPANY.
PLEASE WELCOME **ANDY LEMON** AND **JEFF KATZENBERG**.
AH
WOW. I DIDN'T EXPECT YOU GUYS TO BE SO, UM...YOUNG.
DESPITE OUR YOUTH, WOODY...
... I CAN ASSURE YOU THAT WE ARE INCREDIBLY MATURE AND CIVILIZED INDIVIDUALS.
I'M NOT SURE YOUR BUDDY WOULD ***PICK*** THE SAME WORDS.
WHAT?

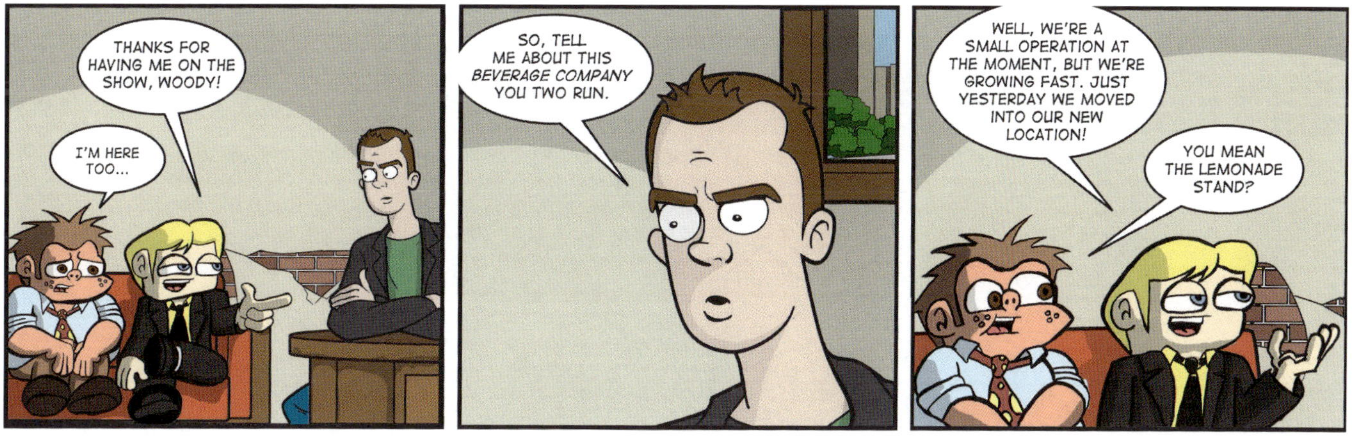
THANKS FOR HAVING ME ON THE SHOW, WOODY!
I'M HERE TOO...
SO, TELL ME ABOUT THIS *BEVERAGE COMPANY* YOU TWO RUN.
WELL, WE'RE A SMALL OPERATION AT THE MOMENT, BUT WE'RE GROWING FAST. JUST YESTERDAY WE MOVED INTO OUR NEW LOCATION!
YOU MEAN THE LEMONADE STAND?

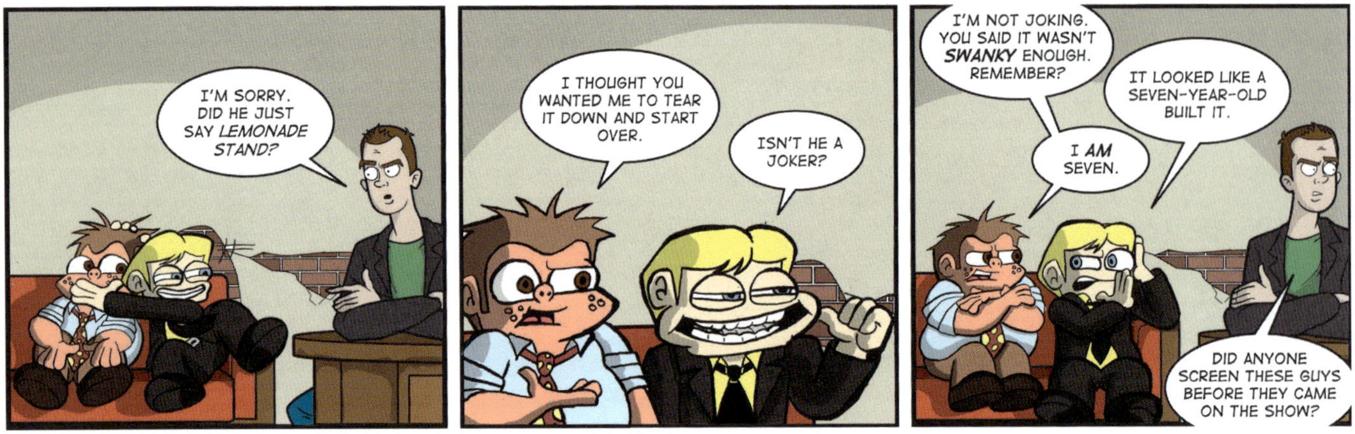
I'M SORRY. DID HE JUST SAY *LEMONADE STAND?*
I THOUGHT YOU WANTED ME TO TEAR IT DOWN AND START OVER.
ISN'T HE A JOKER?
I'M NOT JOKING. YOU SAID IT WASN'T **SWANKY** ENOUGH. REMEMBER?
IT LOOKED LIKE A SEVEN-YEAR-OLD BUILT IT.
I ***AM*** SEVEN.
DID ANYONE SCREEN THESE GUYS BEFORE THEY CAME ON THE SHOW?

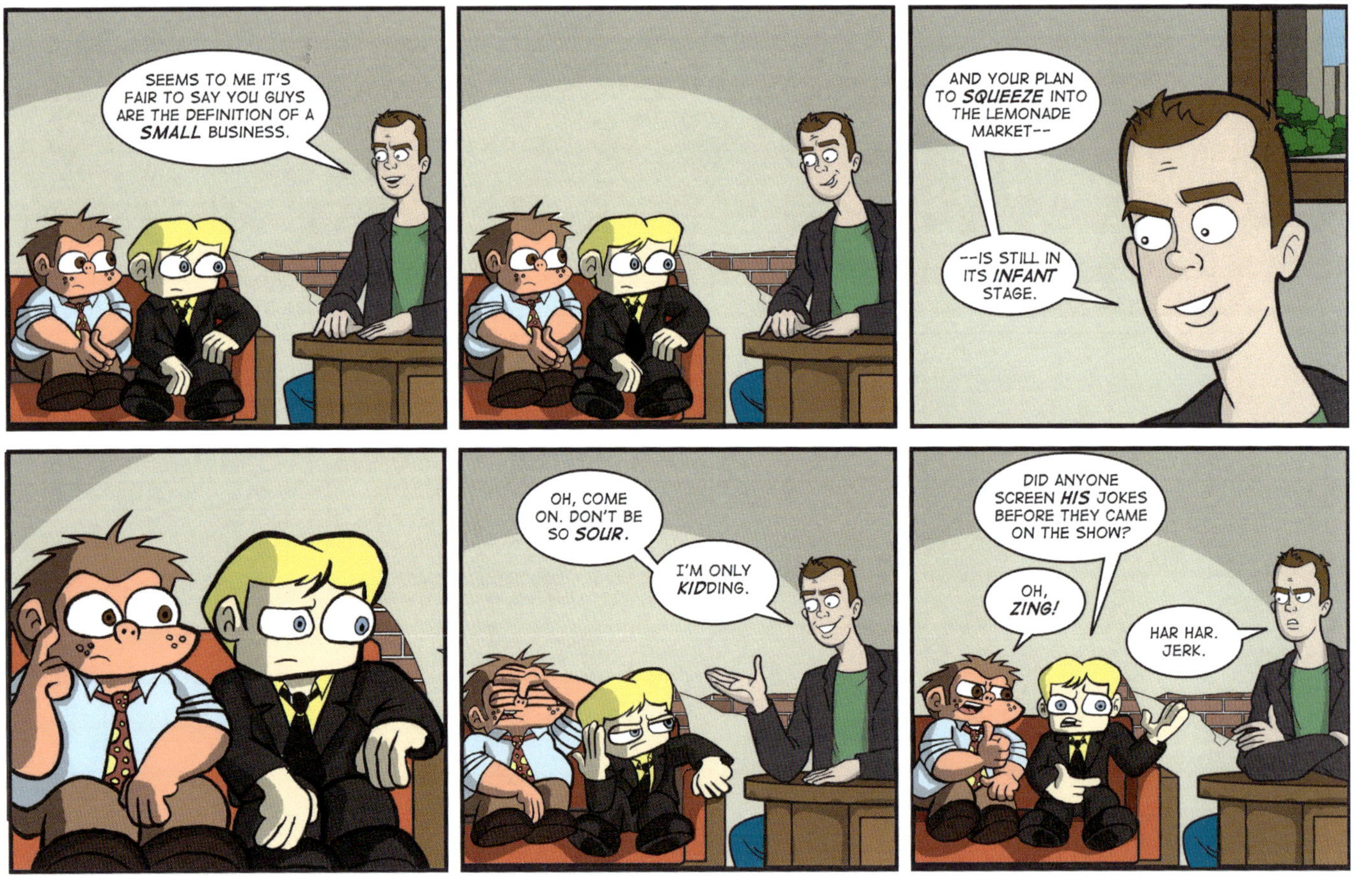
SEEMS TO ME IT'S FAIR TO SAY YOU GUYS ARE THE DEFINITION OF A **SMALL** BUSINESS.
AND YOUR PLAN TO **SQUEEZE** INTO THE LEMONADE MARKET--
--IS STILL IN ITS ***INFANT*** STAGE.
OH, COME ON. DON'T BE SO **SOUR**.
I'M ONLY *KID*DING.
DID ANYONE SCREEN **HIS** JOKES BEFORE THEY CAME ON THE SHOW?
OH, ***ZING!***
HAR HAR. JERK.

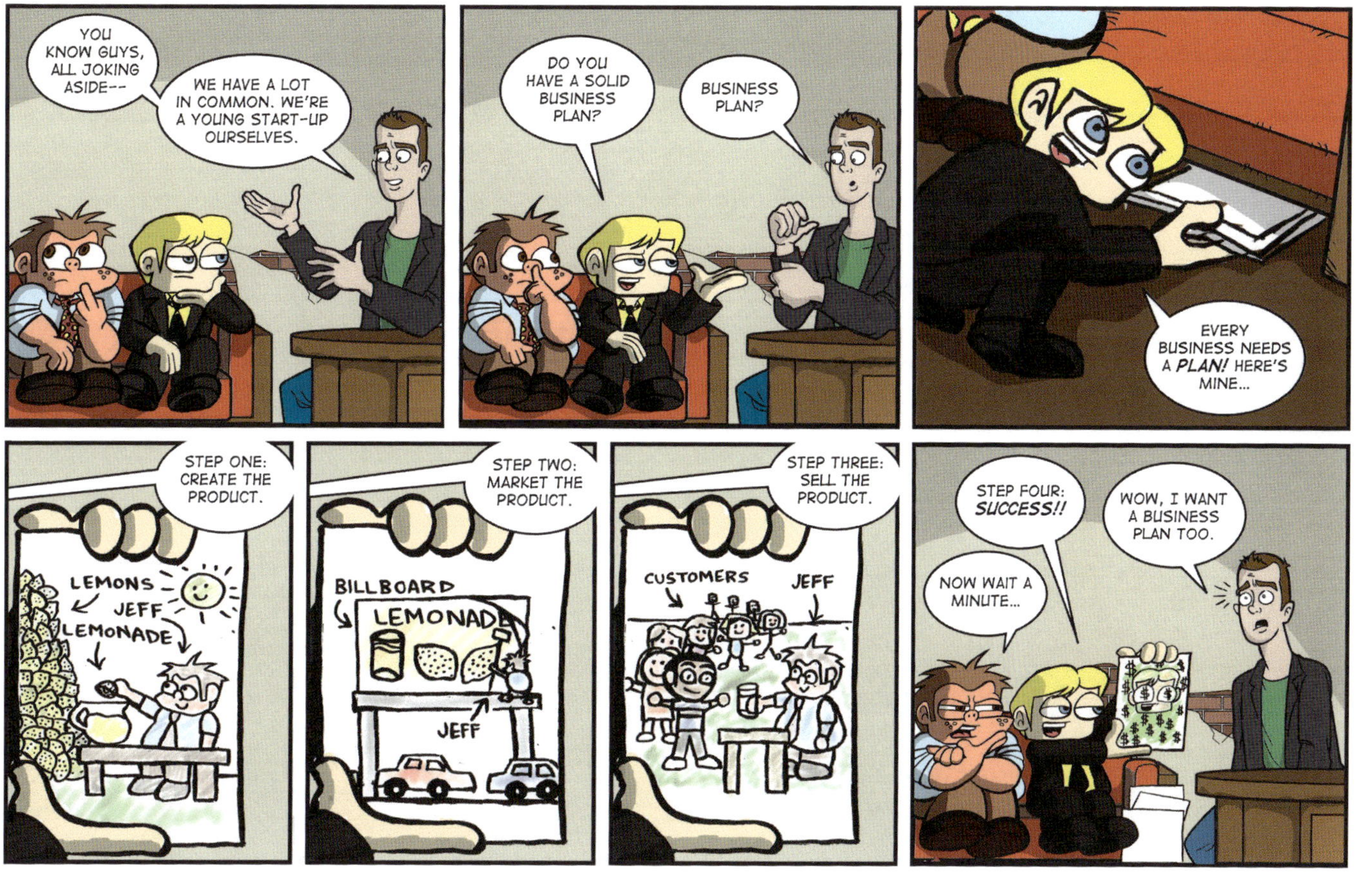
YOU KNOW GUYS, ALL JOKING ASIDE--
WE HAVE A LOT IN COMMON. WE'RE A YOUNG START-UP OURSELVES.
DO YOU HAVE A SOLID BUSINESS PLAN?
BUSINESS PLAN?
EVERY BUSINESS NEEDS A *PLAN!* HERE'S MINE...
STEP ONE: CREATE THE PRODUCT.
LEMONS
JEFF
LEMONADE
STEP TWO: MARKET THE PRODUCT.
BILLBOARD
LEMONAD
JEFF
STEP THREE: SELL THE PRODUCT.
CUSTOMERS
JEFF
STEP FOUR: *SUCCESS!!*
NOW WAIT A MINUTE...
WOW, I WANT A BUSINESS PLAN TOO.

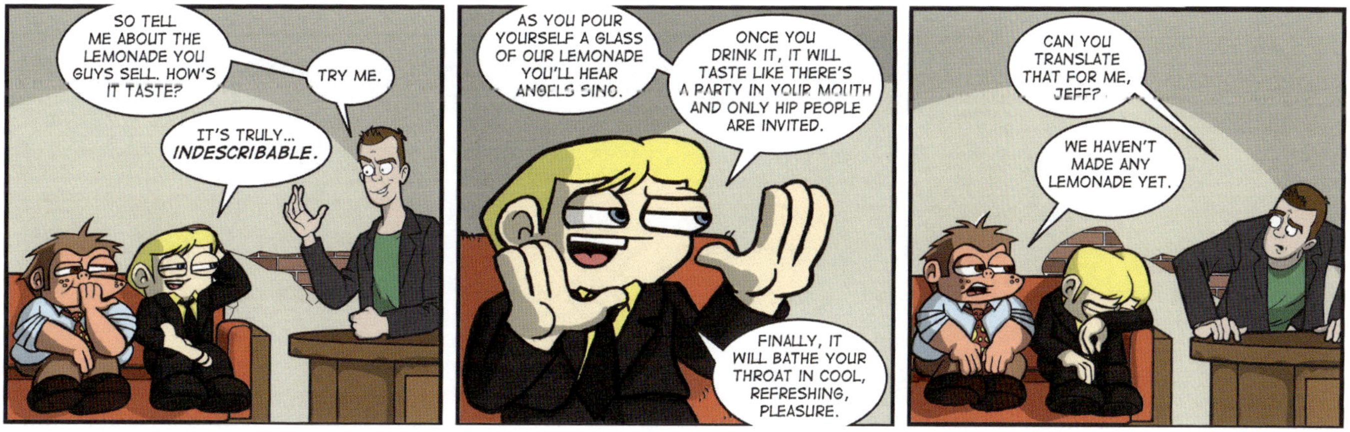
SO TELL ME ABOUT THE LEMONADE YOU GUYS SELL. HOW'S IT TASTE?
TRY ME.
IT'S TRULY... *INDESCRIBABLE.*
AS YOU POUR YOURSELF A GLASS OF OUR LEMONADE YOU'LL HEAR ANGELS SING.
ONCE YOU DRINK IT, IT WILL TASTE LIKE THERE'S A PARTY IN YOUR MOUTH AND ONLY HIP PEOPLE ARE INVITED.
FINALLY, IT WILL BATHE YOUR THROAT IN COOL, REFRESHING, PLEASURE.
CAN YOU TRANSLATE THAT FOR ME, JEFF?
WE HAVEN'T MADE ANY LEMONADE YET.

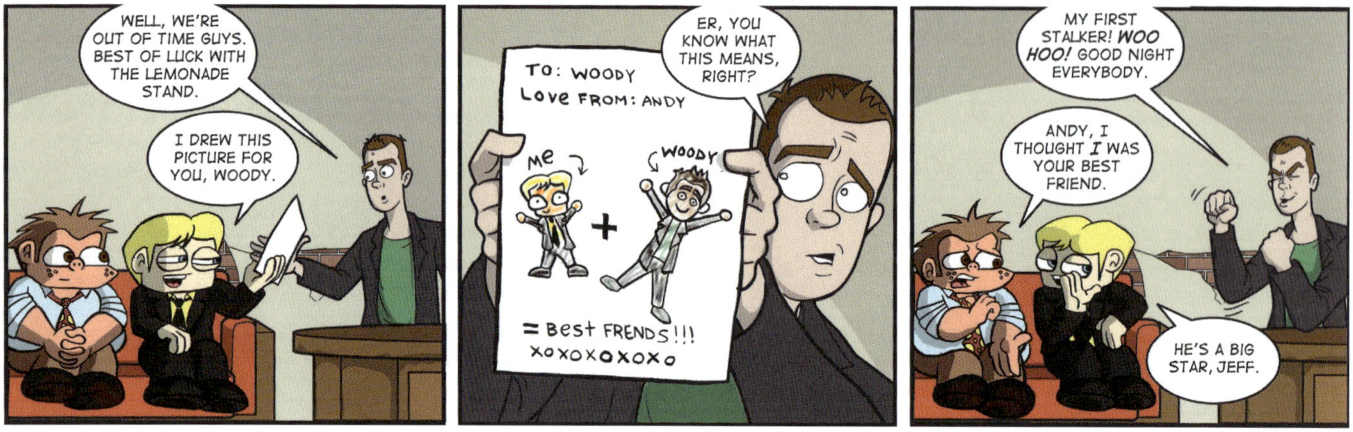
WELL, WE'RE OUT OF TIME GUYS. BEST OF LUCK WITH THE LEMONADE STAND.
I DREW THIS PICTURE FOR YOU, WOODY.
ER, YOU KNOW WHAT THIS MEANS, RIGHT?
TO: WOODY
LOVE FROM: ANDY
ME
WOODY
= BEST FRENDS!!!
XOXOXOXOXO
MY FIRST STALKER! WOO HOO! GOOD NIGHT EVERYBODY.
ANDY, I THOUGHT I WAS YOUR BEST FRIEND.
HE'S A BIG STAR, JEFF.

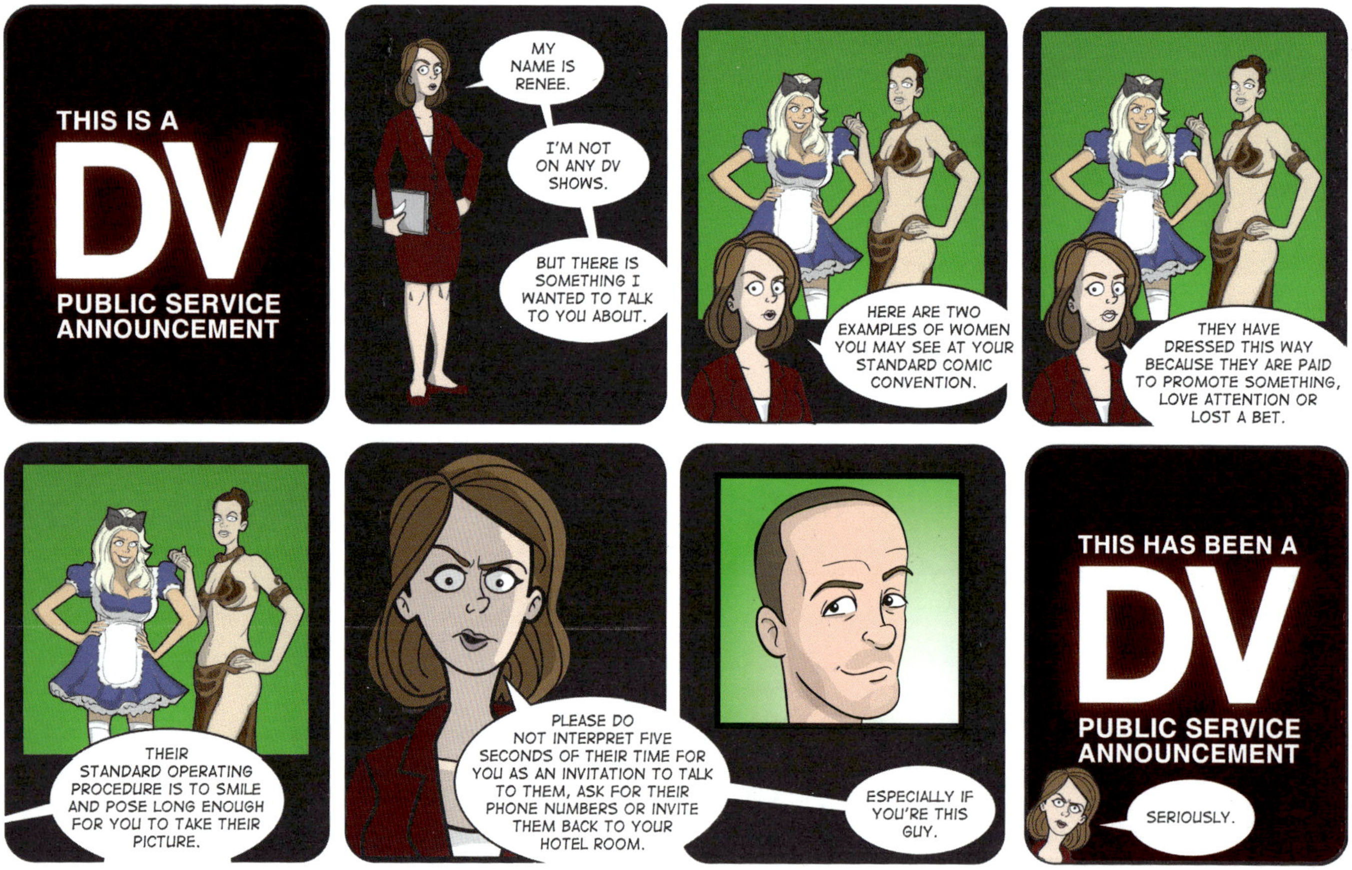
THIS IS A
DV
PUBLIC SERVICE ANNOUNCEMENT
MY NAME IS RENEE.
I'M NOT ON ANY DV SHOWS.
BUT THERE IS SOMETHING I WANTED TO TALK TO YOU ABOUT.
HERE ARE TWO EXAMPLES OF WOMEN YOU MAY SEE AT YOUR STANDARD COMIC CONVENTION.
THEY HAVE DRESSED THIS WAY BECAUSE THEY ARE PAID TO PROMOTE SOMETHING, LOVE ATTENTION OR LOST A BET.
THEIR STANDARD OPERATING PROCEDURE IS TO SMILE AND POSE LONG ENOUGH FOR YOU TO TAKE THEIR PICTURE.
PLEASE DO NOT INTERPRET FIVE SECONDS OF THEIR TIME FOR YOU AS AN INVITATION TO TALK TO THEM, ASK FOR THEIR PHONE NUMBERS OR INVITE THEM BACK TO YOUR HOTEL ROOM.
ESPECIALLY IF YOU'RE THIS GUY.
THIS HAS BEEN A
DV
PUBLIC SERVICE ANNOUNCEMENT
SERIOUSLY.

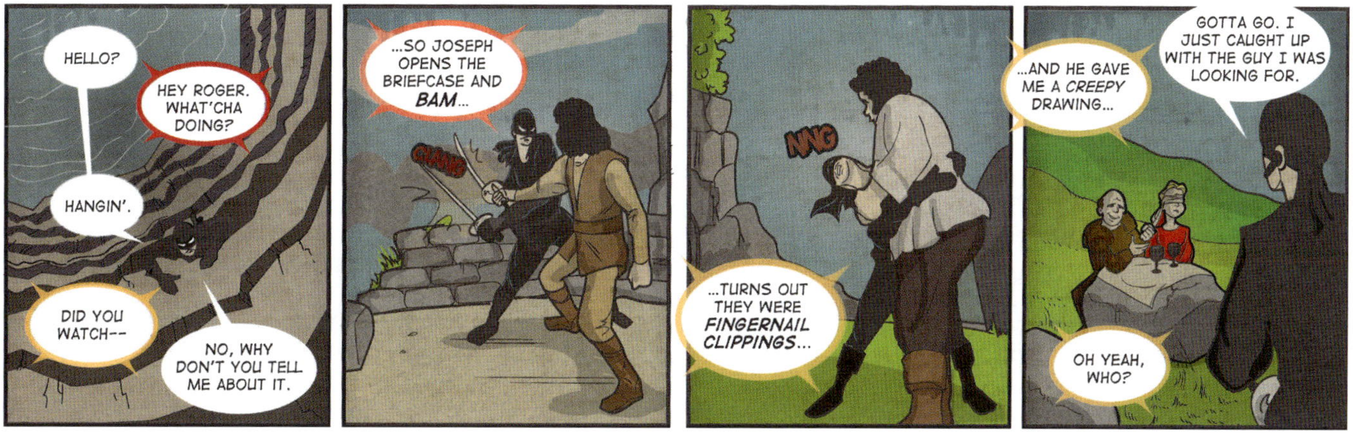
HELLO?
HEY ROGER. WHAT'CHA DOING?
HANGIN'.
DID YOU WATCH--
NO, WHY DON'T YOU TELL ME ABOUT IT.
...SO JOSEPH OPENS THE BRIEFCASE AND *BAM*...
CLANG
NNG
...TURNS OUT THEY WERE *FINGERNAIL CLIPPINGS*...
...AND HE GAVE ME A *CREEPY* DRAWING...
GOTTA GO. I JUST CAUGHT UP WITH THE GUY I WAS LOOKING FOR.
OH YEAH, WHO?

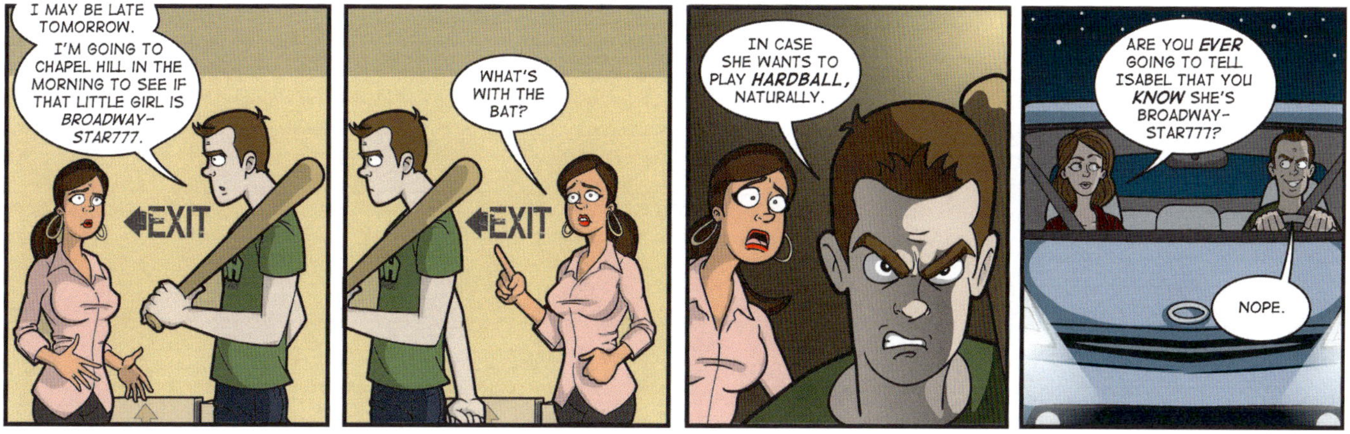
I MAY BE LATE TOMORROW.
I'M GOING TO CHAPEL HILL IN THE MORNING TO SEE IF THAT LITTLE GIRL IS *BROADWAY-STAR777*.
EXIT
WHAT'S WITH THE BAT?
EXIT
IN CASE SHE WANTS TO PLAY *HARDBALL*, NATURALLY.
ARE YOU *EVER* GOING TO TELL ISABEL THAT YOU *KNOW* SHE'S BROADWAY-STAR777?
NOPE.

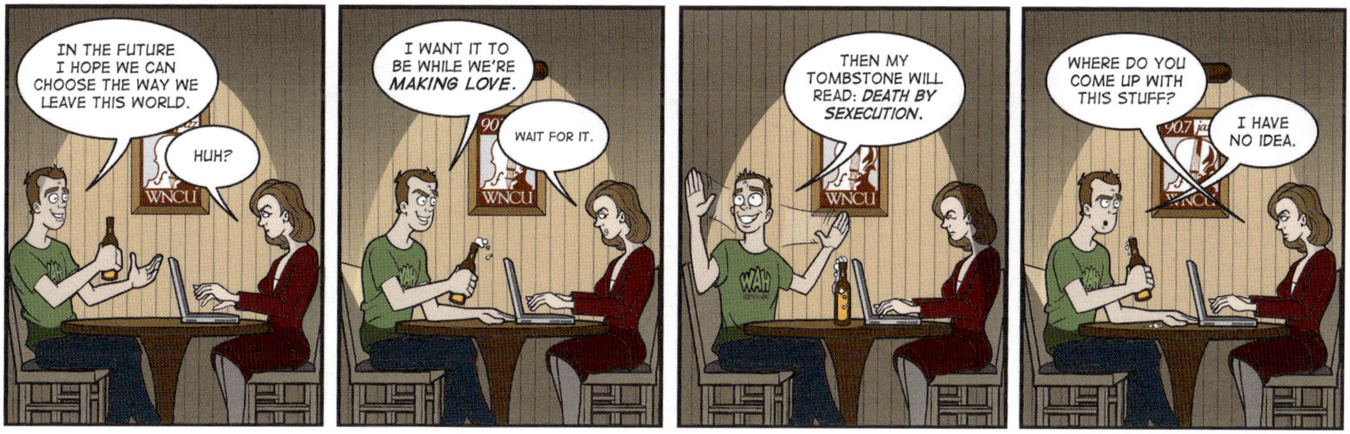
IN THE FUTURE I HOPE WE CAN CHOOSE THE WAY WE LEAVE THIS WORLD.
HUH?
WNCU
I WANT IT TO BE WHILE WE'RE *MAKING LOVE*.
WAIT FOR IT.
WNCU
THEN MY TOMBSTONE WILL READ: *DEATH BY SEXECUTION*.
WNCU
WHERE DO YOU COME UP WITH THIS STUFF?
I HAVE NO IDEA.

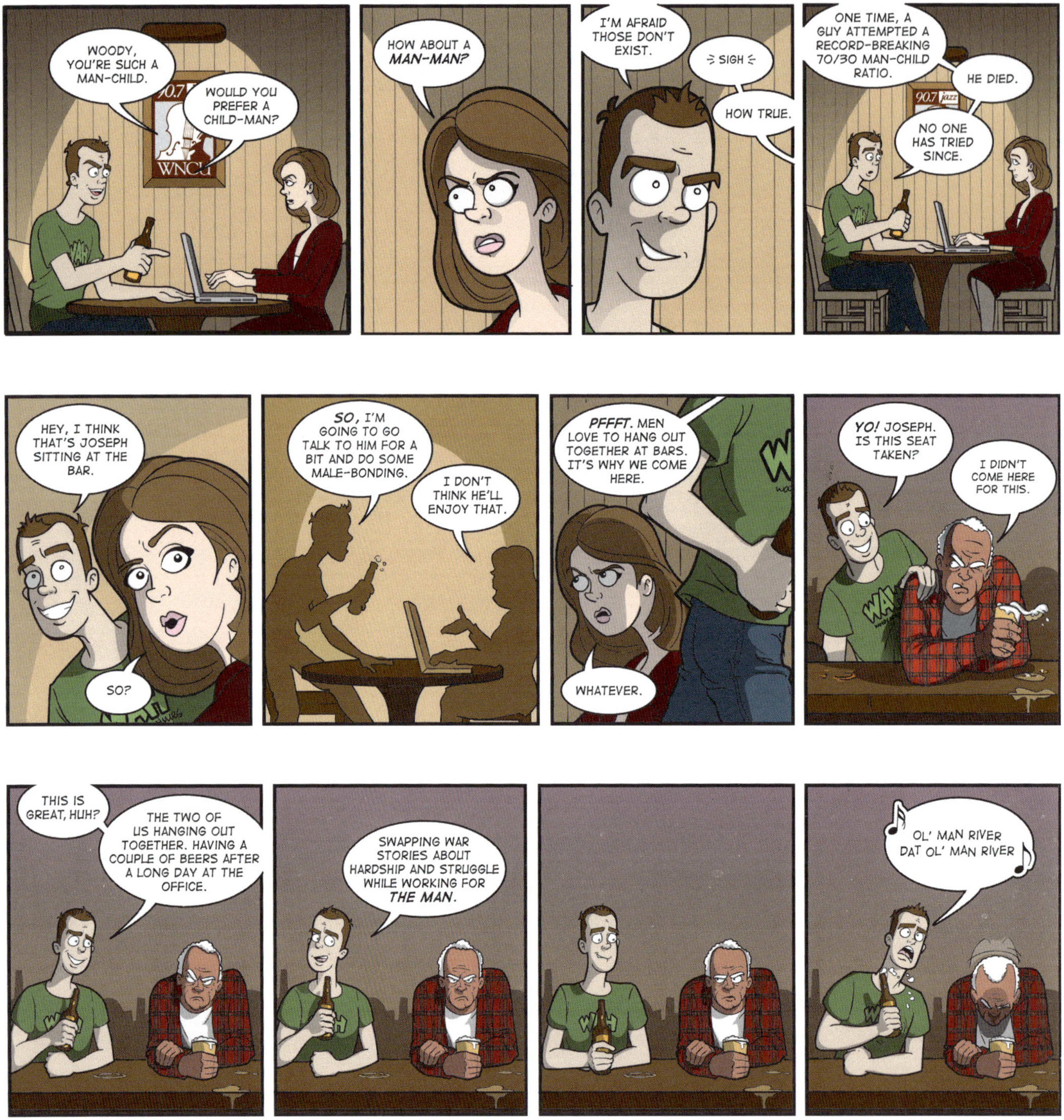

WOODY, YOU'RE SUCH A MAN-CHILD.
WOULD YOU PREFER A CHILD-MAN?
90.7
WNCU
HOW ABOUT A *MAN-MAN?*
I'M AFRAID THOSE DON'T EXIST.
SIGH
HOW TRUE.
ONE TIME, A GUY ATTEMPTED A RECORD-BREAKING 70/30 MAN-CHILD RATIO.
HE DIED.
NO ONE HAS TRIED SINCE.
90.7 jazz
HEY, I THINK THAT'S JOSEPH SITTING AT THE BAR.
SO?
SO, I'M GOING TO GO TALK TO HIM FOR A BIT AND DO SOME MALE-BONDING.
I DON'T THINK HE'LL ENJOY THAT.
PFFFT. MEN LOVE TO HANG OUT TOGETHER AT BARS. IT'S WHY WE COME HERE.
WHATEVER.
YO! JOSEPH. IS THIS SEAT TAKEN?
I DIDN'T COME HERE FOR THIS.
THIS IS GREAT, HUH?
THE TWO OF US HANGING OUT TOGETHER. HAVING A COUPLE OF BEERS AFTER A LONG DAY AT THE OFFICE.
SWAPPING WAR STORIES ABOUT HARDSHIP AND STRUGGLE WHILE WORKING FOR ***THE MAN.***
OL' MAN RIVER DAT OL' MAN RIVER

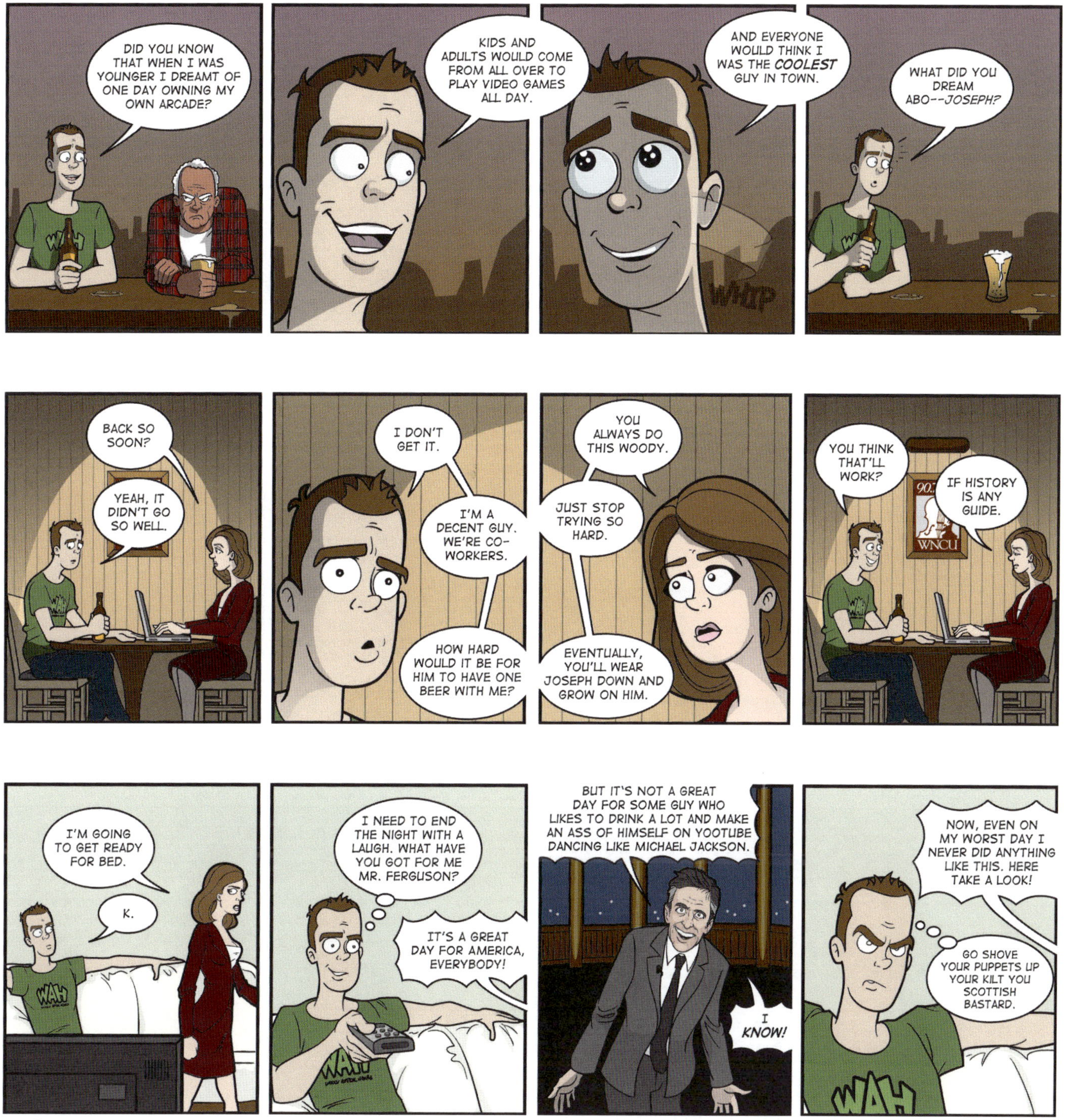
DID YOU KNOW THAT WHEN I WAS YOUNGER I DREAMT OF ONE DAY OWNING MY OWN ARCADE?
KIDS AND ADULTS WOULD COME FROM ALL OVER TO PLAY VIDEO GAMES ALL DAY.
AND EVERYONE WOULD THINK I WAS THE *COOLEST* GUY IN TOWN.
WHIP
WHAT DID YOU DREAM ABO--*JOSEPH?*
BACK SO SOON?
YEAH, IT DIDN'T GO SO WELL.
I DON'T GET IT.
I'M A DECENT GUY. WE'RE CO-WORKERS.
HOW HARD WOULD IT BE FOR HIM TO HAVE ONE BEER WITH ME?
YOU ALWAYS DO THIS WOODY.
JUST STOP TRYING SO HARD.
EVENTUALLY, YOU'LL WEAR JOSEPH DOWN AND GROW ON HIM.
YOU THINK THAT'LL WORK?
WNCU
IF HISTORY IS ANY GUIDE.
I'M GOING TO GET READY FOR BED.
K.
I NEED TO END THE NIGHT WITH A LAUGH. WHAT HAVE YOU GOT FOR ME MR. FERGUSON?
IT'S A GREAT DAY FOR AMERICA, EVERYBODY!
BUT IT'S NOT A GREAT DAY FOR SOME GUY WHO LIKES TO DRINK A LOT AND MAKE AN ASS OF HIMSELF ON YOUTUBE DANCING LIKE MICHAEL JACKSON.
I *KNOW!*
NOW, EVEN ON MY WORST DAY I NEVER DID ANYTHING LIKE THIS. HERE TAKE A LOOK!
GO SHOVE YOUR PUPPETS UP YOUR KILT YOU SCOTTISH BASTARD.

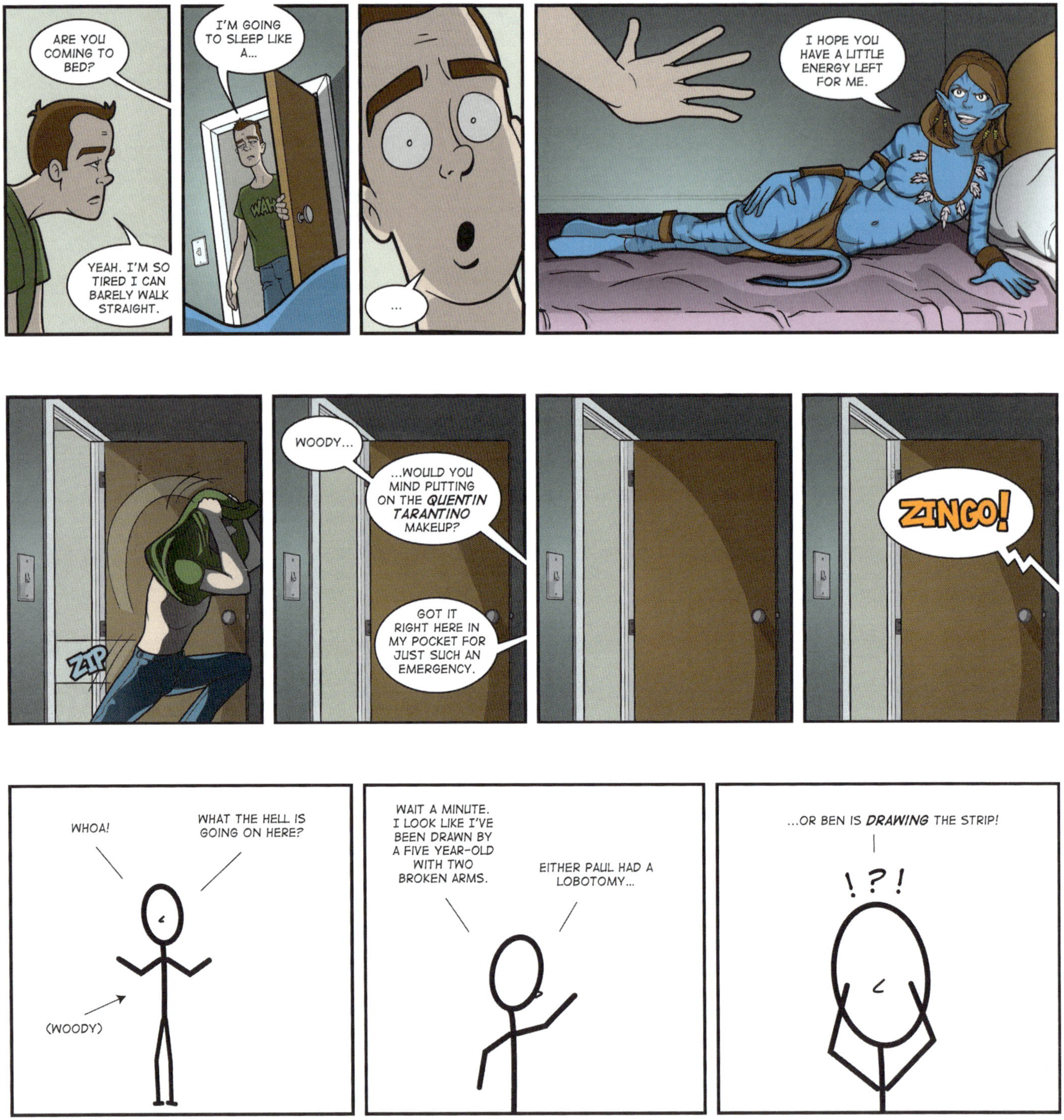
ARE YOU COMING TO BED?
YEAH. I'M SO TIRED I CAN BARELY WALK STRAIGHT.
I'M GOING TO SLEEP LIKE A...
WAH
...
I HOPE YOU HAVE A LITTLE ENERGY LEFT FOR ME.
ZIP
WOODY...
...WOULD YOU MIND PUTTING ON THE *QUENTIN TARANTINO* MAKEUP?
GOT IT RIGHT HERE IN MY POCKET FOR JUST SUCH AN EMERGENCY.
ZINGO!
WHOA!
WHAT THE HELL IS GOING ON HERE?
(WOODY)
WAIT A MINUTE. I LOOK LIKE I'VE BEEN DRAWN BY A FIVE YEAR-OLD WITH TWO BROKEN ARMS.
EITHER PAUL HAD A LOBOTOMY...
...OR BEN IS *DRAWING* THE STRIP!
!?!

LETTING BEN WRITE *AND* DRAW THE STRIP IS LIKE PUTTING THE LUNATICS IN CHARGE OF THE ASYLUM.

TECHNICALLY, *ANYTHING* COULD HAPPEN HERE.

NO MATTER HOW BIZARRE.

OR STUPID.

MEOW.

WHAT'S THIS?

"DEAR WOODY. CONGRATULATIONS. YOU NOW HAVE THE ABILITY TO FLY – BEN."

WELL ALLLLLLRIGHT.

UP, UP AND A....

"SUCKA."

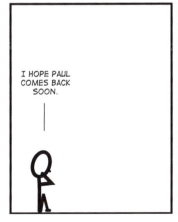

I HOPE PAUL COMES BACK SOON.

BEN'S INABILITY TO DRAW WORTH A $#!] MAKES THIS PLACE REALLY BORING.

I'M SO LONELY.

NOT HELPING!

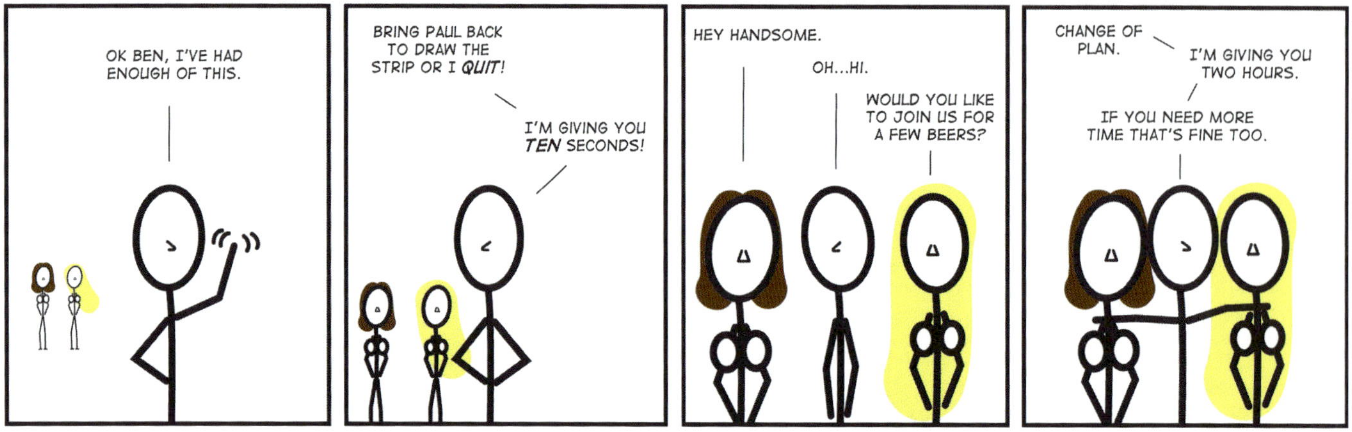
OK BEN, I'VE HAD ENOUGH OF THIS.
BRING PAUL BACK TO DRAW THE STRIP OR I QUIT!
I'M GIVING YOU TEN SECONDS!
HEY HANDSOME.
OH...HI.
WOULD YOU LIKE TO JOIN US FOR A FEW BEERS?
CHANGE OF PLAN.
I'M GIVING YOU TWO HOURS.
IF YOU NEED MORE TIME THAT'S FINE TOO.

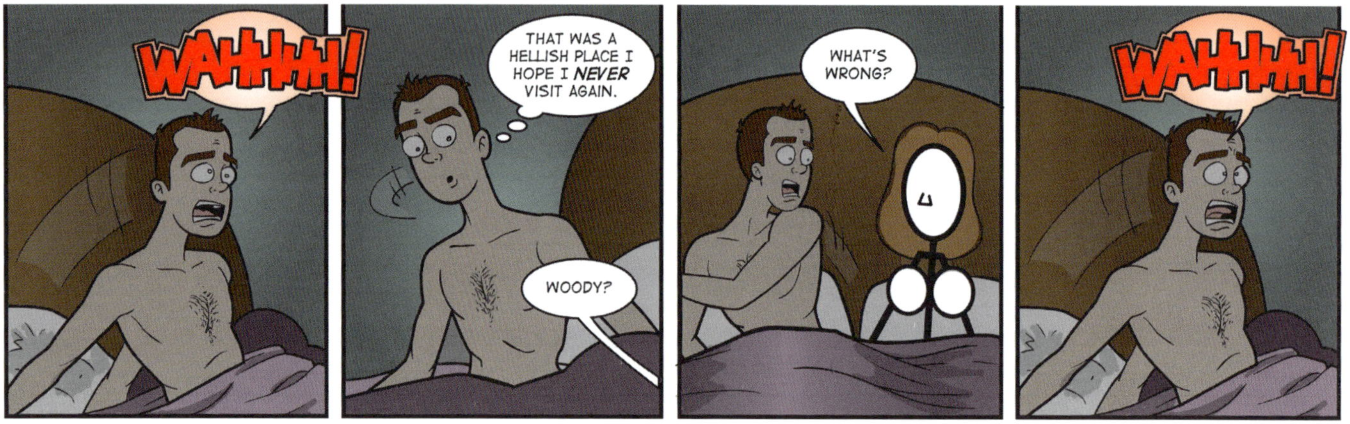
WAHHHH!
THAT WAS A HELLISH PLACE I HOPE I NEVER VISIT AGAIN.
WOODY?
WHAT'S WRONG?
WAHHHH!

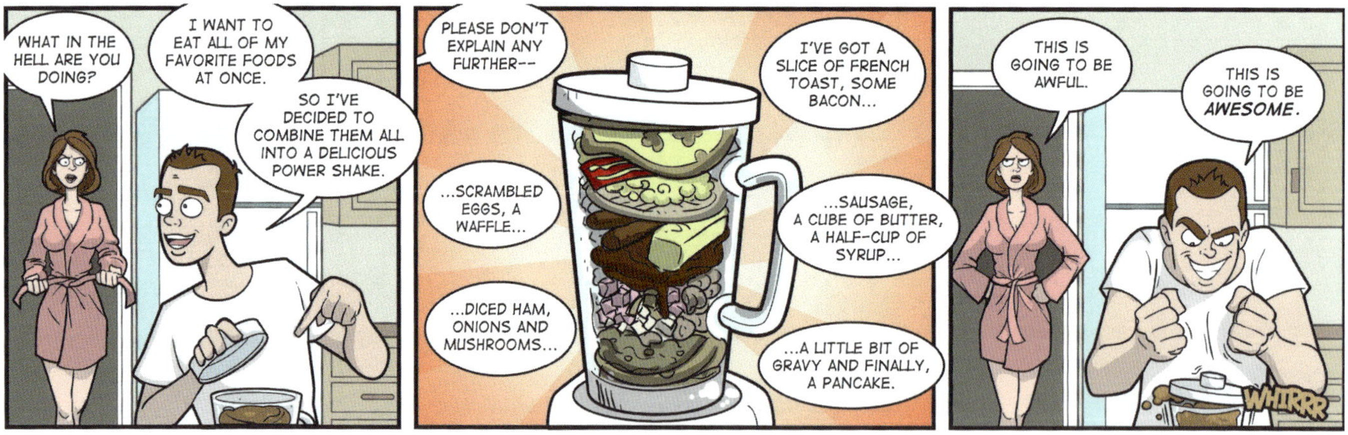
WHAT IN THE HELL ARE YOU DOING?
I WANT TO EAT ALL OF MY FAVORITE FOODS AT ONCE.
SO I'VE DECIDED TO COMBINE THEM ALL INTO A DELICIOUS POWER SHAKE.
PLEASE DON'T EXPLAIN ANY FURTHER--
I'VE GOT A SLICE OF FRENCH TOAST, SOME BACON...
...SCRAMBLED EGGS, A WAFFLE...
...SAUSAGE, A CUBE OF BUTTER, A HALF-CUP OF SYRUP...
...DICED HAM, ONIONS AND MUSHROOMS...
...A LITTLE BIT OF GRAVY AND FINALLY, A PANCAKE.
THIS IS GOING TO BE AWFUL.
THIS IS GOING TO BE AWESOME.
WHIRRR

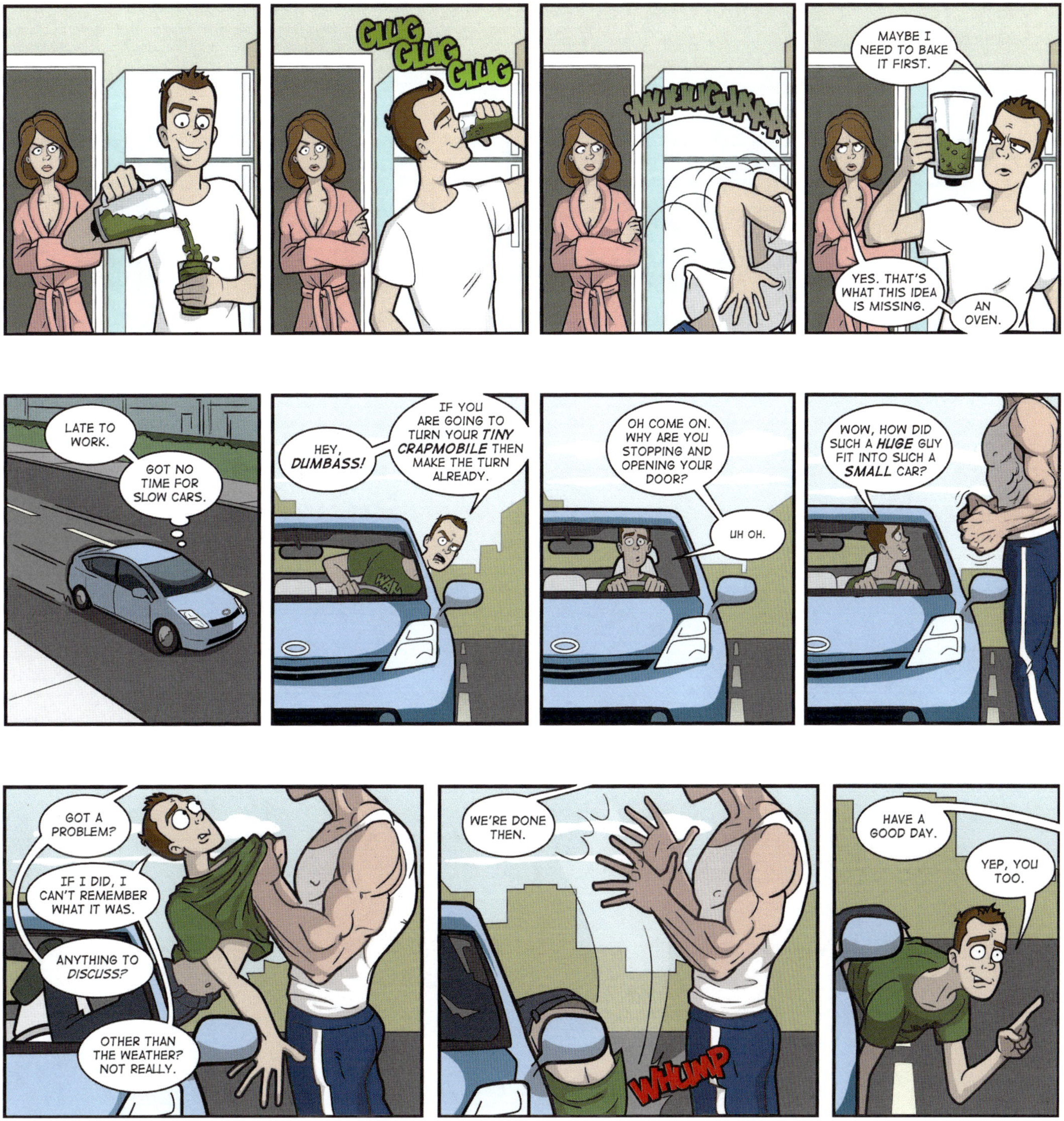
GLUG
GLUG
GLUG
MAYBE I NEED TO BAKE IT FIRST.
YES. THAT'S WHAT THIS IDEA IS MISSING.
AN OVEN.
LATE TO WORK.
GOT NO TIME FOR SLOW CARS.
HEY, DUMBASS!
IF YOU ARE GOING TO TURN YOUR TINY CRAPMOBILE THEN MAKE THE TURN ALREADY.
OH COME ON. WHY ARE YOU STOPPING AND OPENING YOUR DOOR?
UH OH.
WOW, HOW DID SUCH A HUGE GUY FIT INTO SUCH A SMALL CAR?
GOT A PROBLEM?
IF I DID, I CAN'T REMEMBER WHAT IT WAS.
ANYTHING TO DISCUSS?
OTHER THAN THE WEATHER? NOT REALLY.
WE'RE DONE THEN.
WHUMP
HAVE A GOOD DAY.
YEP, YOU TOO.

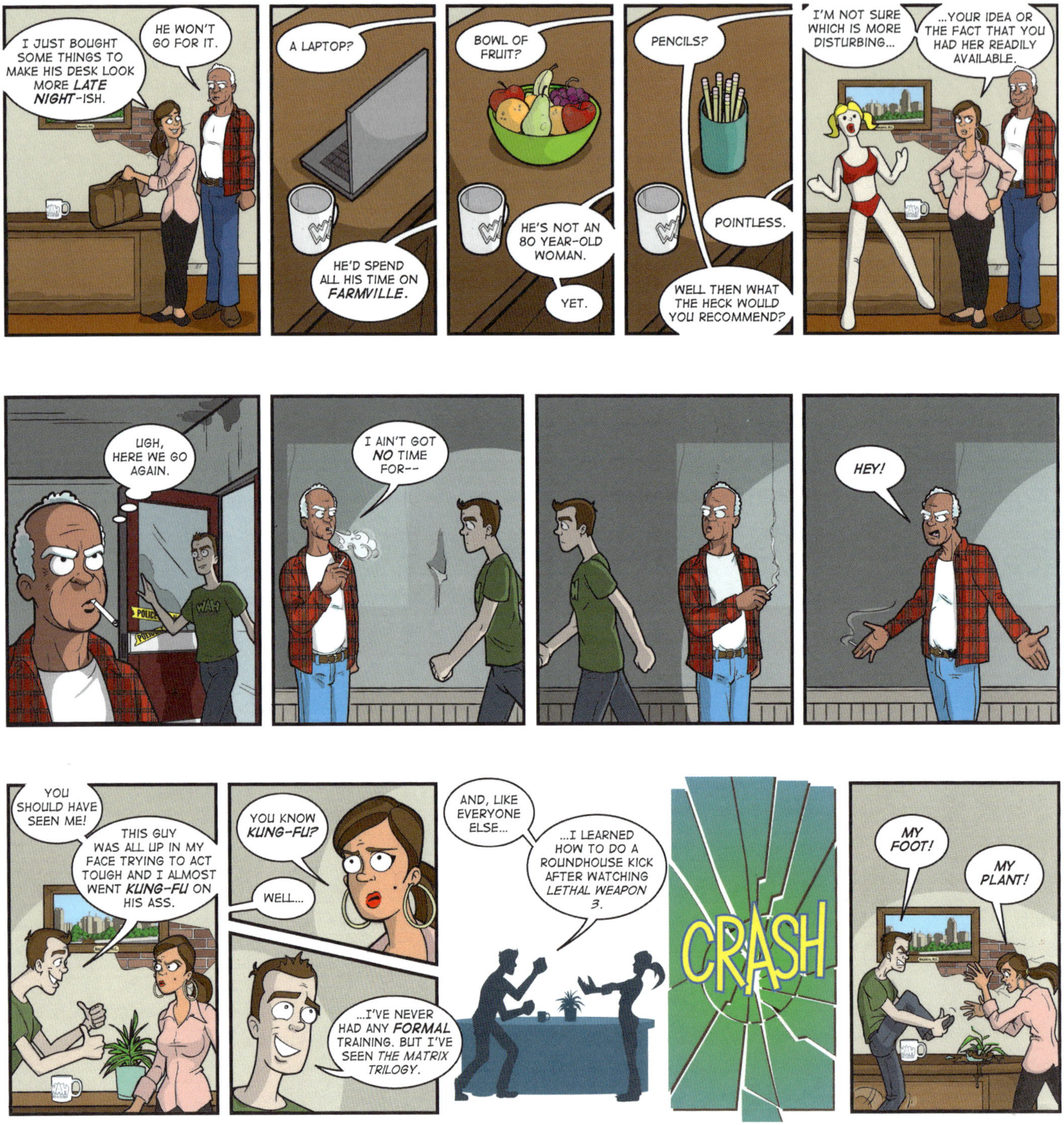
I JUST BOUGHT SOME THINGS TO MAKE HIS DESK LOOK MORE LATE NIGHT-ISH.
HE WON'T GO FOR IT.
A LAPTOP?
HE'D SPEND ALL HIS TIME ON FARMVILLE.
BOWL OF FRUIT?
HE'S NOT AN 80 YEAR-OLD WOMAN.
YET.
PENCILS?
POINTLESS.
WELL THEN WHAT THE HECK WOULD YOU RECOMMEND?
I'M NOT SURE WHICH IS MORE DISTURBING...
...YOUR IDEA OR THE FACT THAT YOU HAD HER READILY AVAILABLE.
UGH, HERE WE GO AGAIN.
I AIN'T GOT NO TIME FOR--
HEY!
YOU SHOULD HAVE SEEN ME!
THIS GUY WAS ALL UP IN MY FACE TRYING TO ACT TOUGH AND I ALMOST WENT KUNG-FU ON HIS ASS.
YOU KNOW KUNG-FU?
WELL...
...I'VE NEVER HAD ANY FORMAL TRAINING. BUT I'VE SEEN THE MATRIX TRILOGY.
AND, LIKE EVERYONE ELSE...
...I LEARNED HOW TO DO A ROUNDHOUSE KICK AFTER WATCHING LETHAL WEAPON 3.
CRASH
MY FOOT!
MY PLANT!

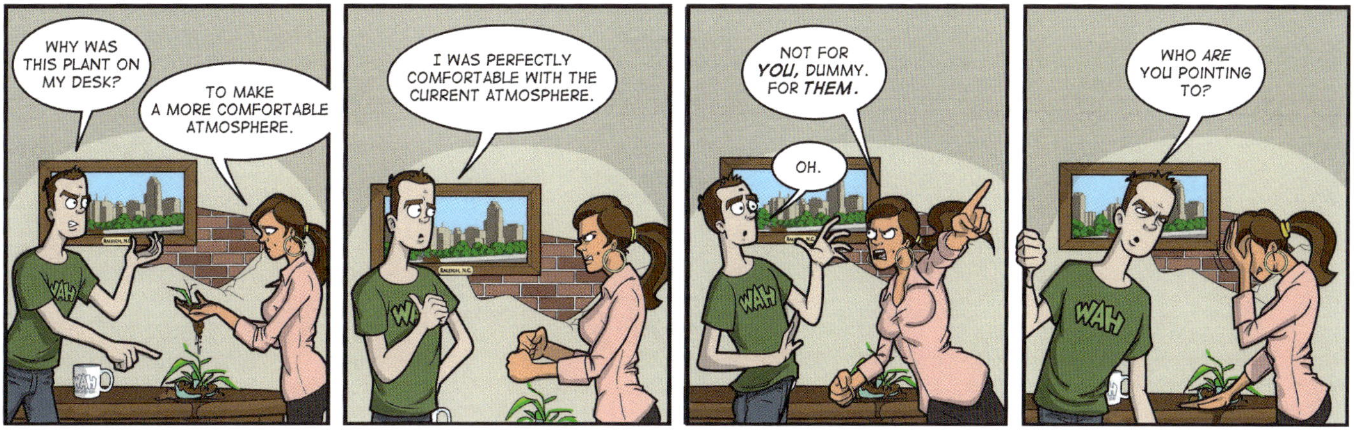
WHY WAS THIS PLANT ON MY DESK?
TO MAKE A MORE COMFORTABLE ATMOSPHERE.
I WAS PERFECTLY COMFORTABLE WITH THE CURRENT ATMOSPHERE.
NOT FOR YOU, DUMMY. FOR THEM.
OH.
WHO ARE YOU POINTING TO?

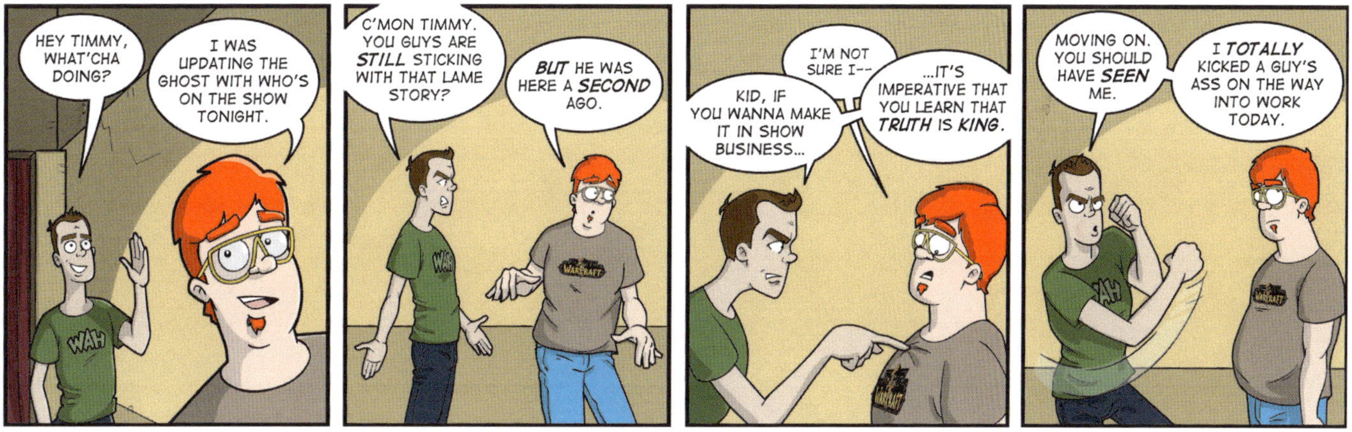
HEY TIMMY, WHAT'CHA DOING?
I WAS UPDATING THE GHOST WITH WHO'S ON THE SHOW TONIGHT.
C'MON TIMMY. YOU GUYS ARE STILL STICKING WITH THAT LAME STORY?
BUT HE WAS HERE A SECOND AGO.
KID, IF YOU WANNA MAKE IT IN SHOW BUSINESS...
I'M NOT SURE I--
...IT'S IMPERATIVE THAT YOU LEARN THAT TRUTH IS KING.
MOVING ON. YOU SHOULD HAVE SEEN ME.
I TOTALLY KICKED A GUY'S ASS ON THE WAY INTO WORK TODAY.

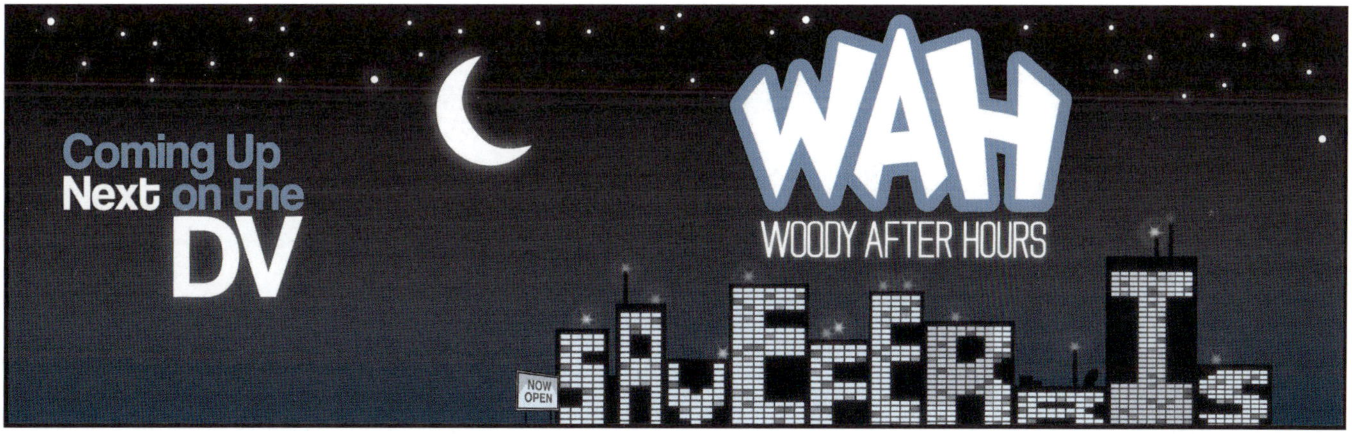
Coming Up Next on the DV
WAH
WOODY AFTER HOURS
NOW OPEN

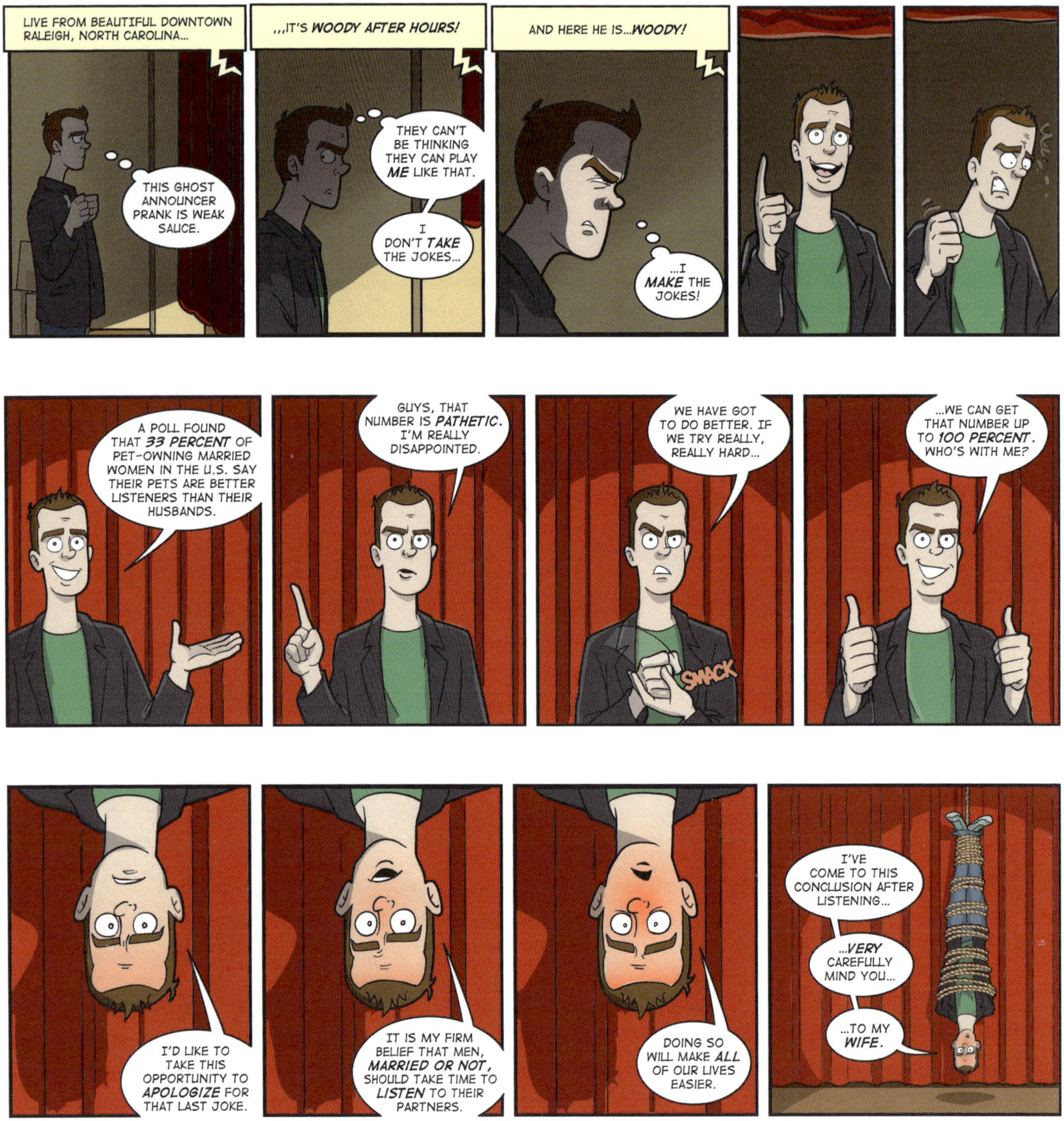
LIVE FROM BEAUTIFUL DOWNTOWN RALEIGH, NORTH CAROLINA...
THIS GHOST ANNOUNCER PRANK IS WEAK SAUCE.
...IT'S WOODY AFTER HOURS!
THEY CAN'T BE THINKING THEY CAN PLAY ME LIKE THAT.
I DON'T TAKE THE JOKES...
AND HERE HE IS...WOODY!
...I MAKE THE JOKES!
A POLL FOUND THAT 33 PERCENT OF PET-OWNING MARRIED WOMEN IN THE U.S. SAY THEIR PETS ARE BETTER LISTENERS THAN THEIR HUSBANDS.
GUYS, THAT NUMBER IS PATHETIC. I'M REALLY DISAPPOINTED.
WE HAVE GOT TO DO BETTER. IF WE TRY REALLY, REALLY HARD...
SMACK
...WE CAN GET THAT NUMBER UP TO 100 PERCENT. WHO'S WITH ME?
I'D LIKE TO TAKE THIS OPPORTUNITY TO APOLOGIZE FOR THAT LAST JOKE.
IT IS MY FIRM BELIEF THAT MEN, MARRIED OR NOT, SHOULD TAKE TIME TO LISTEN TO THEIR PARTNERS.
DOING SO WILL MAKE ALL OF OUR LIVES EASIER.
I'VE COME TO THIS CONCLUSION AFTER LISTENING...
...VERY CAREFULLY MIND YOU...
...TO MY WIFE.

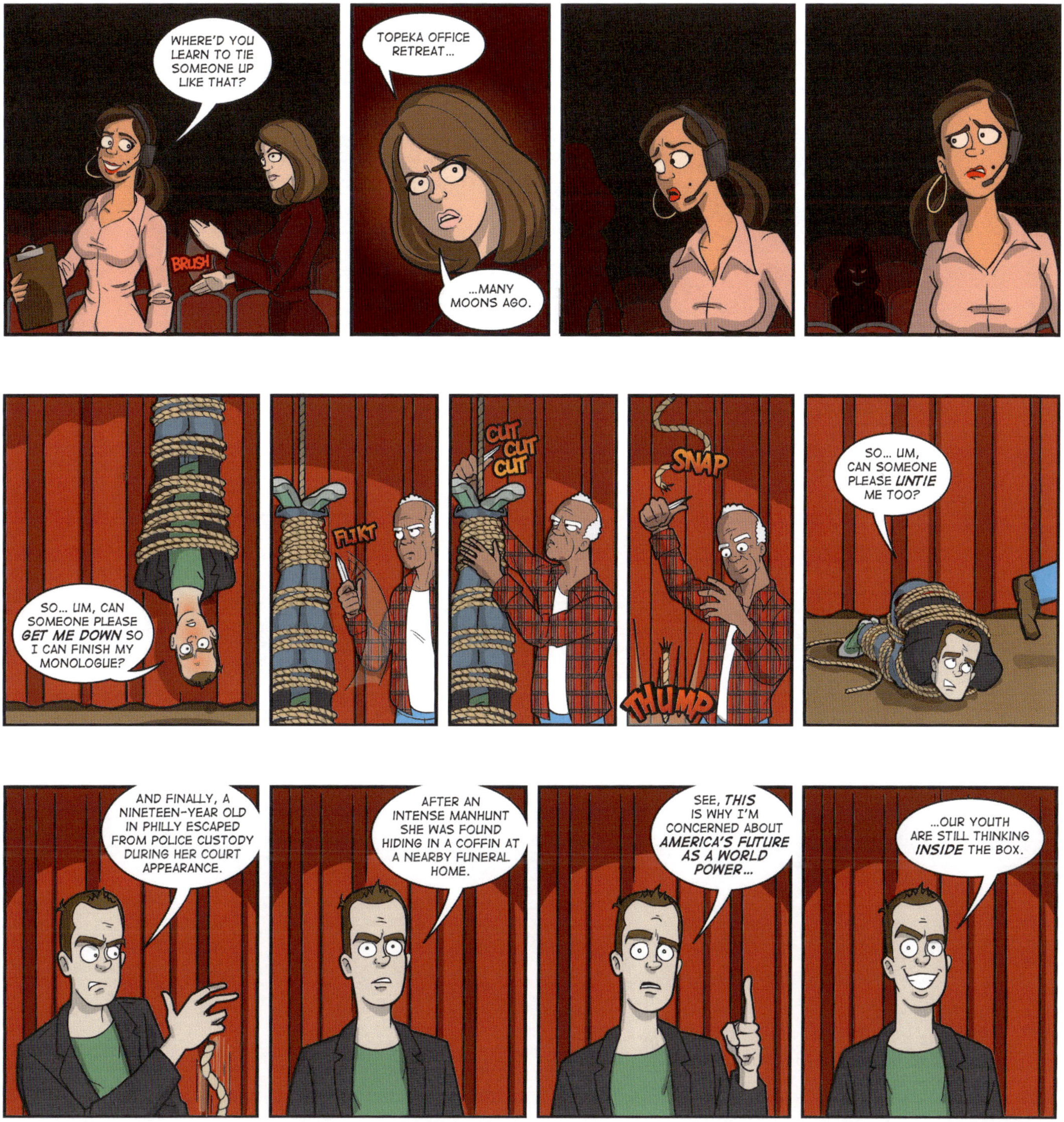
WHERE'D YOU LEARN TO TIE SOMEONE UP LIKE THAT?
BRUSH
TOPEKA OFFICE RETREAT...
...MANY MOONS AGO.
SO... UM, CAN SOMEONE PLEASE GET ME DOWN SO I CAN FINISH MY MONOLOGUE?
FLIKT
CUT CUT CUT
SNAP
THUMP
SO... UM, CAN SOMEONE PLEASE UNTIE ME TOO?
AND FINALLY, A NINETEEN-YEAR OLD IN PHILLY ESCAPED FROM POLICE CUSTODY DURING HER COURT APPEARANCE.
AFTER AN INTENSE MANHUNT SHE WAS FOUND HIDING IN A COFFIN AT A NEARBY FUNERAL HOME.
SEE, THIS IS WHY I'M CONCERNED ABOUT AMERICA'S FUTURE AS A WORLD POWER...
...OUR YOUTH ARE STILL THINKING INSIDE THE BOX.

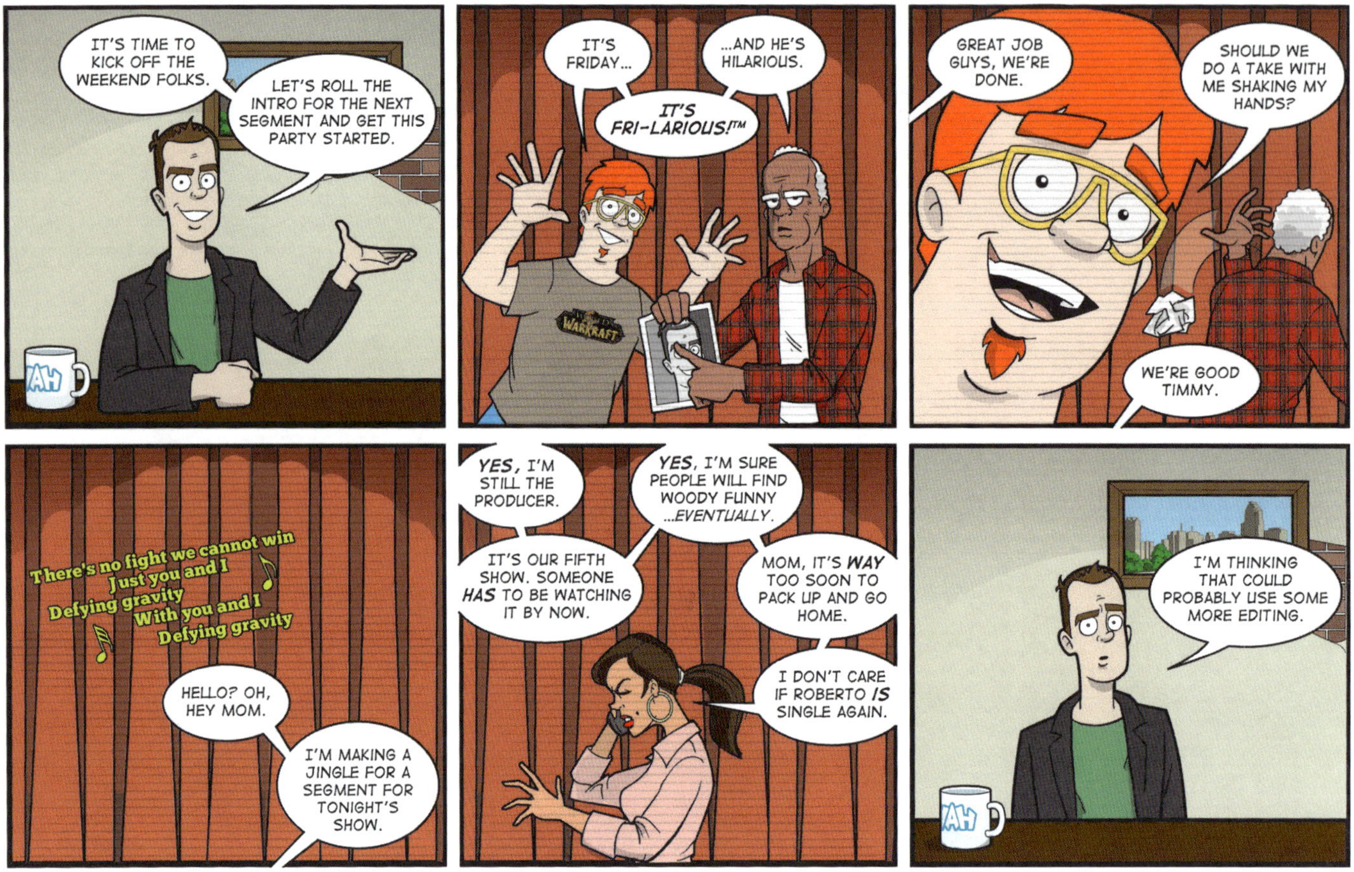
IT'S TIME TO KICK OFF THE WEEKEND FOLKS.
LET'S ROLL THE INTRO FOR THE NEXT SEGMENT AND GET THIS PARTY STARTED.
IT'S FRIDAY...
...AND HE'S HILARIOUS.
IT'S FRI-LARIOUS!™
GREAT JOB GUYS, WE'RE DONE.
SHOULD WE DO A TAKE WITH ME SHAKING MY HANDS?
WE'RE GOOD TIMMY.
There's no fight we cannot win
Just you and I
Defying gravity
With you and I
Defying gravity
HELLO? OH, HEY MOM.
I'M MAKING A JINGLE FOR A SEGMENT FOR TONIGHT'S SHOW.
YES, I'M STILL THE PRODUCER.
IT'S OUR FIFTH SHOW. SOMEONE HAS TO BE WATCHING IT BY NOW.
YES, I'M SURE PEOPLE WILL FIND WOODY FUNNY ...EVENTUALLY.
MOM, IT'S WAY TOO SOON TO PACK UP AND GO HOME.
I DON'T CARE IF ROBERTO IS SINGLE AGAIN.
I'M THINKING THAT COULD PROBABLY USE SOME MORE EDITING.

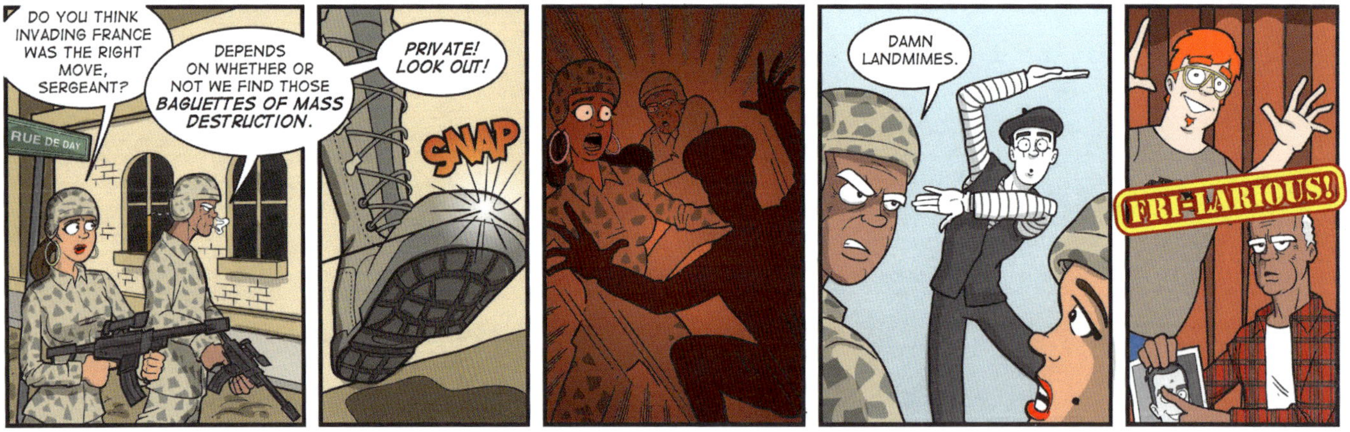
DO YOU THINK INVADING FRANCE WAS THE RIGHT MOVE, SERGEANT?
DEPENDS ON WHETHER OR NOT WE FIND THOSE BAGUETTES OF MASS DESTRUCTION.
RUE DE DAY
PRIVATE! LOOK OUT!
SNAP
DAMN LANDMIMES.
FRI-LARIOUS!

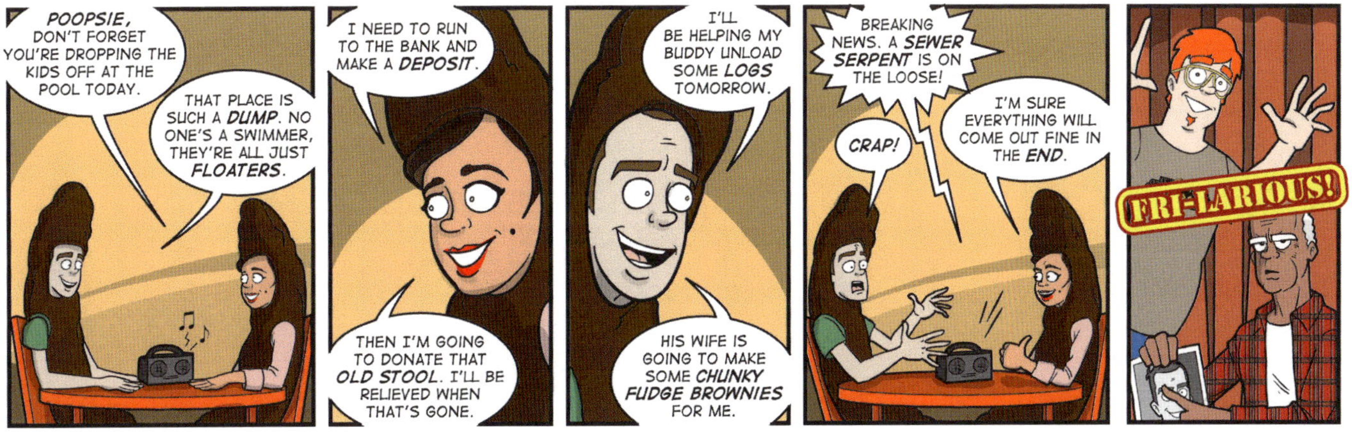
POOPSIE, DON'T FORGET YOU'RE DROPPING THE KIDS OFF AT THE POOL TODAY.
THAT PLACE IS SUCH A DUMP. NO ONE'S A SWIMMER, THEY'RE ALL JUST FLOATERS.
I NEED TO RUN TO THE BANK AND MAKE A DEPOSIT.
THEN I'M GOING TO DONATE THAT OLD STOOL. I'LL BE RELIEVED WHEN THAT'S GONE.
I'LL BE HELPING MY BUDDY UNLOAD SOME LOGS TOMORROW.
HIS WIFE IS GOING TO MAKE SOME CHUNKY FUDGE BROWNIES FOR ME.
BREAKING NEWS. A SEWER SERPENT IS ON THE LOOSE!
CRAP!
I'M SURE EVERYTHING WILL COME OUT FINE IN THE END.
FRI-LARIOUS!

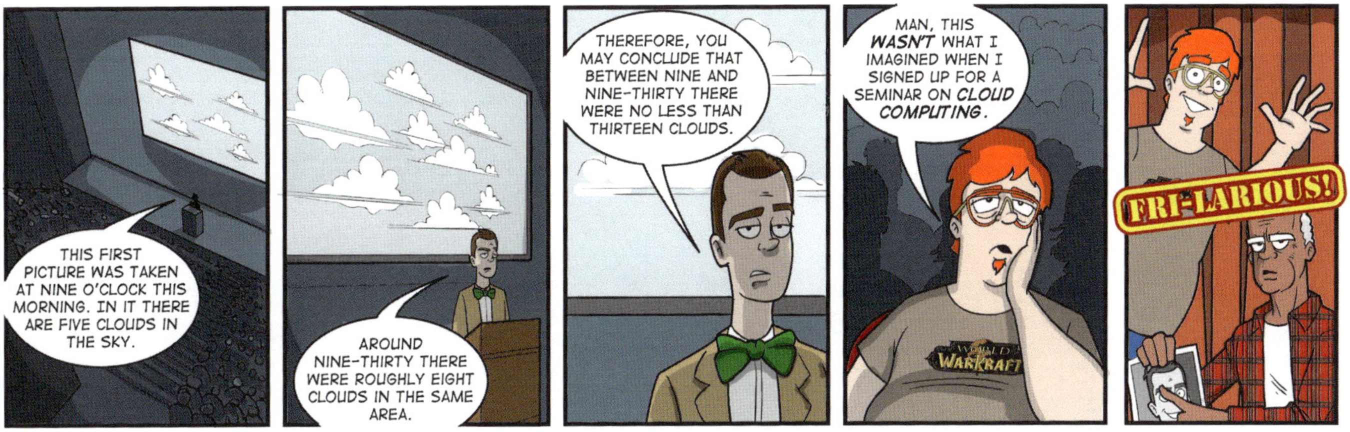
THIS FIRST PICTURE WAS TAKEN AT NINE O'CLOCK THIS MORNING. IN IT THERE ARE FIVE CLOUDS IN THE SKY.
AROUND NINE-THIRTY THERE WERE ROUGHLY EIGHT CLOUDS IN THE SAME AREA.
THEREFORE, YOU MAY CONCLUDE THAT BETWEEN NINE AND NINE-THIRTY THERE WERE NO LESS THAN THIRTEEN CLOUDS.
MAN, THIS WASN'T WHAT I IMAGINED WHEN I SIGNED UP FOR A SEMINAR ON CLOUD COMPUTING.
WARKRAFT
FRI-LARIOUS!

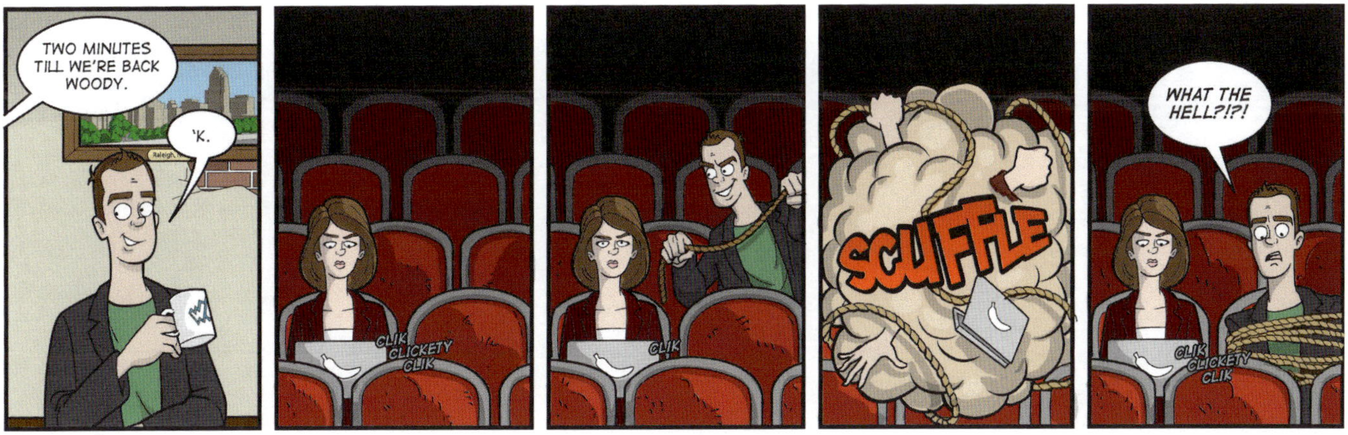
TWO MINUTES TILL WE'RE BACK WOODY.
'K.
CLIK CLICKETY CLIK
CLIK
SCUFFLE
WHAT THE HELL?!?!
CLIK CLICKETY CLIK

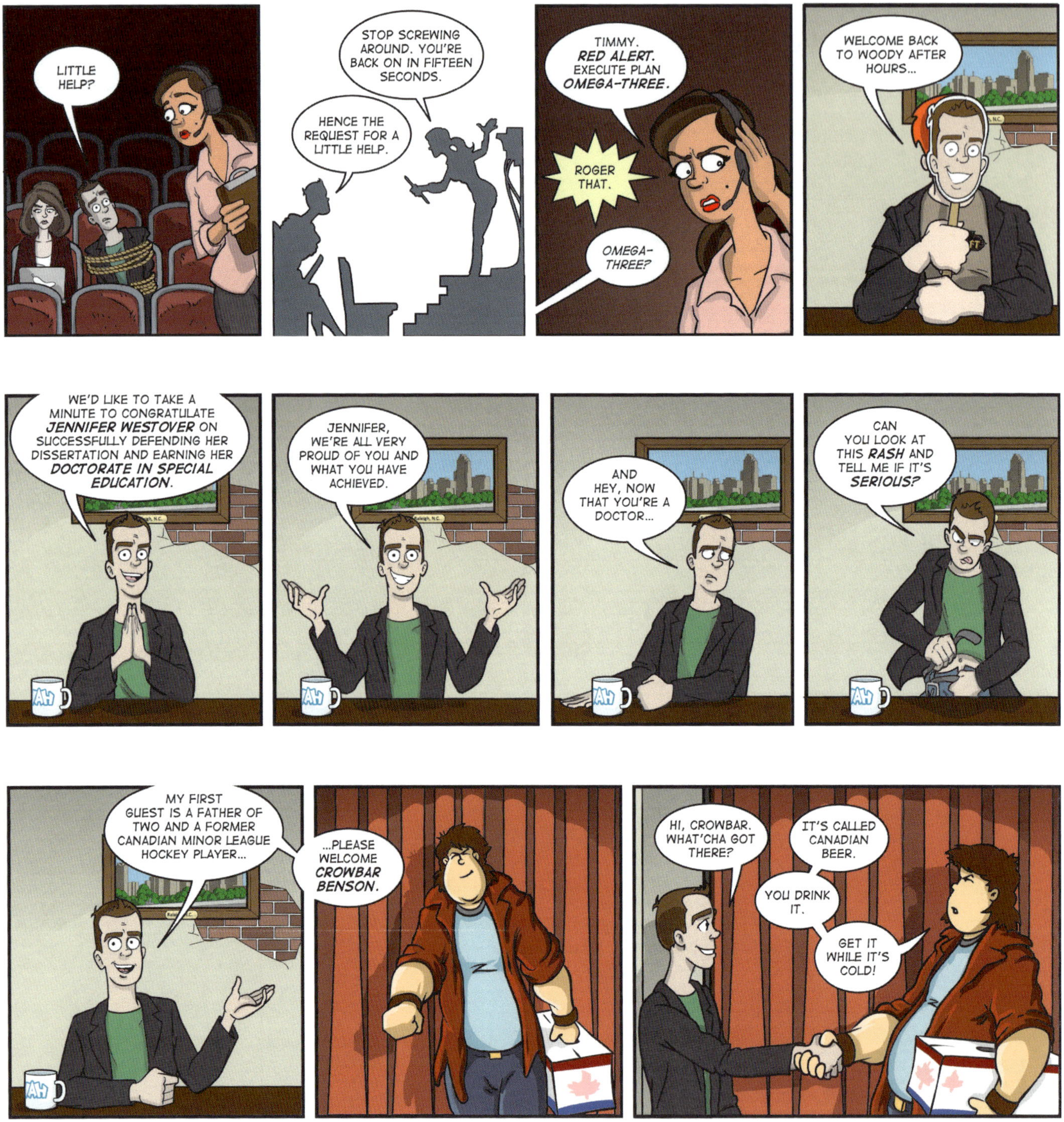
LITTLE HELP?
STOP SCREWING AROUND. YOU'RE BACK ON IN FIFTEEN SECONDS.
HENCE THE REQUEST FOR A LITTLE HELP.
TIMMY. RED ALERT. EXECUTE PLAN OMEGA-THREE.
ROGER THAT.
OMEGA-THREE?
WELCOME BACK TO WOODY AFTER HOURS...
WE'D LIKE TO TAKE A MINUTE TO CONGRATULATE JENNIFER WESTOVER ON SUCCESSFULLY DEFENDING HER DISSERTATION AND EARNING HER DOCTORATE IN SPECIAL EDUCATION.
JENNIFER, WE'RE ALL VERY PROUD OF YOU AND WHAT YOU HAVE ACHIEVED.
AND HEY, NOW THAT YOU'RE A DOCTOR...
CAN YOU LOOK AT THIS RASH AND TELL ME IF IT'S SERIOUS?
MY FIRST GUEST IS A FATHER OF TWO AND A FORMER CANADIAN MINOR LEAGUE HOCKEY PLAYER...
...PLEASE WELCOME CROWBAR BENSON.
HI, CROWBAR. WHAT'CHA GOT THERE?
IT'S CALLED CANADIAN BEER.
YOU DRINK IT.
GET IT WHILE IT'S COLD!

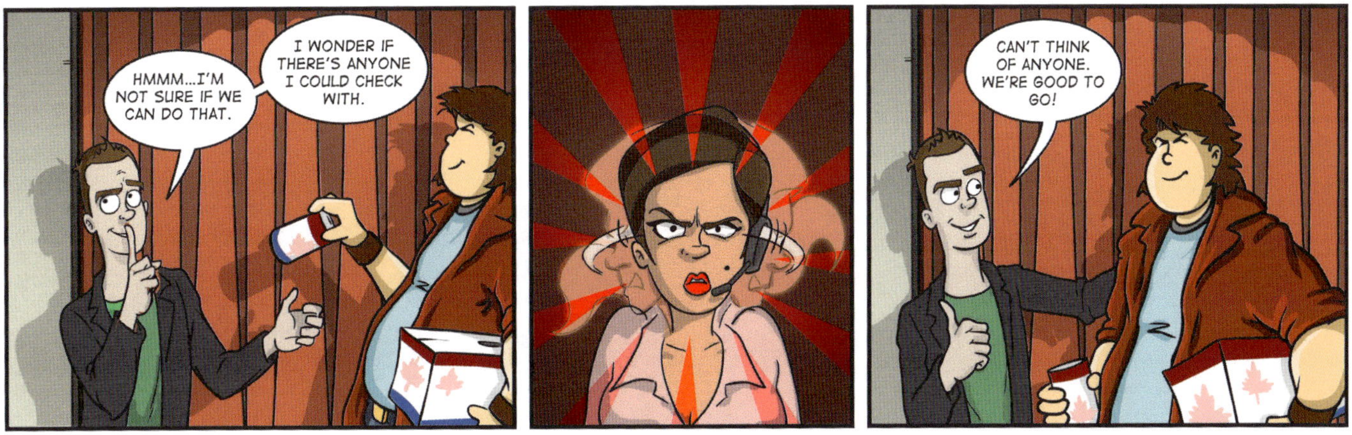
HMMM...I'M NOT SURE IF WE CAN DO THAT.
I WONDER IF THERE'S ANYONE I COULD CHECK WITH.
CAN'T THINK OF ANYONE. WE'RE GOOD TO GO!

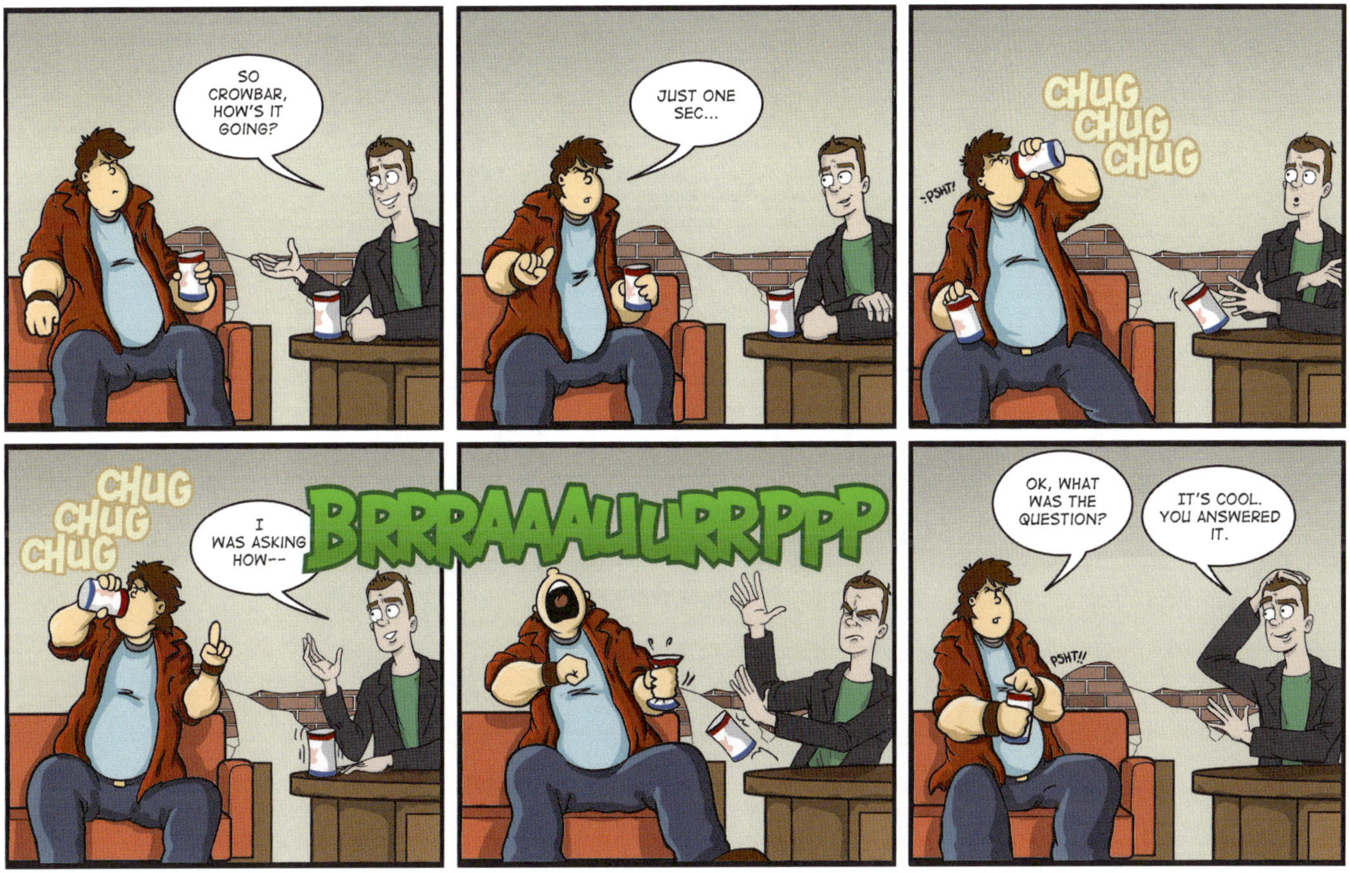
SO CROWBAR, HOW'S IT GOING?
JUST ONE SEC...
CHUG CHUG CHUG
PSHT!
CHUG CHUG CHUG
I WAS ASKING HOW--
BRRRAAAUURRPPP
PSHT!!
OK, WHAT WAS THE QUESTION?
IT'S COOL. YOU ANSWERED IT.

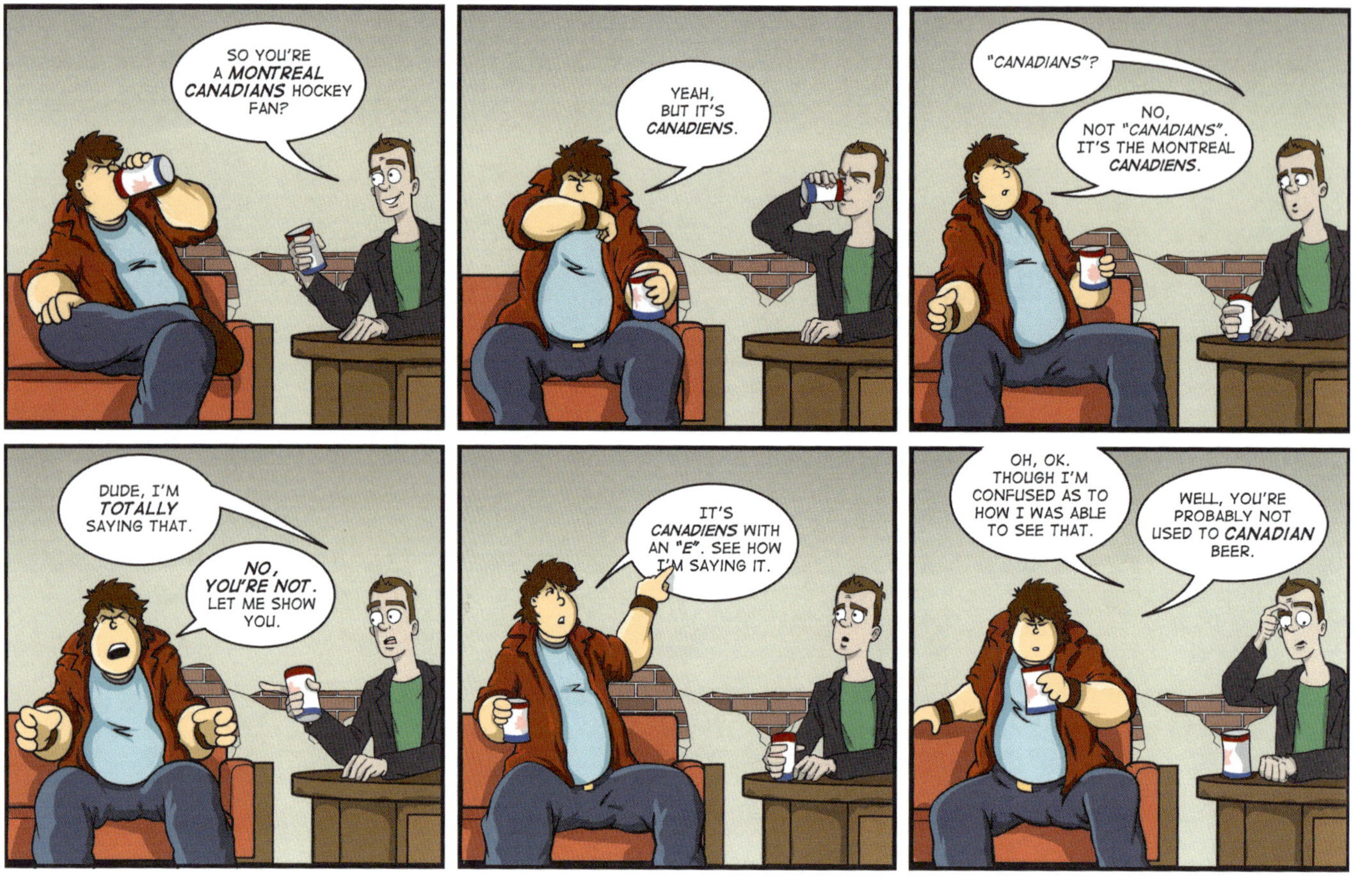
SO YOU'RE A MONTREAL CANADIANS HOCKEY FAN?
YEAH, BUT IT'S CANADIENS.
"CANADIANS"?
NO, NOT "CANADIANS". IT'S THE MONTREAL CANADIENS.
DUDE, I'M TOTALLY SAYING THAT.
NO, YOU'RE NOT. LET ME SHOW YOU.
IT'S CANADIENS WITH AN "E". SEE HOW I'M SAYING IT.
OH, OK. THOUGH I'M CONFUSED AS TO HOW I WAS ABLE TO SEE THAT.
WELL, YOU'RE PROBABLY NOT USED TO CANADIAN BEER.

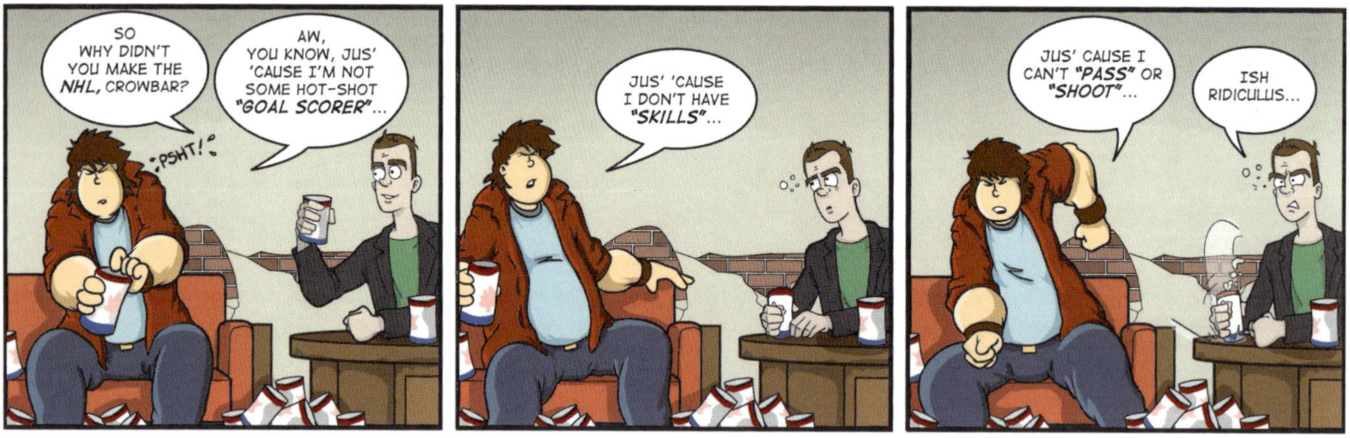
SO WHY DIDN'T YOU MAKE THE NHL, CROWBAR?
AW, YOU KNOW, JUS' 'CAUSE I'M NOT SOME HOT-SHOT "GOAL SCORER"...
PSHT!
JUS' 'CAUSE I DON'T HAVE "SKILLS"...
JUS' CAUSE I CAN'T "PASS" OR "SHOOT"...
ISH RIDICULUS...

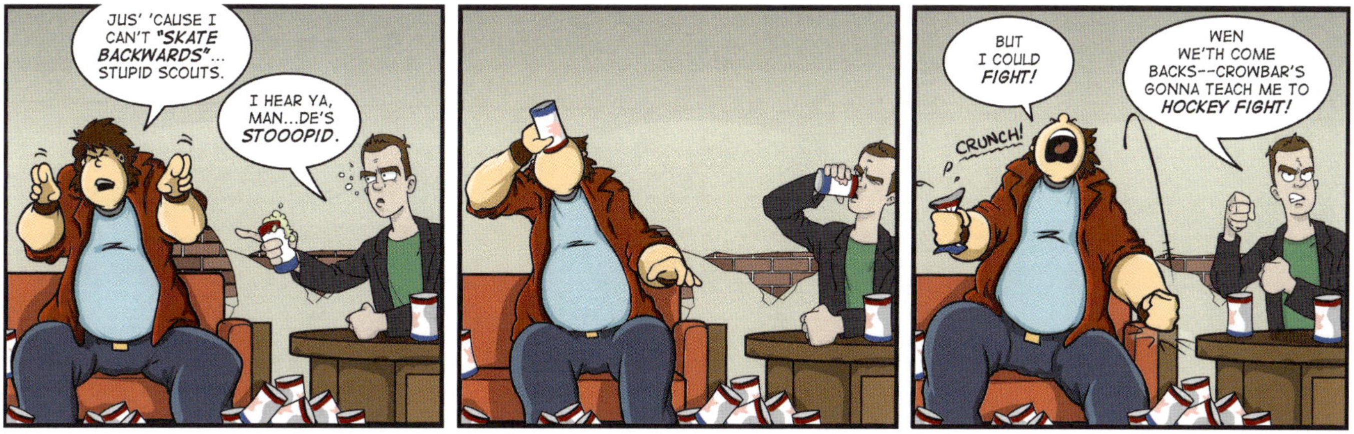
JUS' 'CAUSE I CAN'T "SKATE BACKWARDS"... STUPID SCOUTS.
I HEAR YA, MAN...DE'S STOOOPID.
BUT I COULD FIGHT!
CRUNCH!
WEN WE'TH COME BACKS--CROWBAR'S GONNA TEACH ME TO HOCKEY FIGHT!

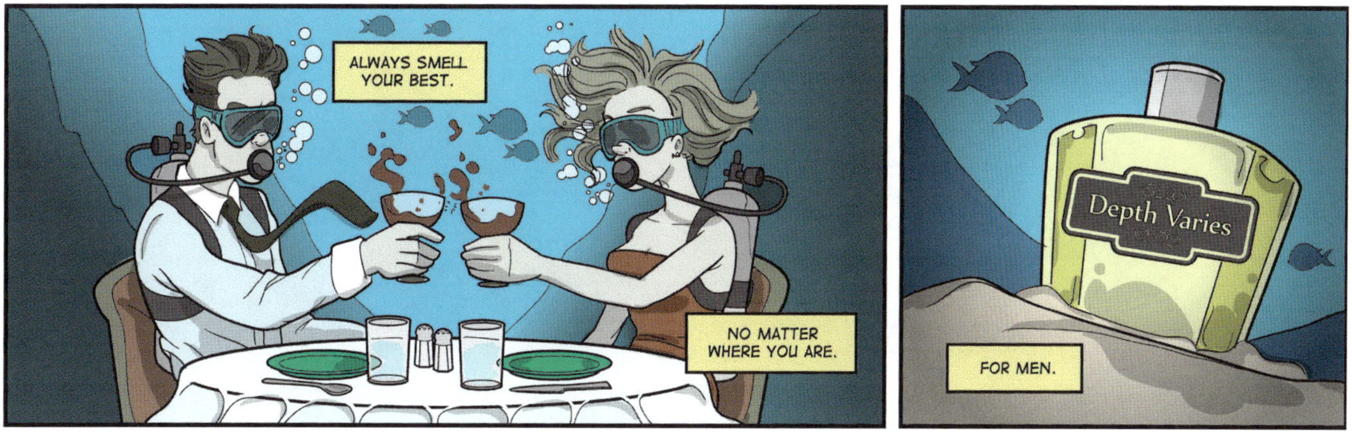
ALWAYS SMELL YOUR BEST.
NO MATTER WHERE YOU ARE.
Depth Varies
FOR MEN.

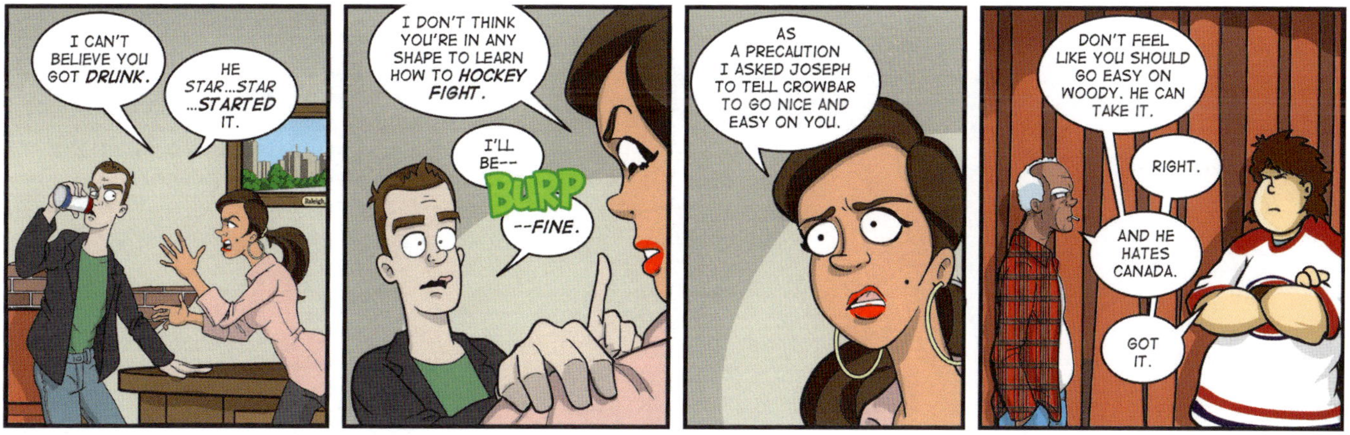
I CAN'T BELIEVE YOU GOT DRUNK.
HE STAR...STAR ...STARTED IT.
I DON'T THINK YOU'RE IN ANY SHAPE TO LEARN HOW TO HOCKEY FIGHT.
I'LL BE--
BURP
--FINE.
AS A PRECAUTION I ASKED JOSEPH TO TELL CROWBAR TO GO NICE AND EASY ON YOU.
DON'T FEEL LIKE YOU SHOULD GO EASY ON WOODY. HE CAN TAKE IT.
RIGHT.
AND HE HATES CANADA.
GOT IT.

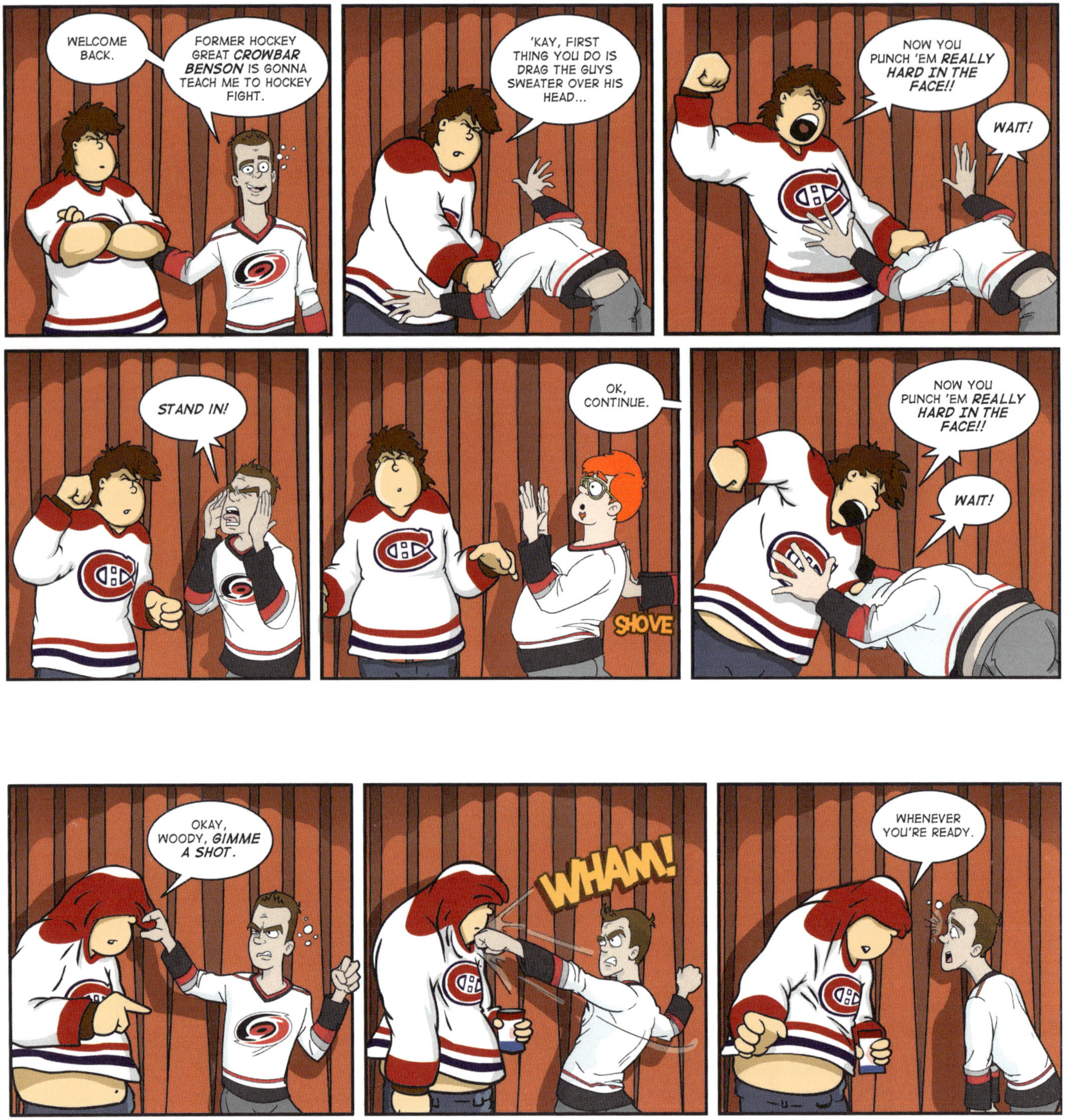
WELCOME BACK.
FORMER HOCKEY GREAT CROWBAR BENSON IS GONNA TEACH ME TO HOCKEY FIGHT.
'KAY, FIRST THING YOU DO IS DRAG THE GUYS SWEATER OVER HIS HEAD...
NOW YOU PUNCH 'EM REALLY HARD IN THE FACE!!
WAIT!
STAND IN!
OK, CONTINUE.
SHOVE
NOW YOU PUNCH 'EM REALLY HARD IN THE FACE!!
WAIT!
OKAY, WOODY, GIMME A SHOT.
WHAM!
WHENEVER YOU'RE READY.

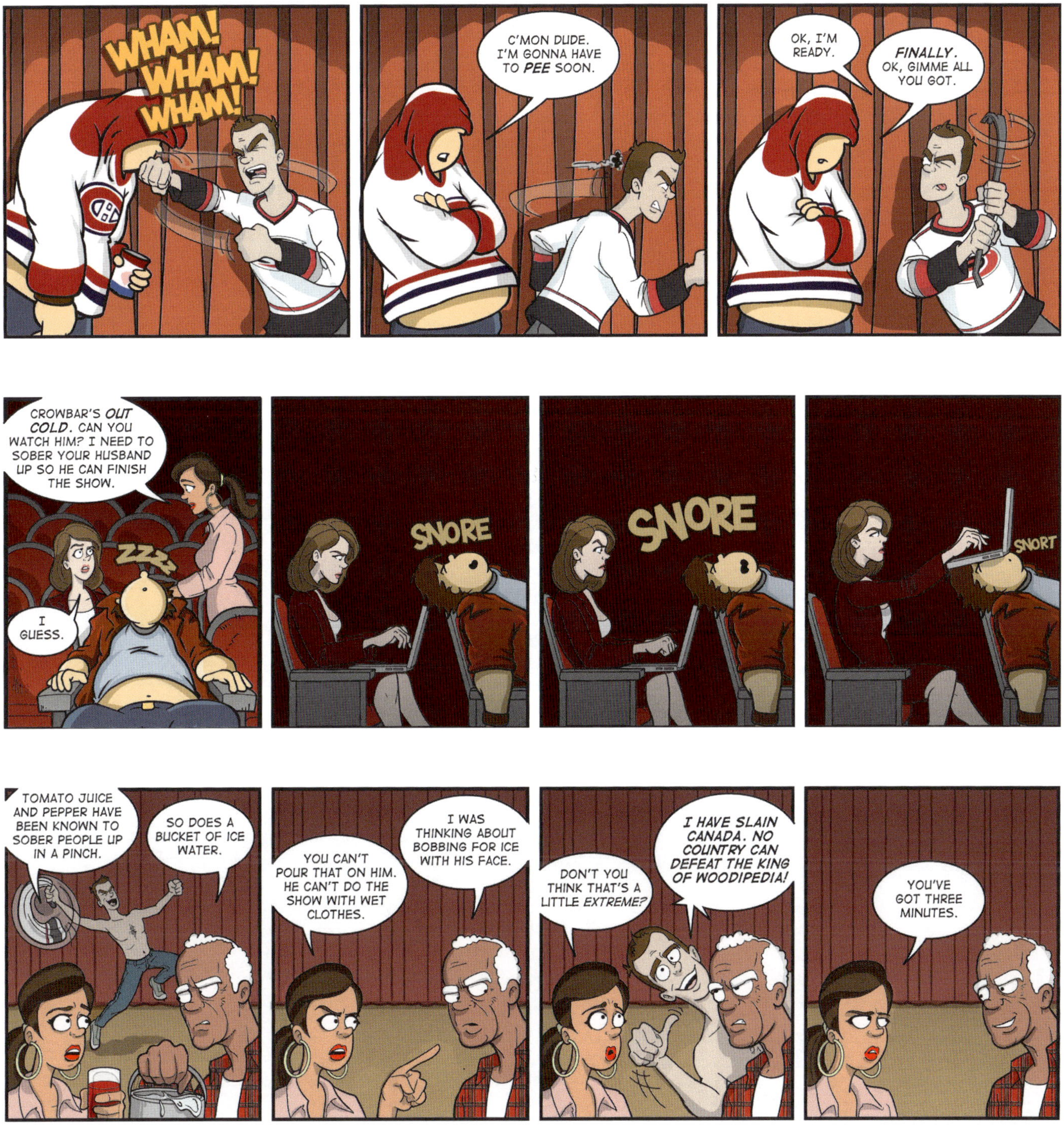
WHAM! WHAM! WHAM!
C'MON DUDE. I'M GONNA HAVE TO PEE SOON.
OK, I'M READY.
FINALLY. OK, GIMME ALL YOU GOT.
CROWBAR'S OUT COLD. CAN YOU WATCH HIM? I NEED TO SOBER YOUR HUSBAND UP SO HE CAN FINISH THE SHOW.
I GUESS.
ZZZ
SNORE
SNORE
SNORT
TOMATO JUICE AND PEPPER HAVE BEEN KNOWN TO SOBER PEOPLE UP IN A PINCH.
SO DOES A BUCKET OF ICE WATER.
YOU CAN'T POUR THAT ON HIM. HE CAN'T DO THE SHOW WITH WET CLOTHES.
I WAS THINKING ABOUT BOBBING FOR ICE WITH HIS FACE.
DON'T YOU THINK THAT'S A LITTLE EXTREME?
I HAVE SLAIN CANADA. NO COUNTRY CAN DEFEAT THE KING OF WOODIPEDIA!
YOU'VE GOT THREE MINUTES.

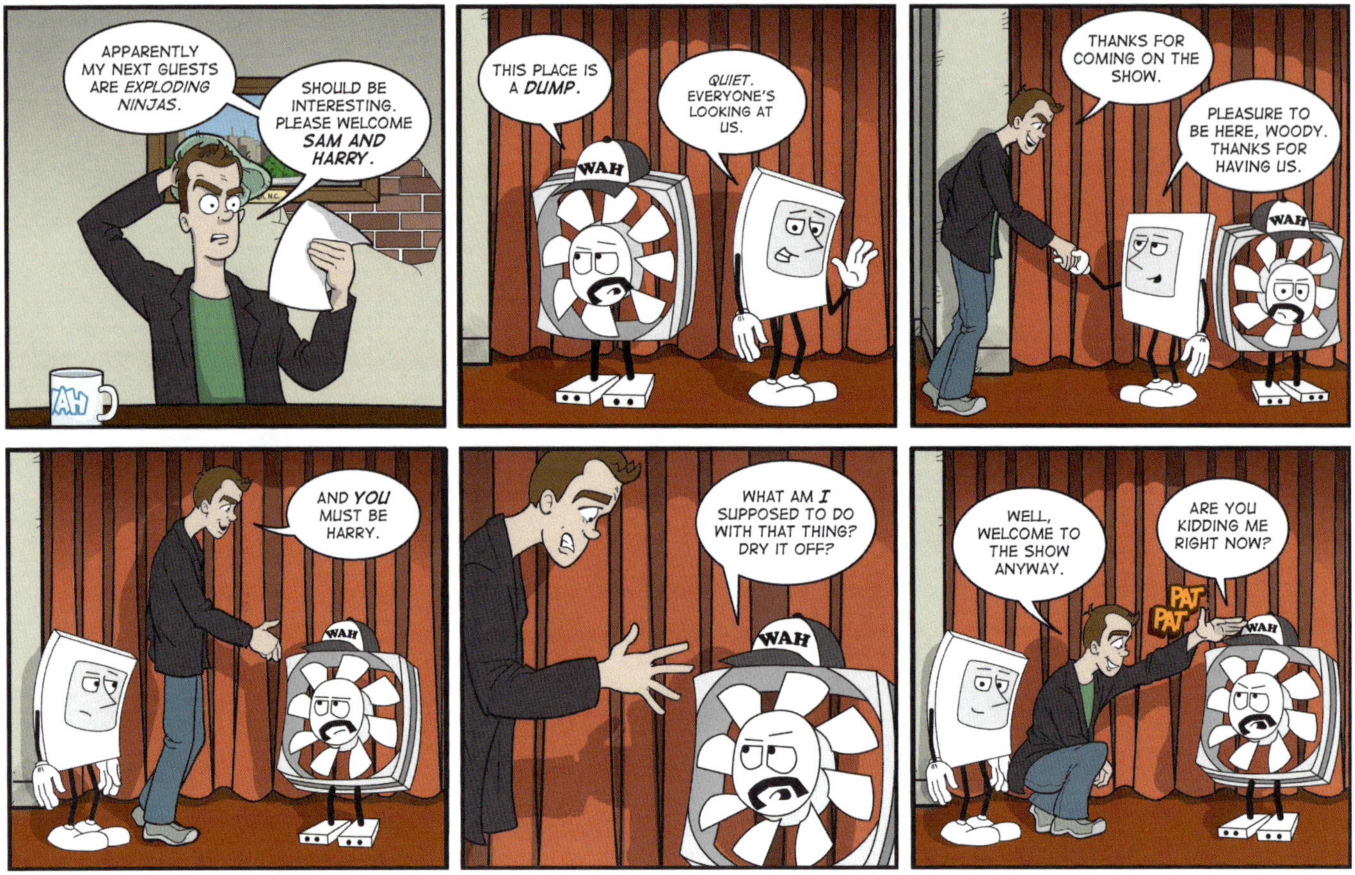
APPARENTLY MY NEXT GUESTS ARE *EXPLODING NINJAS*.
SHOULD BE INTERESTING. PLEASE WELCOME **SAM AND HARRY**.
THIS PLACE IS A **DUMP**.
QUIET. EVERYONE'S LOOKING AT US.
WAH
THANKS FOR COMING ON THE SHOW.
PLEASURE TO BE HERE, WOODY. THANKS FOR HAVING US.
AND *YOU* MUST BE HARRY.
WHAT AM *I* SUPPOSED TO DO WITH THAT THING? DRY IT OFF?
WELL, WELCOME TO THE SHOW ANYWAY.
PAT PAT
ARE YOU KIDDING ME RIGHT NOW?

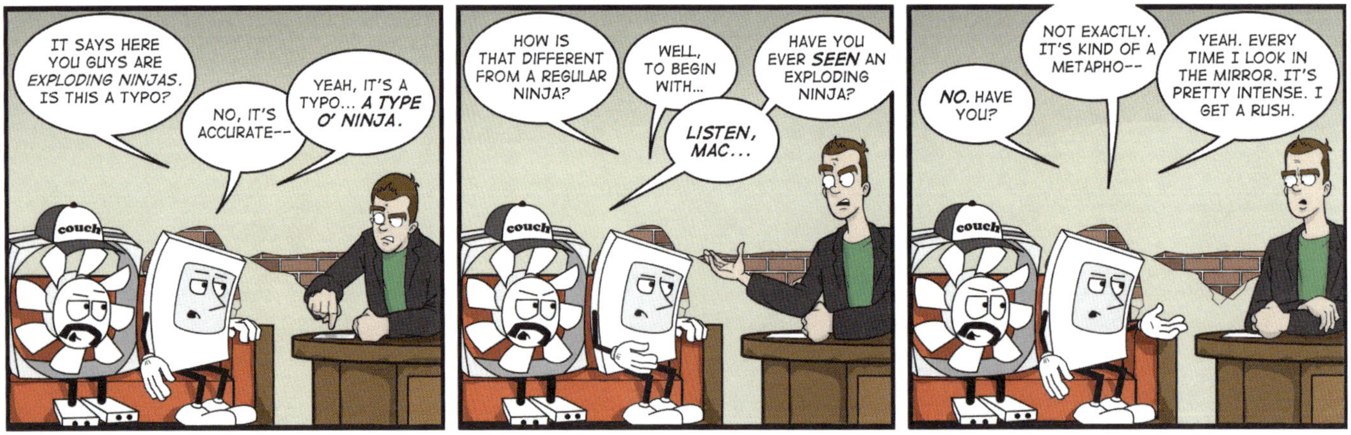
IT SAYS HERE YOU GUYS ARE *EXPLODING NINJAS*. IS THIS A TYPO?
NO, IT'S ACCURATE--
YEAH, IT'S A TYPO... ***A TYPE O' NINJA***.
couch
HOW IS THAT DIFFERENT FROM A REGULAR NINJA?
WELL, TO BEGIN WITH...
HAVE YOU EVER ***SEEN*** AN EXPLODING NINJA?
LISTEN, MAC...
NO. HAVE YOU?
NOT EXACTLY. IT'S KIND OF A METAPHO--
YEAH. EVERY TIME I LOOK IN THE MIRROR. IT'S PRETTY INTENSE. I GET A RUSH.

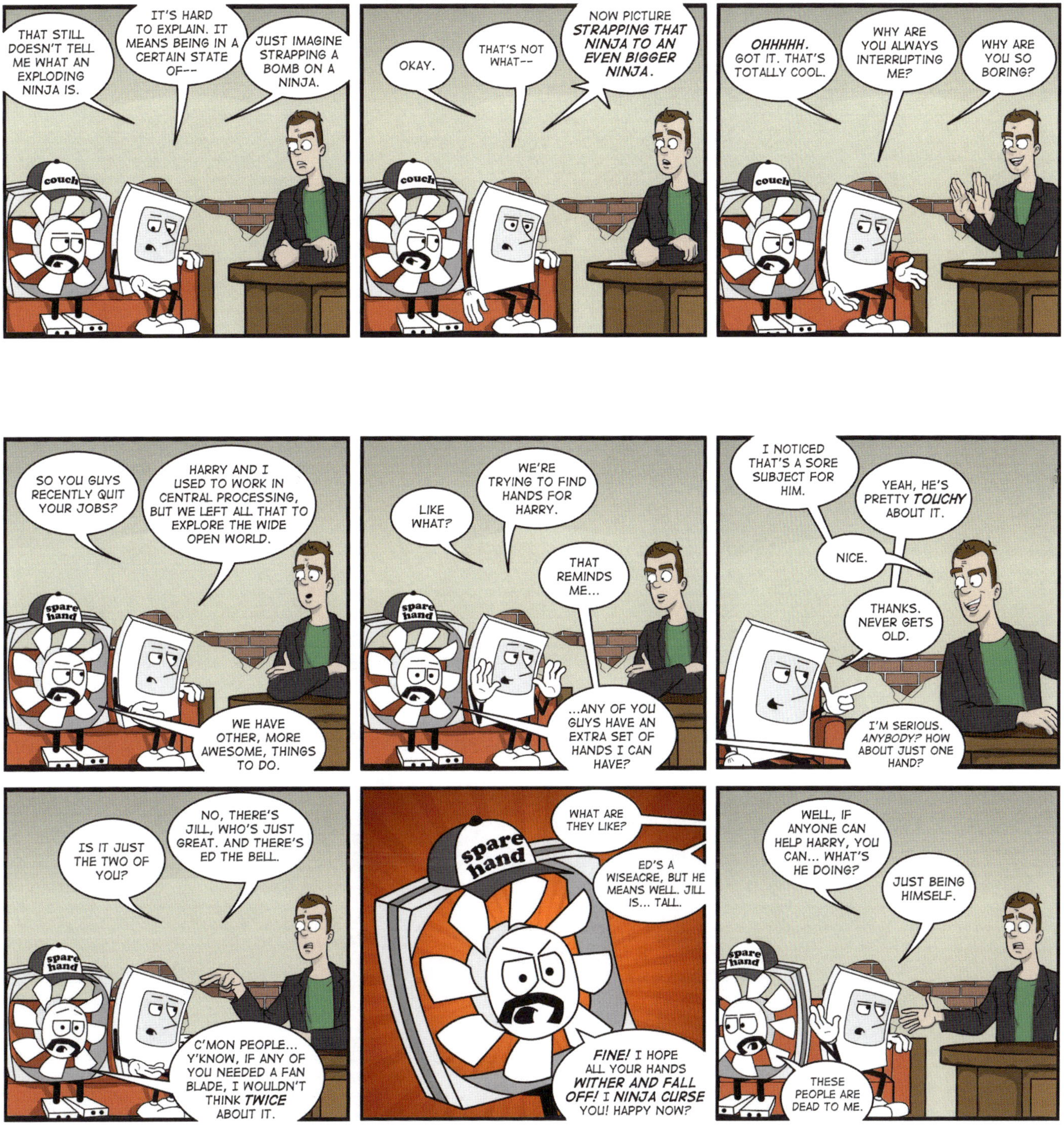
THAT STILL DOESN'T TELL ME WHAT AN EXPLODING NINJA IS.
IT'S HARD TO EXPLAIN. IT MEANS BEING IN A CERTAIN STATE OF--
JUST IMAGINE STRAPPING A BOMB ON A NINJA.
couch
OKAY.
THAT'S NOT WHAT--
NOW PICTURE STRAPPING THAT NINJA TO AN EVEN BIGGER NINJA.
OHHHHH. GOT IT. THAT'S TOTALLY COOL.
WHY ARE YOU ALWAYS INTERRUPTING ME?
WHY ARE YOU SO BORING?
SO YOU GUYS RECENTLY QUIT YOUR JOBS?
HARRY AND I USED TO WORK IN CENTRAL PROCESSING, BUT WE LEFT ALL THAT TO EXPLORE THE WIDE OPEN WORLD.
spare hand
WE HAVE OTHER, MORE AWESOME, THINGS TO DO.
LIKE WHAT?
WE'RE TRYING TO FIND HANDS FOR HARRY.
THAT REMINDS ME...
...ANY OF YOU GUYS HAVE AN EXTRA SET OF HANDS I CAN HAVE?
I NOTICED THAT'S A SORE SUBJECT FOR HIM.
YEAH, HE'S PRETTY TOUCHY ABOUT IT.
NICE.
THANKS. NEVER GETS OLD.
I'M SERIOUS. ANYBODY? HOW ABOUT JUST ONE HAND?
IS IT JUST THE TWO OF YOU?
NO, THERE'S JILL, WHO'S JUST GREAT. AND THERE'S ED THE BELL.
C'MON PEOPLE... Y'KNOW, IF ANY OF YOU NEEDED A FAN BLADE, I WOULDN'T THINK TWICE ABOUT IT.
WHAT ARE THEY LIKE?
ED'S A WISEACRE, BUT HE MEANS WELL. JILL IS... TALL.
FINE! I HOPE ALL YOUR HANDS WITHER AND FALL OFF! I NINJA CURSE YOU! HAPPY NOW?
WELL, IF ANYONE CAN HELP HARRY, YOU CAN... WHAT'S HE DOING?
JUST BEING HIMSELF.
THESE PEOPLE ARE DEAD TO ME.

IT WAS A REAL PLEASURE HAVING YOU GUYS ON MY SHOW.
PLEASE, YOU'RE GOING TO MAKE HARRY BLUSH.
PFFT! I DON'T EVEN KNOW THE MEANING OF THE WORD "BLUSH."
IT'S TRUE... HE DOESN'T. BUT SERIOUSLY, THE PLEASURE IS ALL MINE.
I KNOW HARRY TOOK NO PLEASURE FROM THIS.
YOU GOT THAT RIGHT.
no fun
I THINK I KNOW HOW TO MAKE IT UP TO YOU, HARRY...
YEAH? TRY ME.
CAN YOU READ THIS TO THE AUDIENCE?
GO AHEAD, HARRY. BE NICE TO THE MAN.
SIGH
FINE. GIVE IT HERE.
AHEM. "HEY, WOODY. YOU'RE A TERRIFIC GUY, AND I LOVE YOUR SHOW."
LADIES AND GENTLEMEN, LET'S HEAR IT FOR MY BIGGEST FAN!
WELL, DUH. THAT OSCILLATING CHUMP IN THE GREEN ROOM AIN'T GOT NOTHING ON ME.

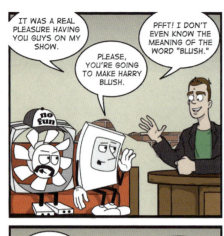

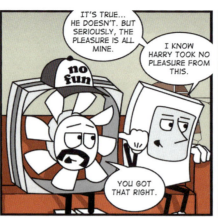

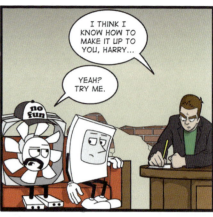

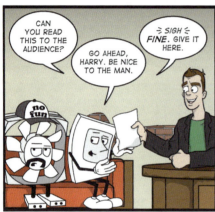

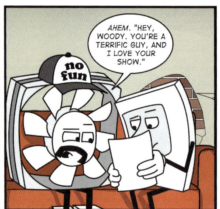

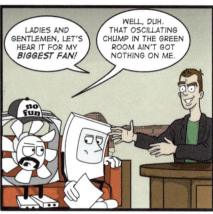

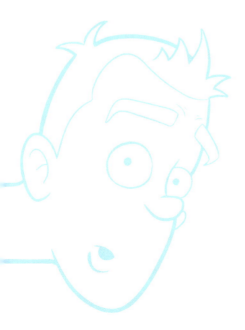

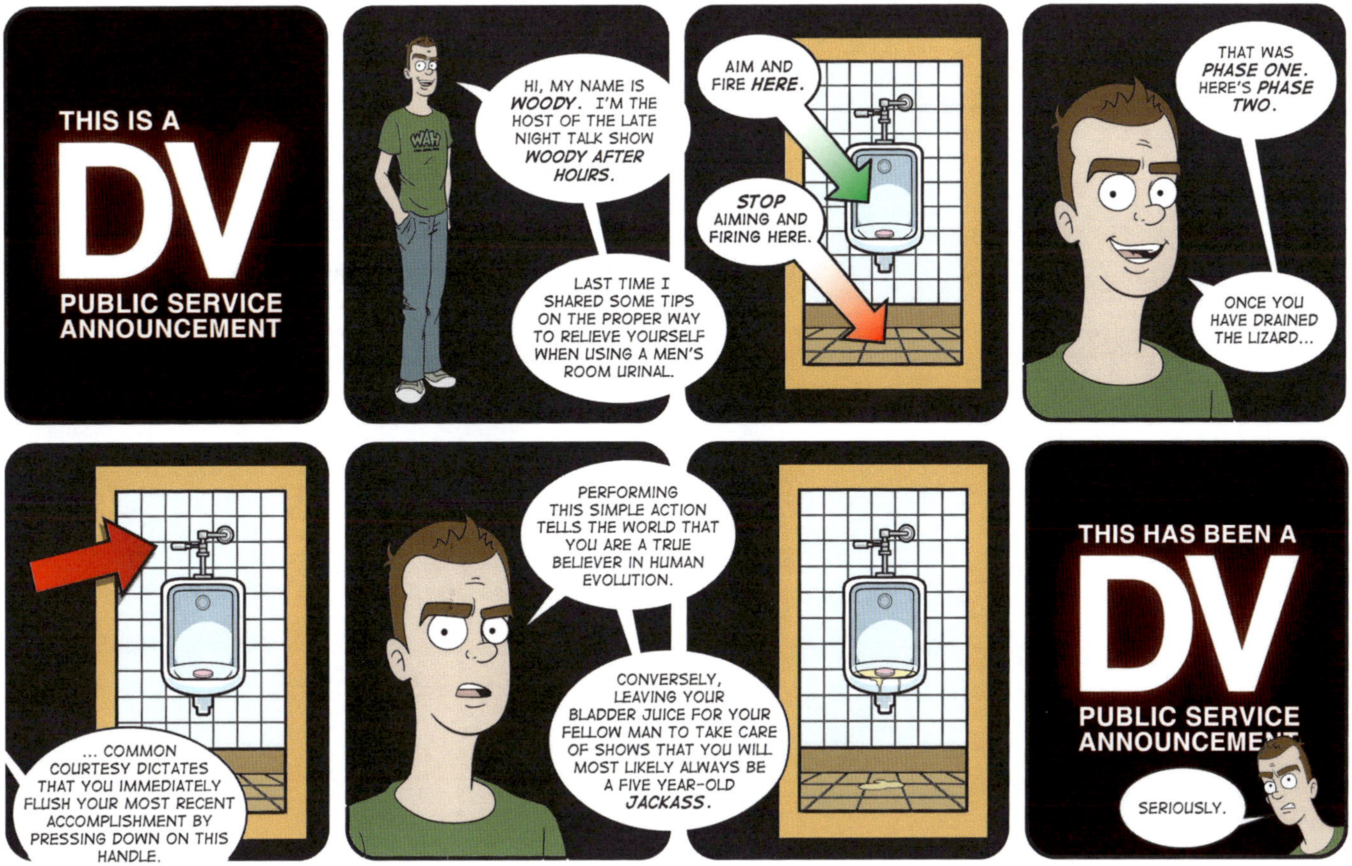
THIS IS A
DV
PUBLIC SERVICE ANNOUNCEMENT
HI, MY NAME IS WOODY. I'M THE HOST OF THE LATE NIGHT TALK SHOW WOODY AFTER HOURS.
LAST TIME I SHARED SOME TIPS ON THE PROPER WAY TO RELIEVE YOURSELF WHEN USING A MEN'S ROOM URINAL.
AIM AND FIRE HERE.
STOP AIMING AND FIRING HERE.
THAT WAS PHASE ONE. HERE'S PHASE TWO.
ONCE YOU HAVE DRAINED THE LIZARD...
... COMMON COURTESY DICTATES THAT YOU IMMEDIATELY FLUSH YOUR MOST RECENT ACCOMPLISHMENT BY PRESSING DOWN ON THIS HANDLE.
PERFORMING THIS SIMPLE ACTION TELLS THE WORLD THAT YOU ARE A TRUE BELIEVER IN HUMAN EVOLUTION.
CONVERSELY, LEAVING YOUR BLADDER JUICE FOR YOUR FELLOW MAN TO TAKE CARE OF SHOWS THAT YOU WILL MOST LIKELY ALWAYS BE A FIVE YEAR-OLD JACKASS.
THIS HAS BEEN A
DV
PUBLIC SERVICE ANNOUNCEMENT
SERIOUSLY.

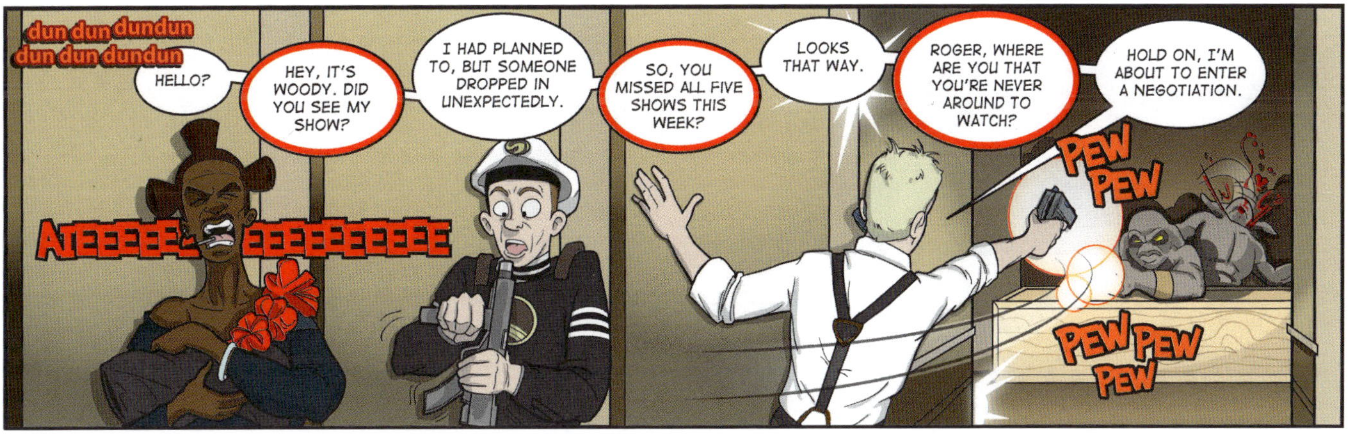
dun dun dundun
dun dun dundun
HELLO?
HEY, IT'S WOODY. DID YOU SEE MY SHOW?
AIEEEEEEEEEEEEEEEEE
I HAD PLANNED TO, BUT SOMEONE DROPPED IN UNEXPECTEDLY.
SO, YOU MISSED ALL FIVE SHOWS THIS WEEK?
LOOKS THAT WAY.
ROGER, WHERE ARE YOU THAT YOU'RE NEVER AROUND TO WATCH?
HOLD ON, I'M ABOUT TO ENTER A NEGOTIATION.
PEW PEW
PEW PEW
PEW

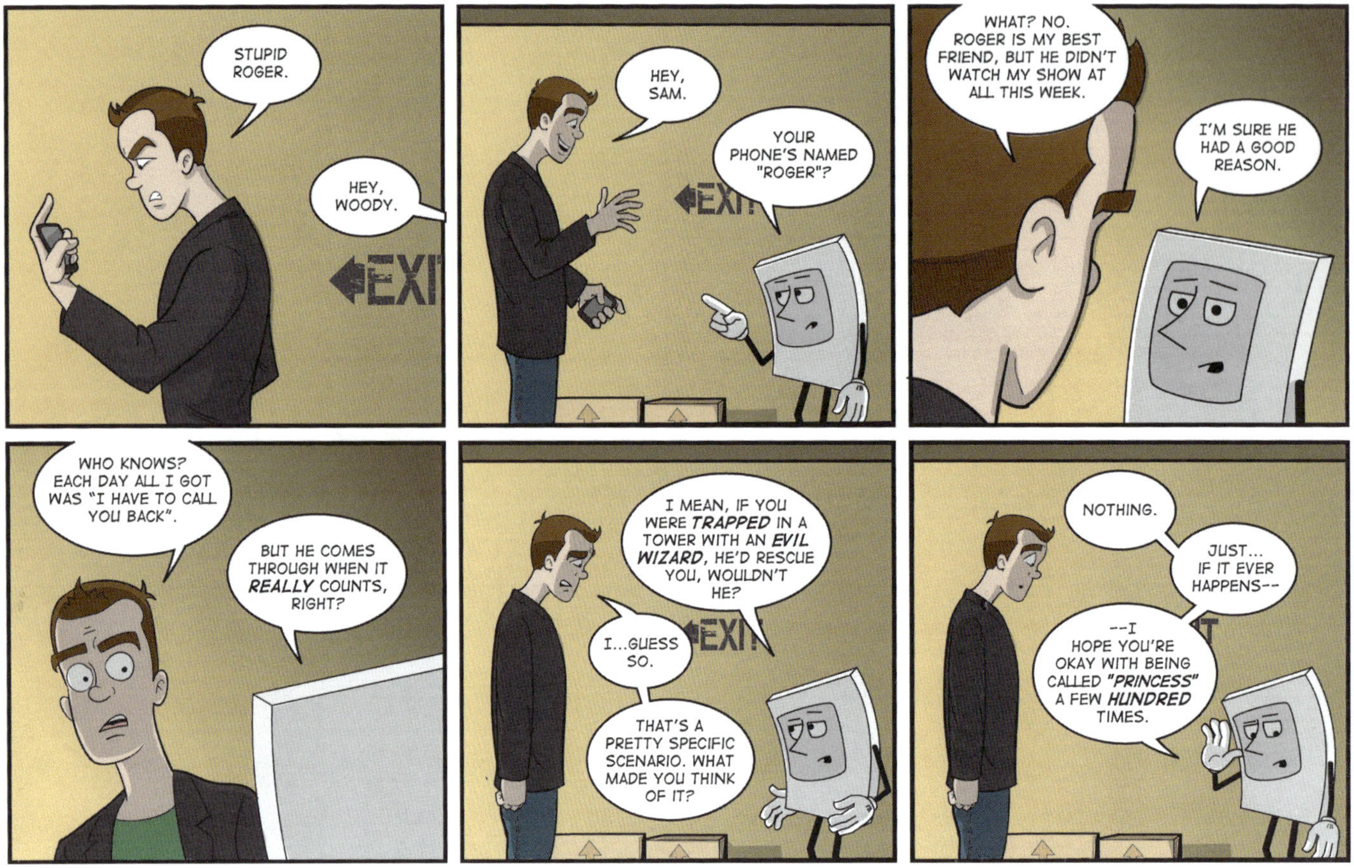
STUPID ROGER.
HEY, WOODY.
HEY, SAM.
YOUR PHONE'S NAMED "ROGER"?
WHAT? NO. ROGER IS MY BEST FRIEND, BUT HE DIDN'T WATCH MY SHOW AT ALL THIS WEEK.
I'M SURE HE HAD A GOOD REASON.
WHO KNOWS? EACH DAY ALL I GOT WAS "I HAVE TO CALL YOU BACK".
BUT HE COMES THROUGH WHEN IT *REALLY* COUNTS, RIGHT?
I MEAN, IF YOU WERE *TRAPPED* IN A TOWER WITH AN *EVIL WIZARD*, HE'D RESCUE YOU, WOULDN'T HE?
I...GUESS SO.
THAT'S A PRETTY SPECIFIC SCENARIO. WHAT MADE YOU THINK OF IT?
NOTHING.
JUST... IF IT EVER HAPPENS--
--I HOPE YOU'RE OKAY WITH BEING CALLED *"PRINCESS"* A FEW *HUNDRED* TIMES.

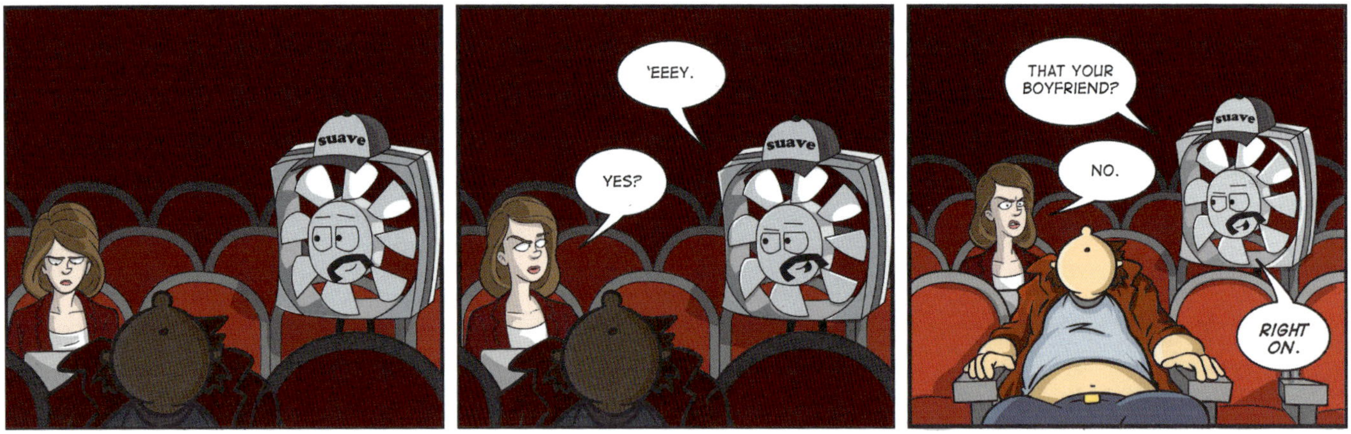
suave
'EEEY.
YES?
THAT YOUR BOYFRIEND?
NO.
RIGHT ON.

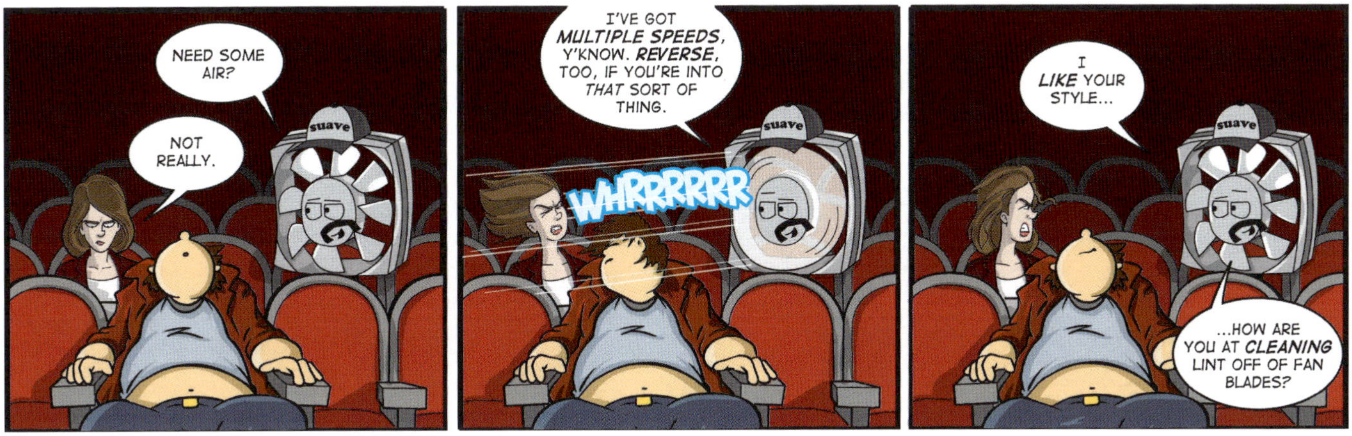
NEED SOME AIR?
NOT REALLY.
suave
I'VE GOT *MULTIPLE SPEEDS*, Y'KNOW. *REVERSE*, TOO, IF YOU'RE INTO *THAT* SORT OF THING.
WHRRRRRR
I *LIKE* YOUR STYLE...
...HOW ARE YOU AT *CLEANING* LINT OFF OF FAN BLADES?

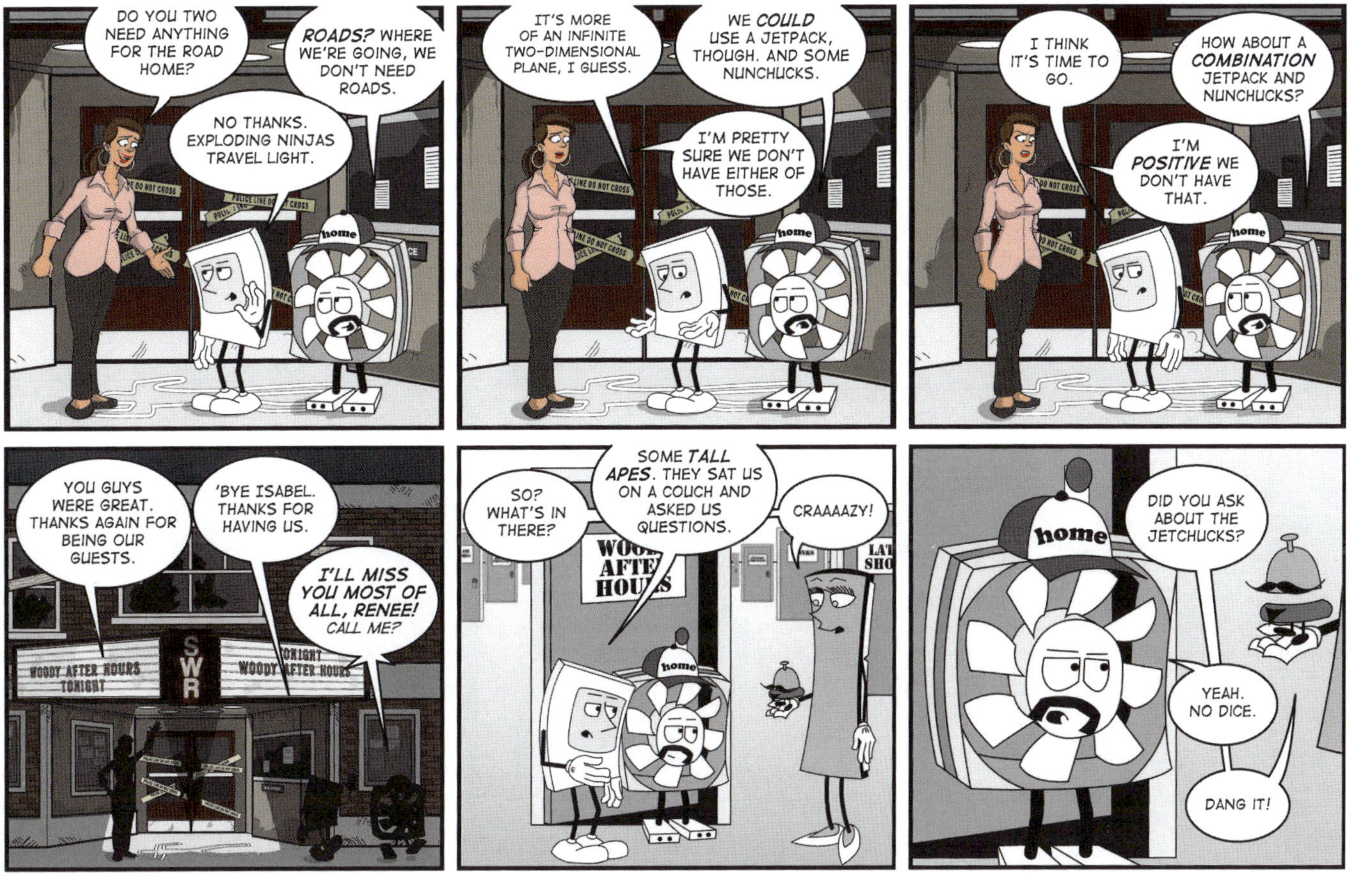
DO YOU TWO NEED ANYTHING FOR THE ROAD HOME?
NO THANKS. EXPLODING NINJAS TRAVEL LIGHT.
ROADS? WHERE WE'RE GOING, WE DON'T NEED ROADS.
home
IT'S MORE OF AN INFINITE TWO-DIMENSIONAL PLANE, I GUESS.
WE *COULD* USE A JETPACK, THOUGH. AND SOME NUNCHUCKS.
I'M PRETTY SURE WE DON'T HAVE EITHER OF THOSE.
I THINK IT'S TIME TO GO.
HOW ABOUT A *COMBINATION* JETPACK AND NUNCHUCKS?
I'M *POSITIVE* WE DON'T HAVE THAT.
YOU GUYS WERE GREAT. THANKS AGAIN FOR BEING OUR GUESTS.
'BYE ISABEL. THANKS FOR HAVING US.
I'LL MISS YOU MOST OF ALL, RENEE! CALL ME?
WOODY AFTER HOURS TONIGHT
SWR
TONIGHT WOODY AFTER HOURS
SO? WHAT'S IN THERE?
SOME *TALL APES*. THEY SAT US ON A COUCH AND ASKED US QUESTIONS.
CRAAAAZY!
DID YOU ASK ABOUT THE JETCHUCKS?
YEAH. NO DICE.
DANG IT!

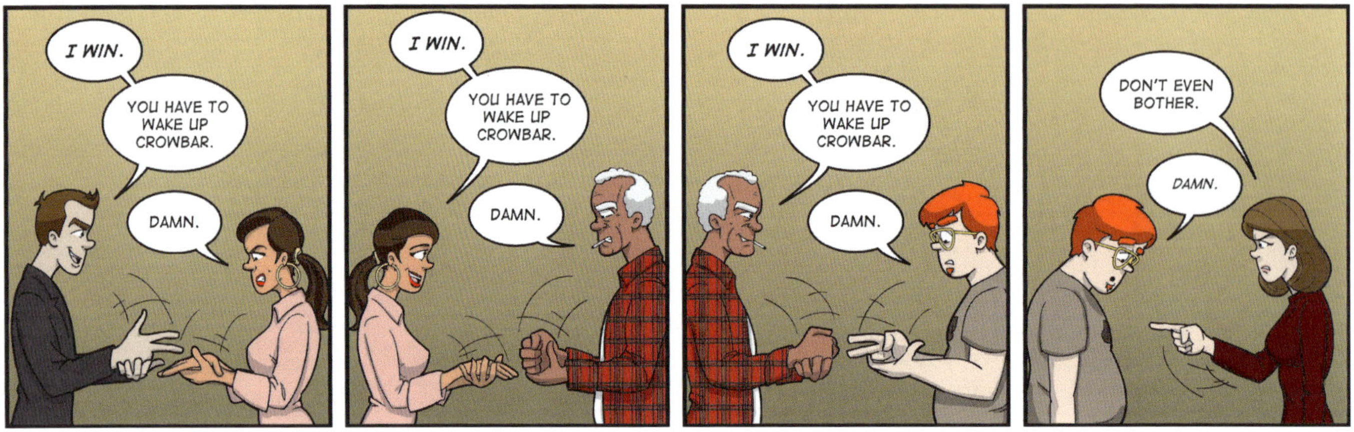
I WIN.
YOU HAVE TO WAKE UP CROWBAR.
DAMN.
I WIN.
YOU HAVE TO WAKE UP CROWBAR.
DAMN.
I WIN.
YOU HAVE TO WAKE UP CROWBAR.
DAMN.
DON'T EVEN BOTHER.
DAMN.

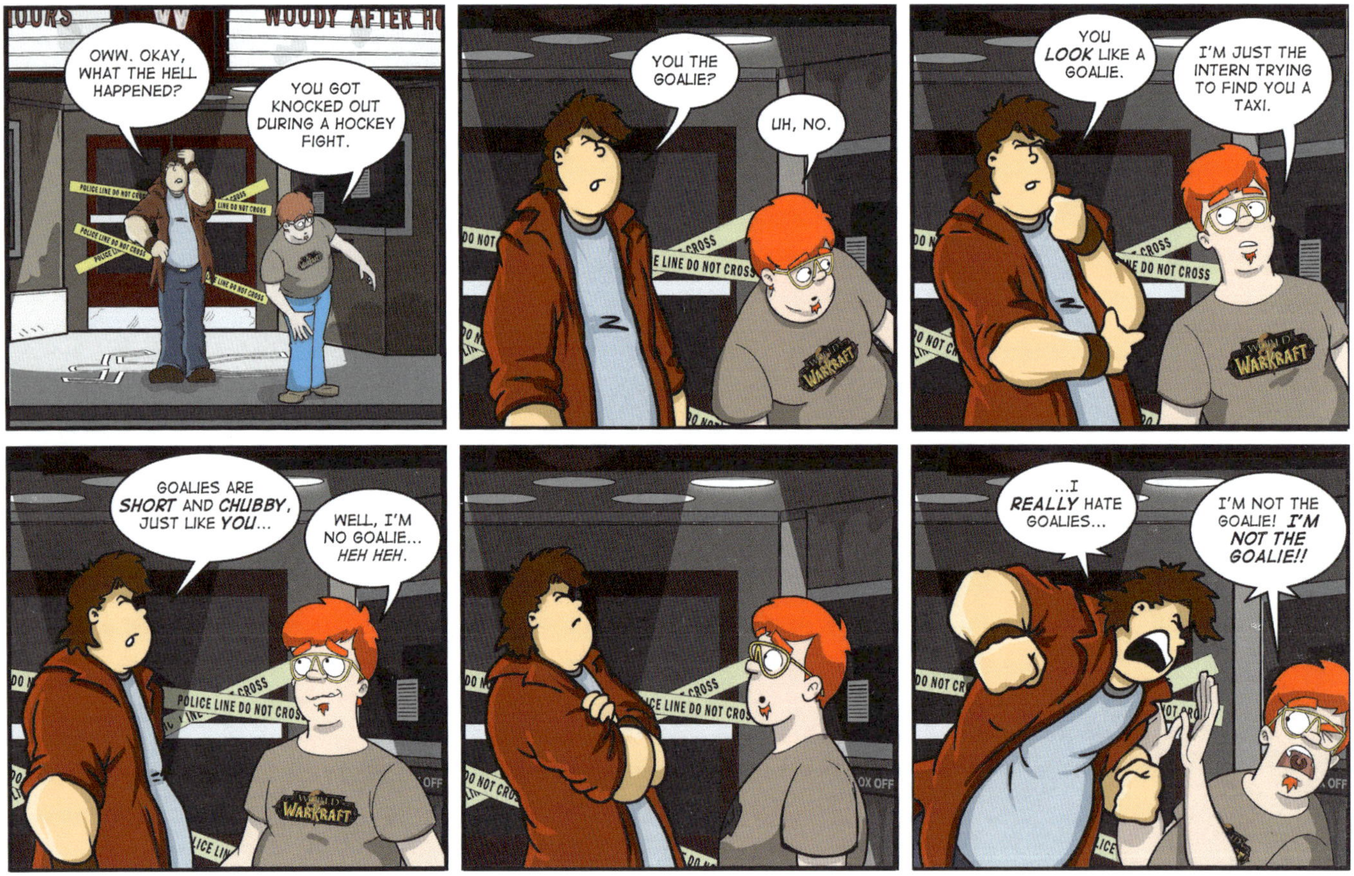
OWW. OKAY, WHAT THE HELL HAPPENED?
YOU GOT KNOCKED OUT DURING A HOCKEY FIGHT.
YOU THE GOALIE?
UH, NO.
YOU *LOOK* LIKE A GOALIE.
I'M JUST THE INTERN TRYING TO FIND YOU A TAXI.
GOALIES ARE ***SHORT*** AND ***CHUBBY***, JUST LIKE ***YOU***...
WELL, I'M NO GOALIE... *HEH HEH.*
...I ***REALLY*** HATE GOALIES...
I'M NOT THE GOALIE! ***I'M NOT THE GOALIE!!***

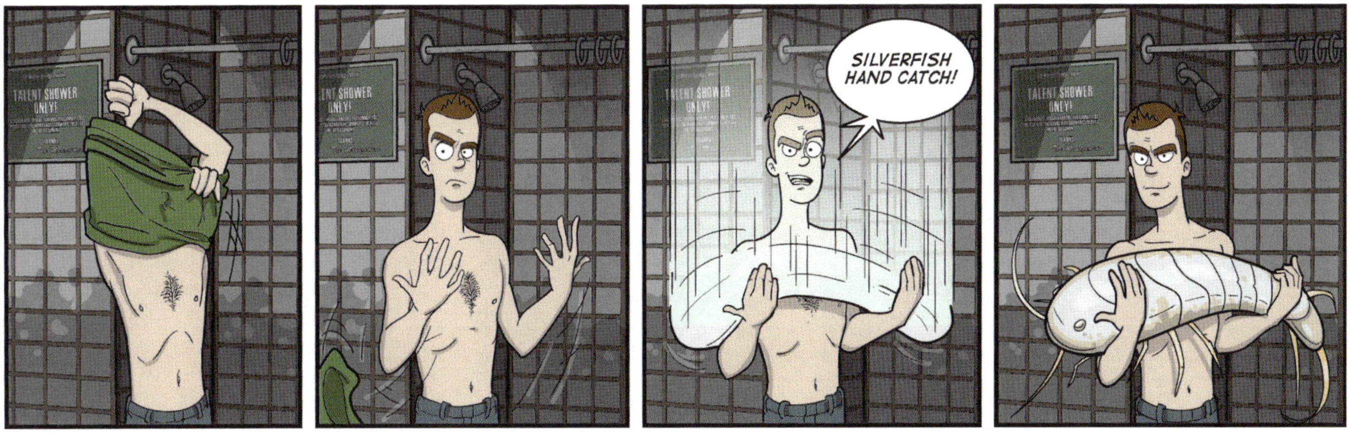
TALENT SHOWER ONLY!
SILVERFISH HAND CATCH!

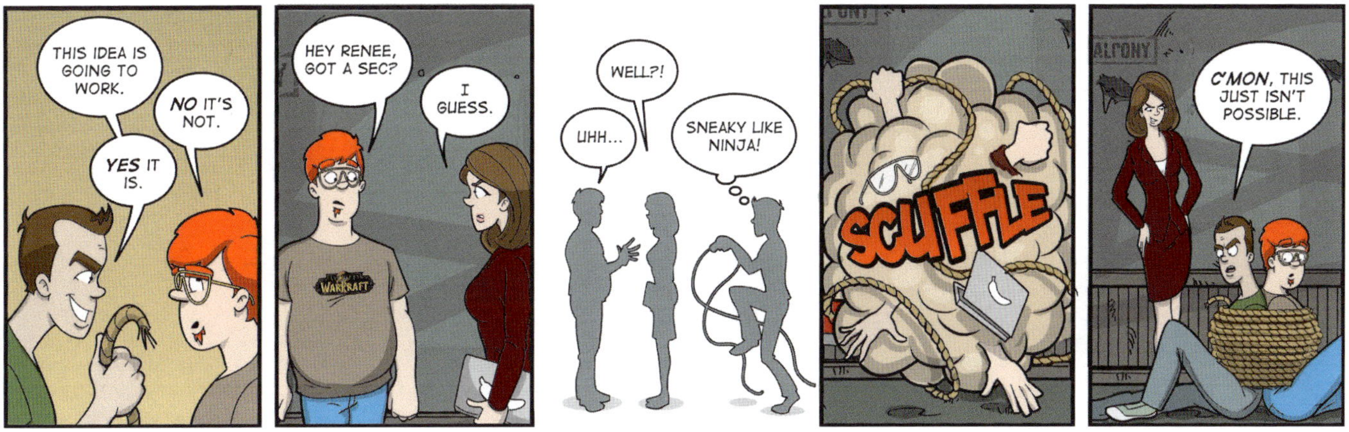
THIS IDEA IS GOING TO WORK.
NO IT'S NOT.
YES IT IS.
HEY RENEE, GOT A SEC?
WARKRAFT
I GUESS.
WELL?!
UHH...
SNEAKY LIKE NINJA!
SCUFFLE
C'MON, THIS JUST ISN'T POSSIBLE.

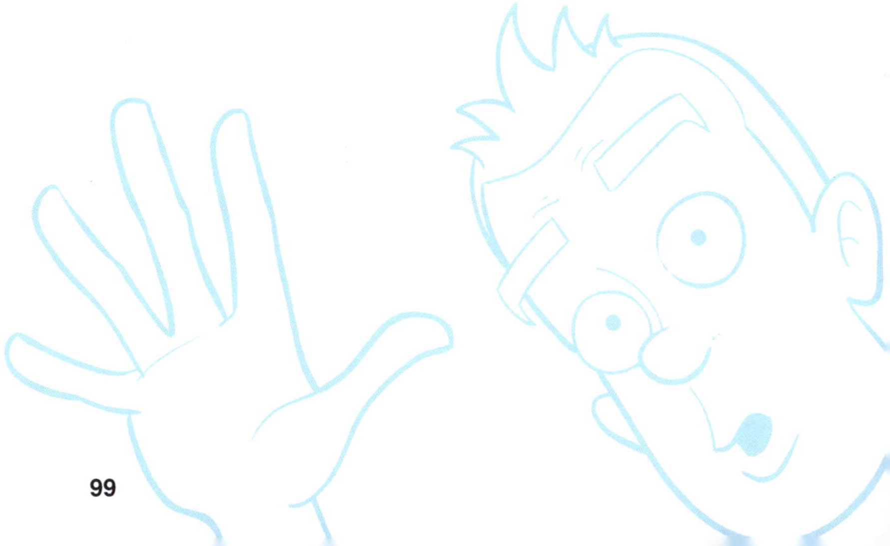

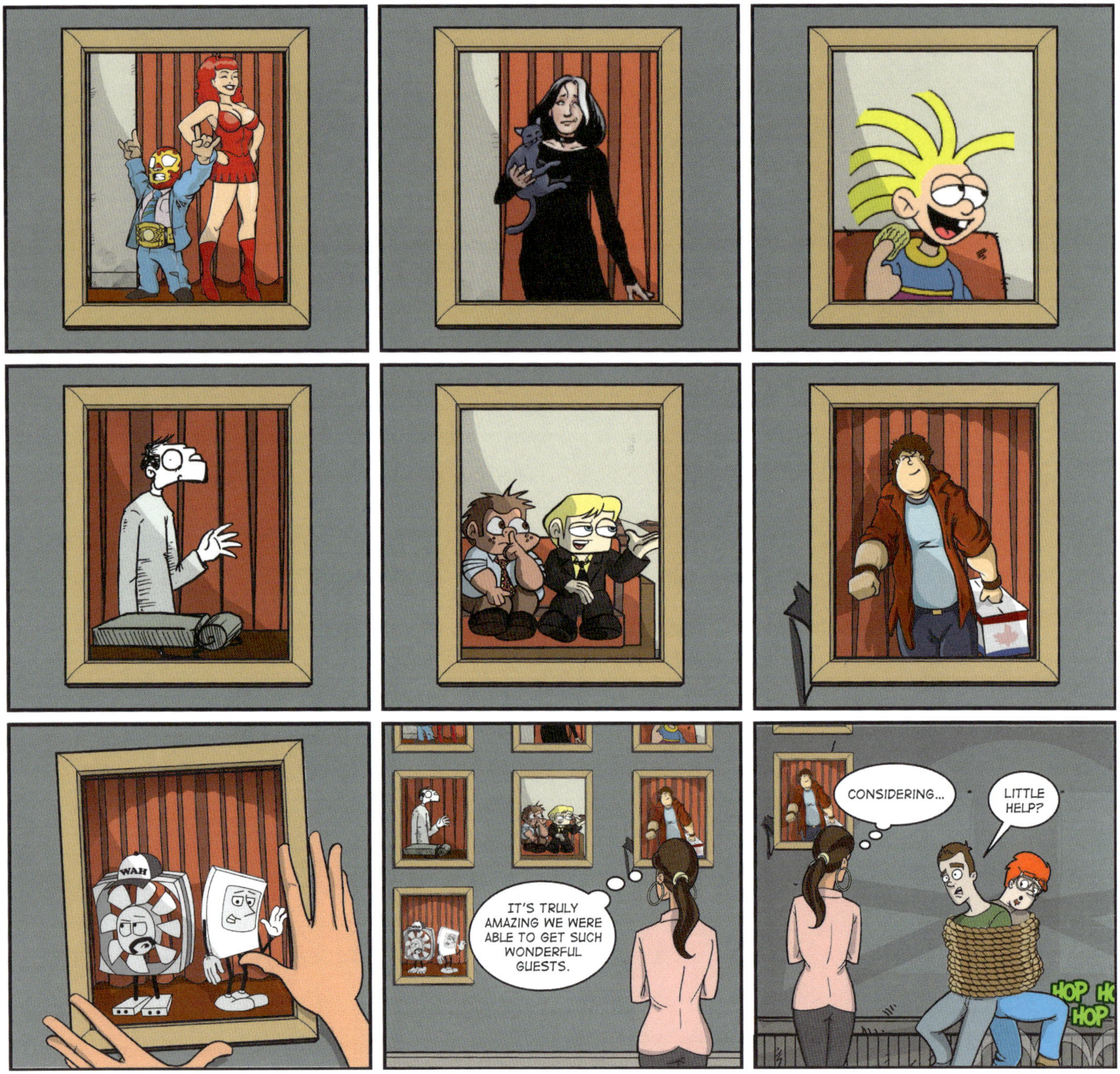
WAH
IT'S TRULY AMAZING WE WERE ABLE TO GET SUCH WONDERFUL GUESTS.
CONSIDERING...
LITTLE HELP?
HOP HO
HOP

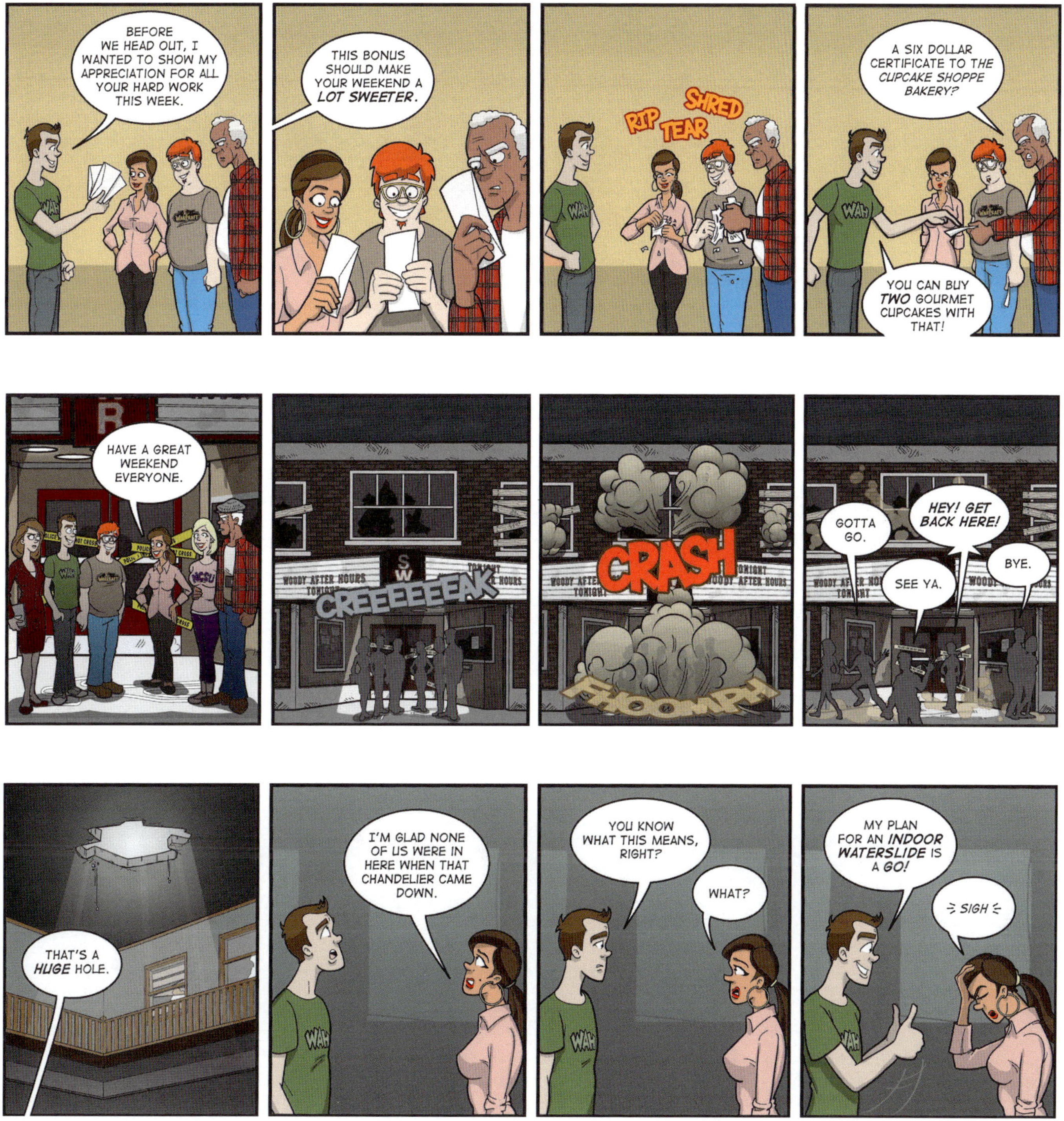

BEFORE WE HEAD OUT, I WANTED TO SHOW MY APPRECIATION FOR ALL YOUR HARD WORK THIS WEEK.
THIS BONUS SHOULD MAKE YOUR WEEKEND A *LOT SWEETER*.
RIP
SHRED
TEAR
A SIX DOLLAR CERTIFICATE TO *THE CUPCAKE SHOPPE BAKERY?*
YOU CAN BUY *TWO* GOURMET CUPCAKES WITH THAT!
HAVE A GREAT WEEKEND EVERYONE.
WOODY AFTER HOURS TONIGHT
CREEEEEEAK
CRASH
FHOOMPH
GOTTA GO.
HEY! GET BACK HERE!
SEE YA.
BYE.
THAT'S A *HUGE* HOLE.
I'M GLAD NONE OF US WERE IN HERE WHEN THAT CHANDELIER CAME DOWN.
YOU KNOW WHAT THIS MEANS, RIGHT?
WHAT?
MY PLAN FOR AN *INDOOR WATERSLIDE* IS A *GO!*
SIGH

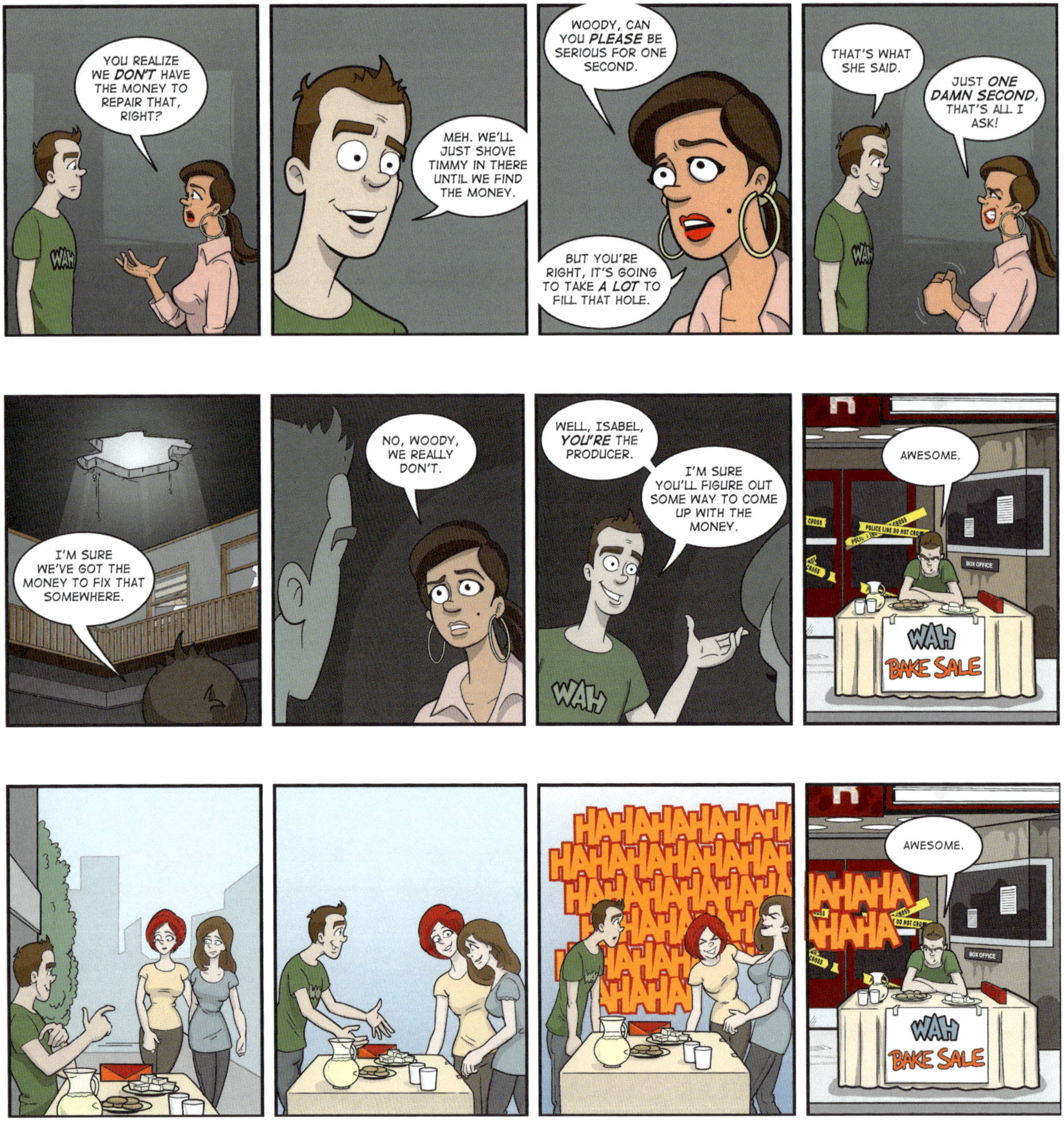
YOU REALIZE WE DON'T HAVE THE MONEY TO REPAIR THAT, RIGHT?
WAH
MEH. WE'LL JUST SHOVE TIMMY IN THERE UNTIL WE FIND THE MONEY.
WOODY, CAN YOU PLEASE BE SERIOUS FOR ONE SECOND.
BUT YOU'RE RIGHT, IT'S GOING TO TAKE A LOT TO FILL THAT HOLE.
THAT'S WHAT SHE SAID.
JUST ONE DAMN SECOND, THAT'S ALL I ASK!
I'M SURE WE'VE GOT THE MONEY TO FIX THAT SOMEWHERE.
NO, WOODY, WE REALLY DON'T.
WELL, ISABEL, YOU'RE THE PRODUCER.
I'M SURE YOU'LL FIGURE OUT SOME WAY TO COME UP WITH THE MONEY.
WAH
AWESOME.
BOX OFFICE
WAH
BAKE SALE
HAHAHAHAHAHAHA
AWESOME.
BOX OFFICE
WAH
BAKE SALE

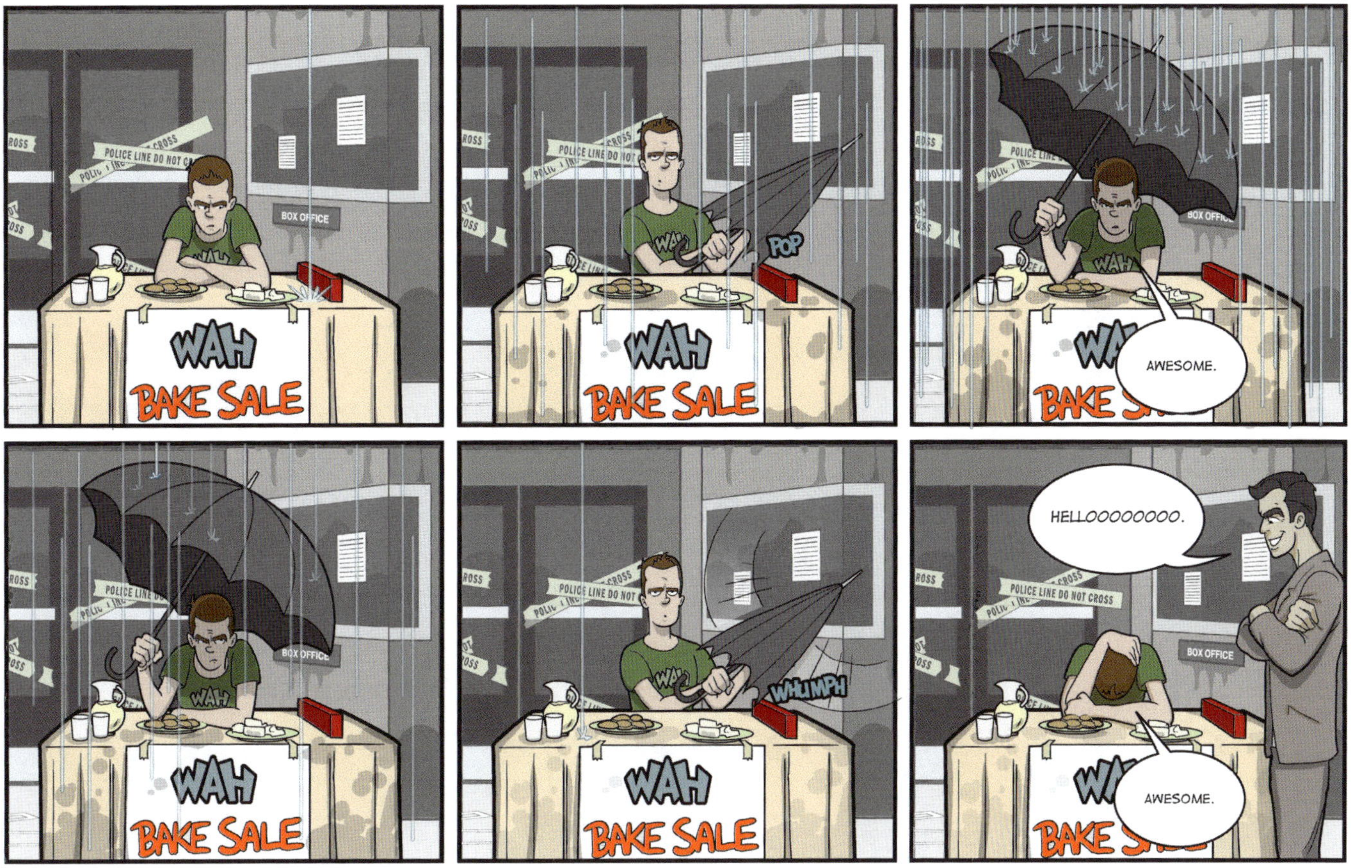
POLICE LINE DO NOT CROSS
BOX OFFICE
WAH
BAKE SALE
POP
AWESOME.
WHUMPH
HELLOOOOOOOO.
AWESOME.

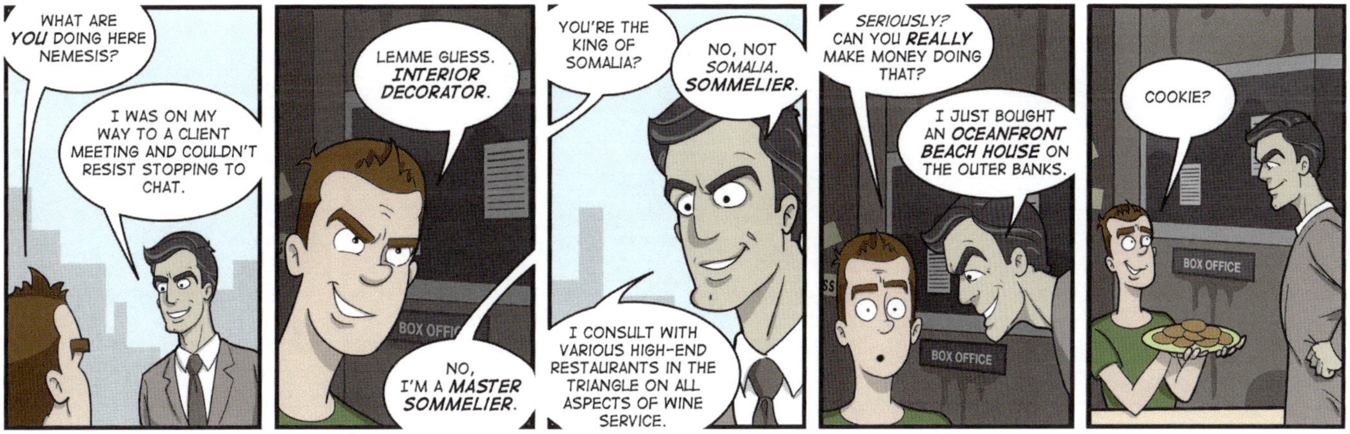
WHAT ARE *YOU* DOING HERE NEMESIS?
I WAS ON MY WAY TO A CLIENT MEETING AND COULDN'T RESIST STOPPING TO CHAT.
LEMME GUESS. ***INTERIOR DECORATOR***.
NO, I'M A ***MASTER SOMMELIER***.
YOU'RE THE KING OF SOMALIA?
NO, NOT *SOMALIA*. ***SOMMELIER***.
I CONSULT WITH VARIOUS HIGH-END RESTAURANTS IN THE TRIANGLE ON ALL ASPECTS OF WINE SERVICE.
SERIOUSLY? CAN YOU ***REALLY*** MAKE MONEY DOING THAT?
I JUST BOUGHT AN ***OCEANFRONT BEACH HOUSE*** ON THE OUTER BANKS.
BOX OFFICE
COOKIE?

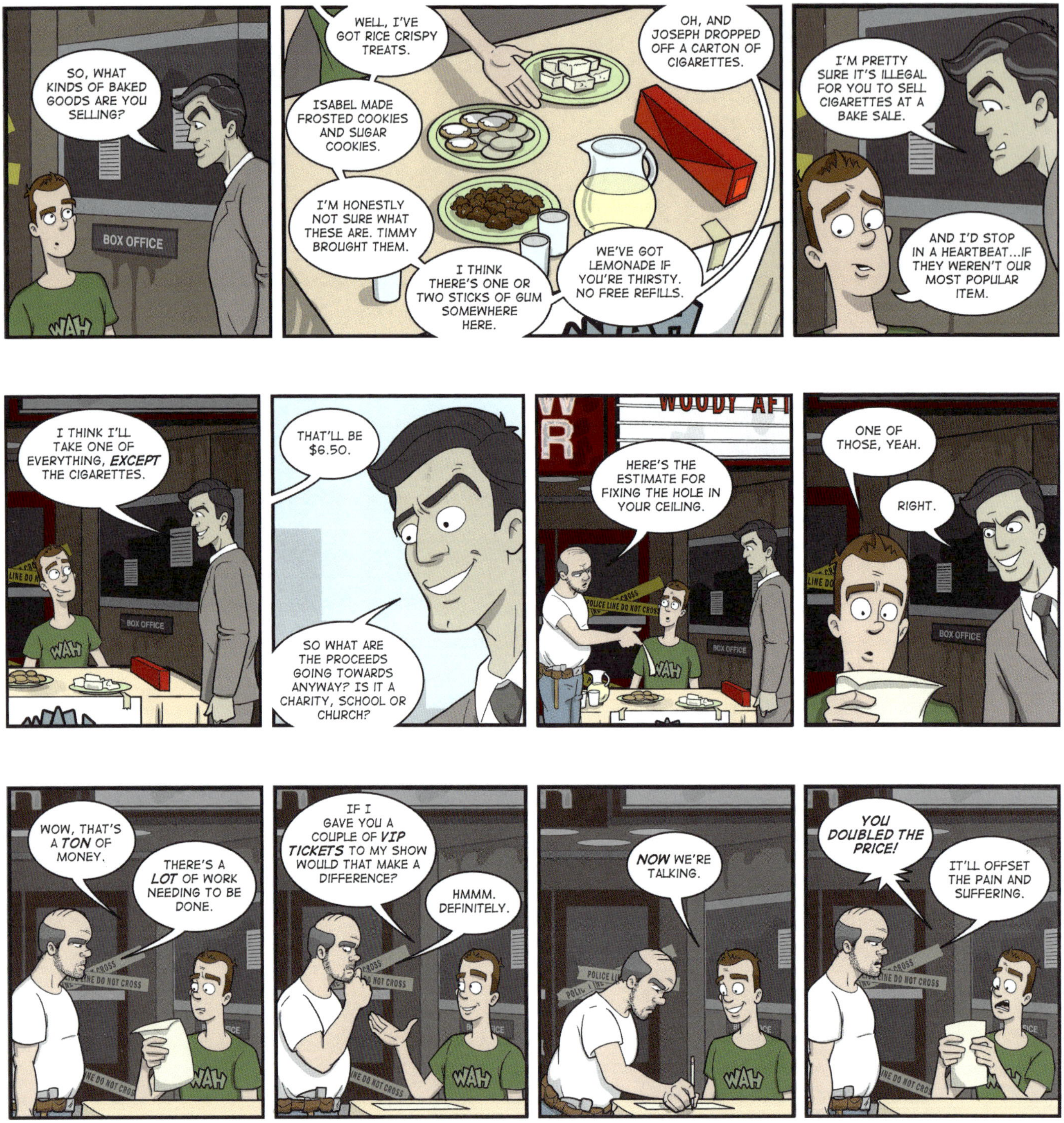
SO, WHAT KINDS OF BAKED GOODS ARE YOU SELLING?
BOX OFFICE
WAH
WELL, I'VE GOT RICE CRISPY TREATS.
ISABEL MADE FROSTED COOKIES AND SUGAR COOKIES.
I'M HONESTLY NOT SURE WHAT THESE ARE. TIMMY BROUGHT THEM.
I THINK THERE'S ONE OR TWO STICKS OF GUM SOMEWHERE HERE.
WE'VE GOT LEMONADE IF YOU'RE THIRSTY. NO FREE REFILLS.
OH, AND JOSEPH DROPPED OFF A CARTON OF CIGARETTES.
I'M PRETTY SURE IT'S ILLEGAL FOR YOU TO SELL CIGARETTES AT A BAKE SALE.
AND I'D STOP IN A HEARTBEAT...IF THEY WEREN'T OUR MOST POPULAR ITEM.
I THINK I'LL TAKE ONE OF EVERYTHING, ***EXCEPT*** THE CIGARETTES.
BOX OFFICE
WAH
THAT'LL BE $6.50.
SO WHAT ARE THE PROCEEDS GOING TOWARDS ANYWAY? IS IT A CHARITY, SCHOOL OR CHURCH?
HERE'S THE ESTIMATE FOR FIXING THE HOLE IN YOUR CEILING.
POLICE LINE DO NOT CROSS
ONE OF THOSE, YEAH.
RIGHT.
BOX OFFICE
WOW, THAT'S A *TON* OF MONEY.
THERE'S A *LOT* OF WORK NEEDING TO BE DONE.
IF I GAVE YOU A COUPLE OF *VIP TICKETS* TO MY SHOW WOULD THAT MAKE A DIFFERENCE?
HMMM. DEFINITELY.
NOW WE'RE TALKING.
YOU DOUBLED THE PRICE!
IT'LL OFFSET THE PAIN AND SUFFERING.

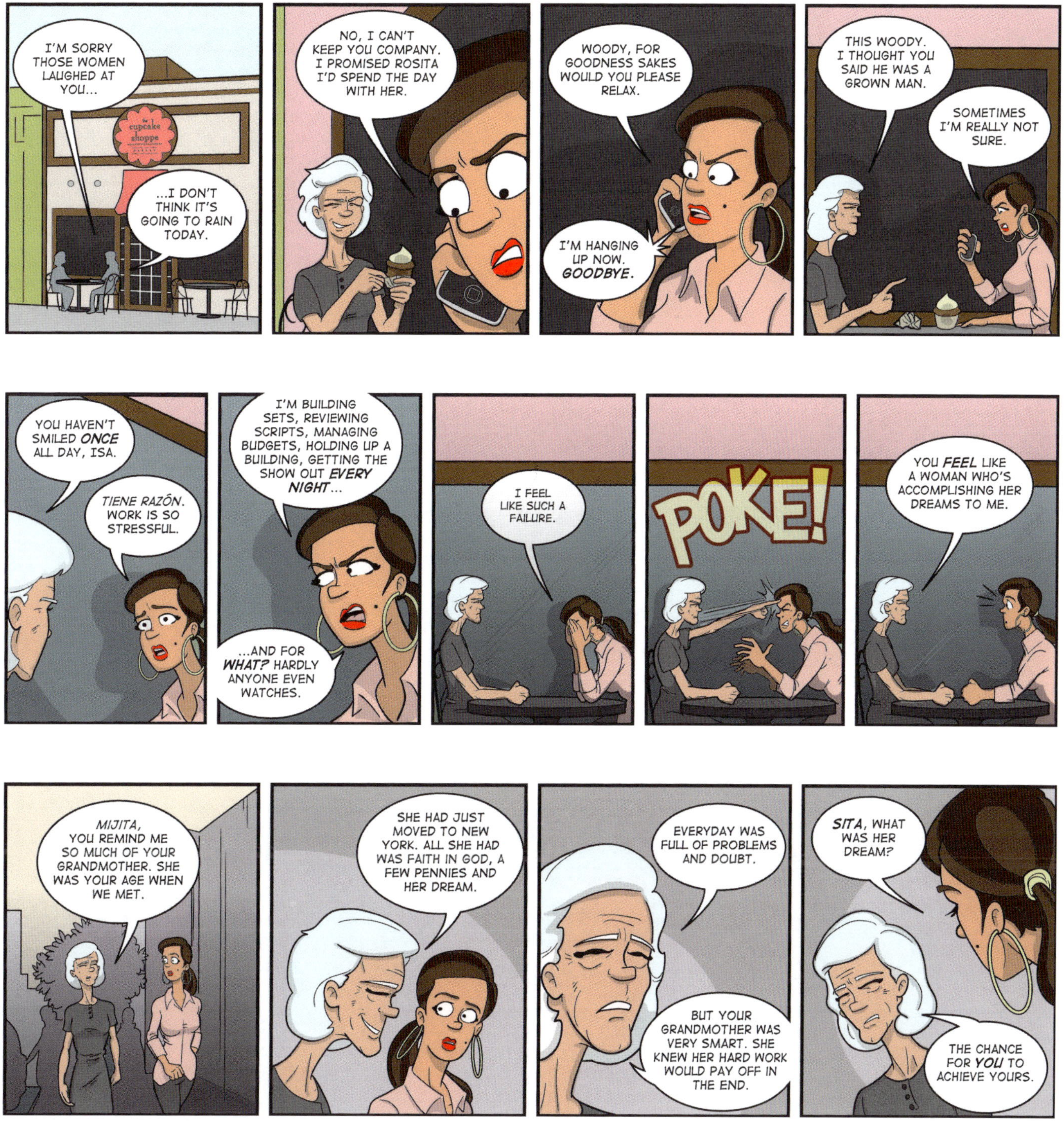
I'M SORRY THOSE WOMEN LAUGHED AT YOU...
...I DON'T THINK IT'S GOING TO RAIN TODAY.
NO, I CAN'T KEEP YOU COMPANY. I PROMISED ROSITA I'D SPEND THE DAY WITH HER.
WOODY, FOR GOODNESS SAKES WOULD YOU PLEASE RELAX.
I'M HANGING UP NOW. GOODBYE.
THIS WOODY. I THOUGHT YOU SAID HE WAS A GROWN MAN.
SOMETIMES I'M REALLY NOT SURE.
YOU HAVEN'T SMILED ONCE ALL DAY, ISA.
TIENE RAZÓN. WORK IS SO STRESSFUL.
I'M BUILDING SETS, REVIEWING SCRIPTS, MANAGING BUDGETS, HOLDING UP A BUILDING, GETTING THE SHOW OUT EVERY NIGHT...
...AND FOR WHAT? HARDLY ANYONE EVEN WATCHES.
I FEEL LIKE SUCH A FAILURE.
POKE!
YOU FEEL LIKE A WOMAN WHO'S ACCOMPLISHING HER DREAMS TO ME.
MIJITA, YOU REMIND ME SO MUCH OF YOUR GRANDMOTHER. SHE WAS YOUR AGE WHEN WE MET.
SHE HAD JUST MOVED TO NEW YORK. ALL SHE HAD WAS FAITH IN GOD, A FEW PENNIES AND HER DREAM.
EVERYDAY WAS FULL OF PROBLEMS AND DOUBT.
BUT YOUR GRANDMOTHER WAS VERY SMART. SHE KNEW HER HARD WORK WOULD PAY OFF IN THE END.
SITA, WHAT WAS HER DREAM?
THE CHANCE FOR YOU TO ACHIEVE YOURS.

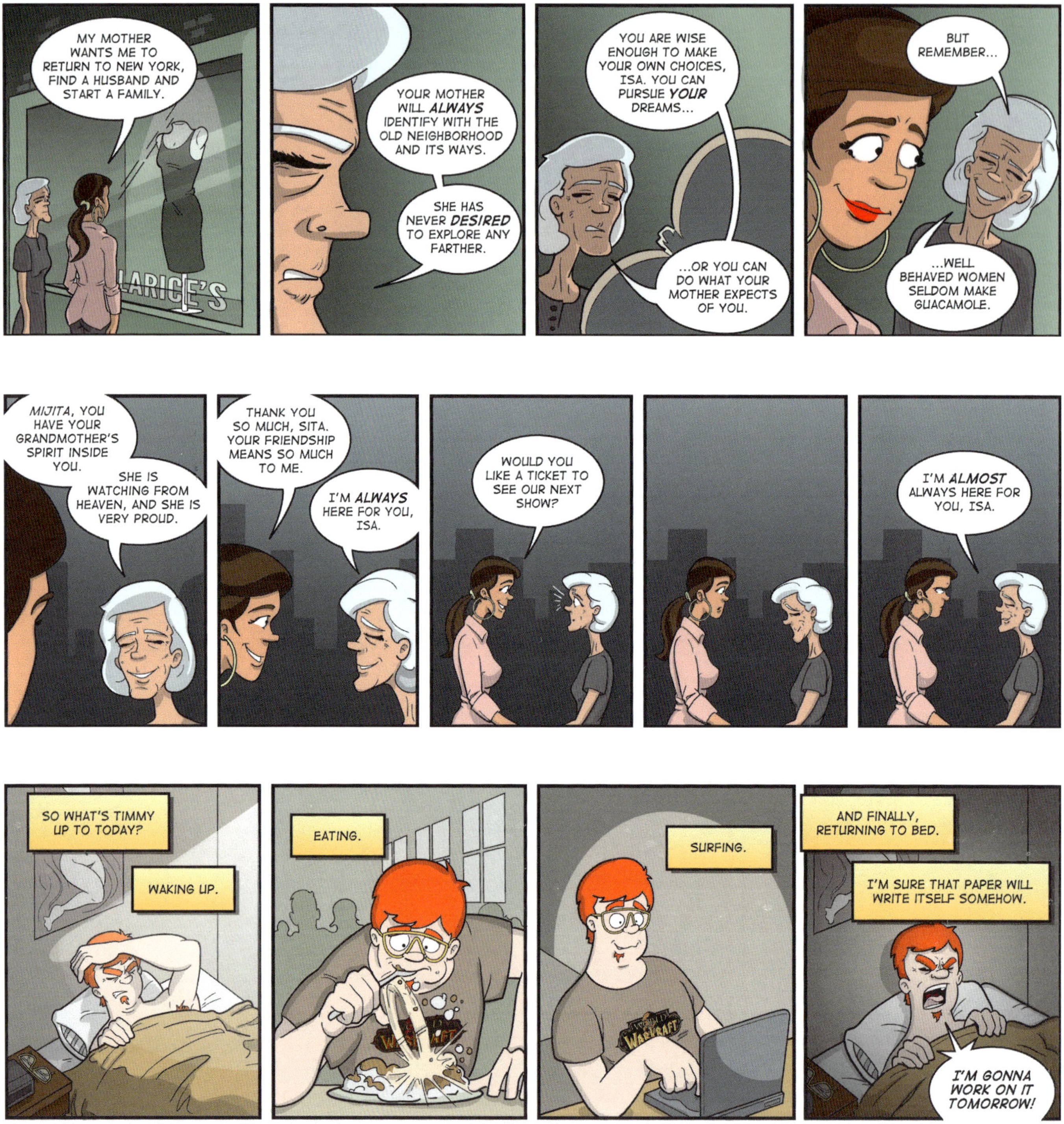
MY MOTHER WANTS ME TO RETURN TO NEW YORK, FIND A HUSBAND AND START A FAMILY.
LARICE'S
YOUR MOTHER WILL *ALWAYS* IDENTIFY WITH THE OLD NEIGHBORHOOD AND ITS WAYS.
SHE HAS NEVER *DESIRED* TO EXPLORE ANY FARTHER.
YOU ARE WISE ENOUGH TO MAKE YOUR OWN CHOICES, ISA. YOU CAN PURSUE *YOUR* DREAMS...
...OR YOU CAN DO WHAT YOUR MOTHER EXPECTS OF YOU.
BUT REMEMBER...
...WELL BEHAVED WOMEN SELDOM MAKE GUACAMOLE.
MIJITA, YOU HAVE YOUR GRANDMOTHER'S SPIRIT INSIDE YOU.
SHE IS WATCHING FROM HEAVEN, AND SHE IS VERY PROUD.
THANK YOU SO MUCH, SITA. YOUR FRIENDSHIP MEANS SO MUCH TO ME.
I'M *ALWAYS* HERE FOR YOU, ISA.
WOULD YOU LIKE A TICKET TO SEE OUR NEXT SHOW?
I'M *ALMOST* ALWAYS HERE FOR YOU, ISA.
SO WHAT'S TIMMY UP TO TODAY?
WAKING UP.
EATING.
SURFING.
AND FINALLY, RETURNING TO BED.
I'M SURE THAT PAPER WILL WRITE ITSELF SOMEHOW.
I'M GONNA WORK ON IT TOMORROW!

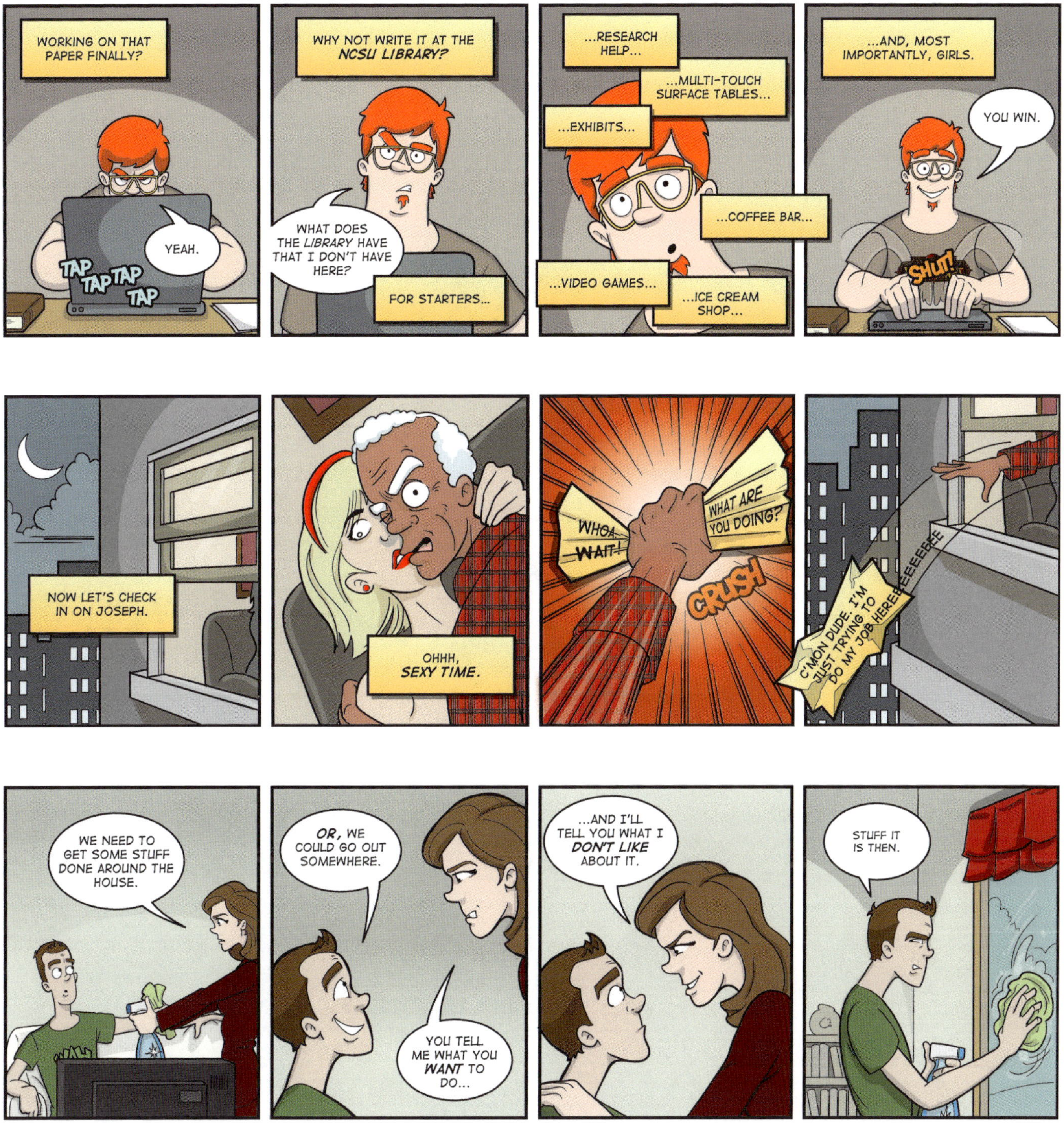
WORKING ON THAT PAPER FINALLY?
TAP TAP TAP TAP
YEAH.
WHY NOT WRITE IT AT THE NCSU LIBRARY?
WHAT DOES THE LIBRARY HAVE THAT I DON'T HAVE HERE?
FOR STARTERS...
...RESEARCH HELP...
...MULTI-TOUCH SURFACE TABLES...
...EXHIBITS...
...COFFEE BAR...
...VIDEO GAMES...
...ICE CREAM SHOP...
...AND, MOST IMPORTANTLY, GIRLS.
YOU WIN.
SHUT!
NOW LET'S CHECK IN ON JOSEPH.
OHHH, SEXY TIME.
WHOA, WAIT!
WHAT ARE YOU DOING?
CRUSH
C'MON DUDE. I'M JUST TRYING TO DO MY JOB HEREEEEEEEEEE
WE NEED TO GET SOME STUFF DONE AROUND THE HOUSE.
OR, WE COULD GO OUT SOMEWHERE.
YOU TELL ME WHAT YOU WANT TO DO...
...AND I'LL TELL YOU WHAT I DON'T LIKE ABOUT IT.
STUFF IT IS THEN.

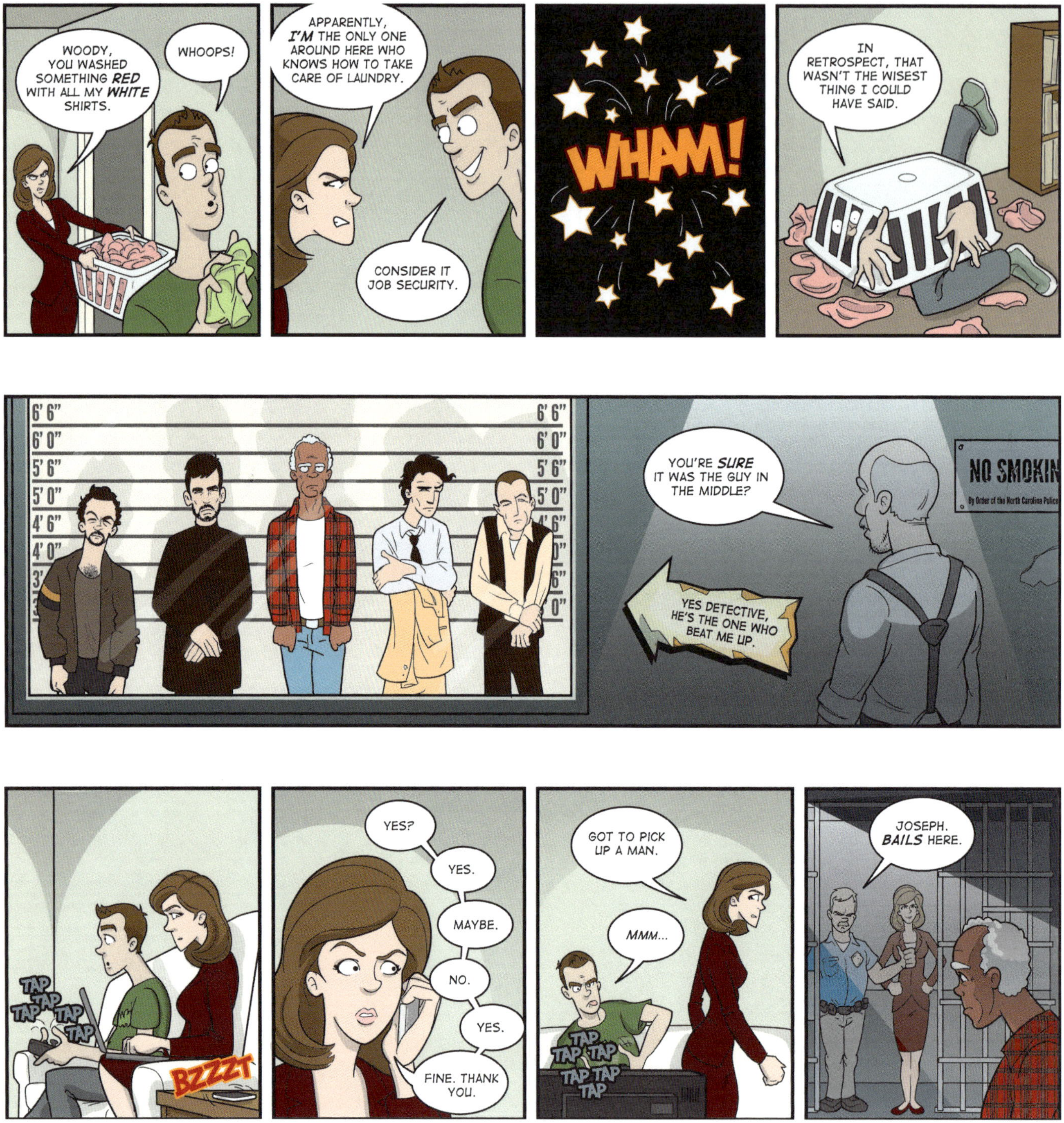
WOODY, YOU WASHED SOMETHING RED WITH ALL MY WHITE SHIRTS.
WHOOPS!
APPARENTLY, I'M THE ONLY ONE AROUND HERE WHO KNOWS HOW TO TAKE CARE OF LAUNDRY.
CONSIDER IT JOB SECURITY.
WHAM!
IN RETROSPECT, THAT WASN'T THE WISEST THING I COULD HAVE SAID.
6' 6"
6' 0"
5' 6"
5' 0"
4' 6"
4' 0"
YOU'RE SURE IT WAS THE GUY IN THE MIDDLE?
NO SMOKIN
By Order of the North Carolina Police
YES DETECTIVE, HE'S THE ONE WHO BEAT ME UP.
TAP TAP TAP TAP TAP
BZZZT
YES?
YES.
MAYBE.
NO.
YES.
FINE. THANK YOU.
GOT TO PICK UP A MAN.
MMM...
TAP TAP TAP TAP TAP TAP
JOSEPH. BAILS HERE.

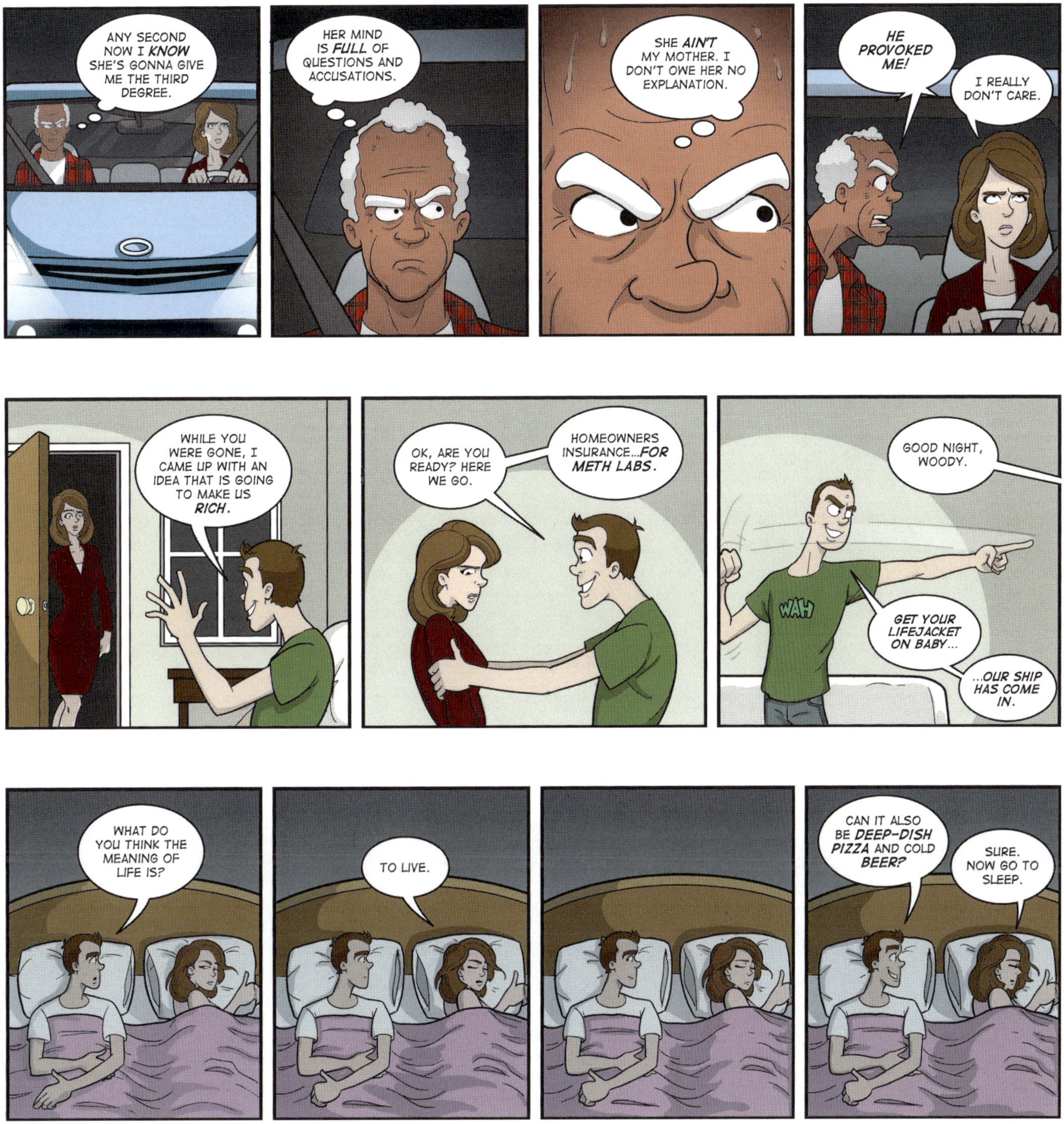
ANY SECOND NOW I KNOW SHE'S GONNA GIVE ME THE THIRD DEGREE.
HER MIND IS FULL OF QUESTIONS AND ACCUSATIONS.
SHE AIN'T MY MOTHER. I DON'T OWE HER NO EXPLANATION.
HE PROVOKED ME!
I REALLY DON'T CARE.
WHILE YOU WERE GONE, I CAME UP WITH AN IDEA THAT IS GOING TO MAKE US RICH.
OK, ARE YOU READY? HERE WE GO.
HOMEOWNERS INSURANCE...FOR METH LABS.
GOOD NIGHT, WOODY.
WAH
GET YOUR LIFEJACKET ON BABY...
...OUR SHIP HAS COME IN.
WHAT DO YOU THINK THE MEANING OF LIFE IS?
TO LIVE.
CAN IT ALSO BE DEEP-DISH PIZZA AND COLD BEER?
SURE. NOW GO TO SLEEP.

TO READ MORE

VISIT US AT
www.woodyafterhours.com

I'VE GOT YER COMMENTARY RIGHT HERE!

OK, WOODY--

--IN TEN SECONDS YOU'RE GOING TO WALK OUT ON THAT STAGE AND START YOUR NEW CAREER.

YOU *CAN* DO THIS.

It Tasted Like a Good Idea at the Time (Strip 2): This is the first *Woody After Hours* strip I ever wrote. It summarizes my view of the *WAH* universe pretty well. This strip was supposed to be the first strip published. At some point the idea for the *WAH* promo strip was born, and that became the first strip instead. Nobody understood the promo strip when WAH debuted on March 9th, 2009. That summarizes my universe pretty well.

The First Phase Of The Mexican Surfboard (Strip 50): *Woody After Hours* would never have made it to the web if not for the contributions of a handful of wonderful individuals. Jesse Justice is one of them. Besides being a great guy, he taught me a lot about making comics, helped me find Paul and was the first artist to lend us his characters for the guest interviews. I will always be grateful for Jesse's role in bringing *WAH* to life.

GO TO COMMERCIAL!

GO TO COMMERCIAL

HELLO?
HEY, WOODY. I WANTED TO LET YOU KNOW THAT DAVE AND I ARE EXPECTING.
EXPECTING WHAT?
TWINS!
PFFFFT

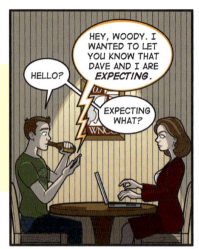

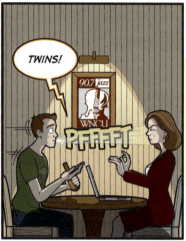

Congratulations Emily and Dave **(Strip 66):** I'm happy to report that Emily and Dave had healthy twin boys. By the time we finally get this book out, they should just about be starting college.

TODAY, I EXPAND MY VAST EMPIRE AND SMITE THOSE WHO OPPOSE MY MIGHTY WILL!
GIVE 'EM HELL!
I SHALL!

Scene At The Crack of Noon **(Strip 72):** This is one of my favorite strips. I like the way it gives us some insight into how Renee perceives herself, Woody and their relationship. Don't get me wrong. I like all of the comics we've created, but there are some I like more, or less, than most. Since these strips aren't my biological children I believe I can get away with this inequality without a state agency being called.

"A GUY CAME IN RECENTLY AND BOUGHT A PINEAPPLE-FLAVORED ONE. HE ATE THE WHOLE THING BY HIMSELF IN ONLY EIGHT DAYS AND EVEN BLOGGED ABOUT IT."
WAH

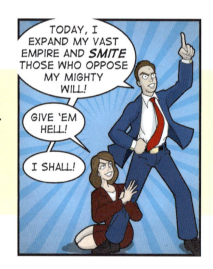

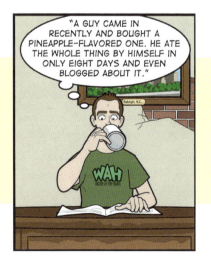

Hey, I Heard That **(Strip 76):** This comic, and this commentary about it, is an example of shameless self-promotion. I did, in fact, eat a pineapple-flavored *World's Largest Gummy Bear™* in eight days and blog about it. If you're interested in reading about my adventures, please put this book down for a few minutes, go to the *WAH* website and check it out. It's full of witty writing and funny pictures. Honest.

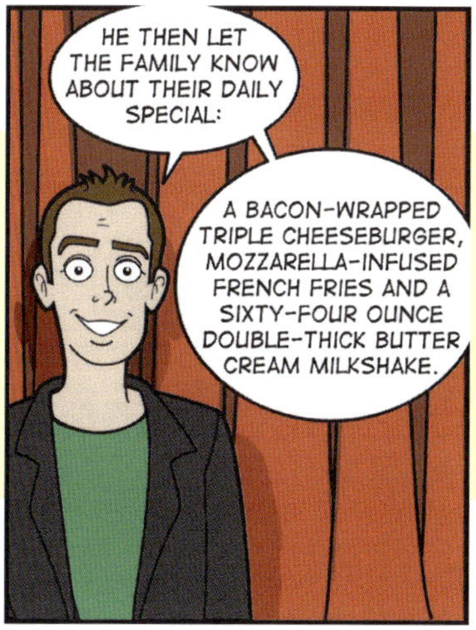
HE THEN LET THE FAMILY KNOW ABOUT THEIR DAILY SPECIAL:
A BACON-WRAPPED TRIPLE CHEESEBURGER, MOZZARELLA-INFUSED FRENCH FRIES AND A SIXTY-FOUR OUNCE DOUBLE-THICK BUTTER CREAM MILKSHAKE.

***That's A Happy Meal I Can Get On Board With* (Strip 84):** What's unique about this one? It receives more spam in the comments section than all other strips combined times three. My hope is that the people who are sending us this stuff will buy my book, see this comment, realize that their handiwork is annoying, feel bad about it and finally stop doing it.

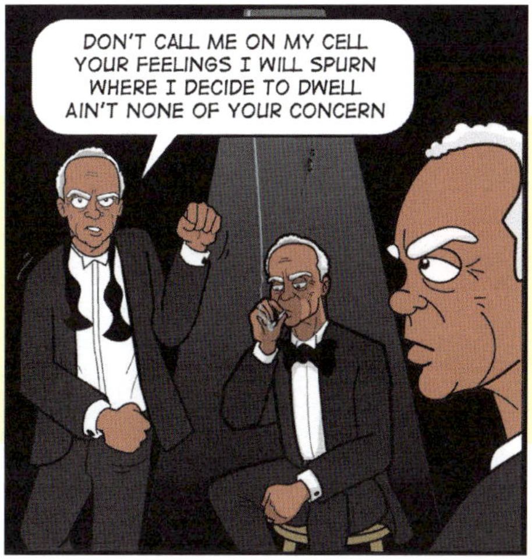
DON'T CALL ME ON MY CELL
YOUR FEELINGS I WILL SPURN
WHERE I DECIDE TO DWELL
AIN'T NONE OF YOUR CONCERN

***A Clear Message* (Strip 89):** This is another one of my favorite strips. It parodies William Shatner's performance of the song *Rocket Man* during the 1978 *Science Fiction Awards*. I recommend watching the clip on the interwebs if you haven't seen it. Spoofing a four minute video in a comic is not easy, but Paul did an absolutely wonderful job.

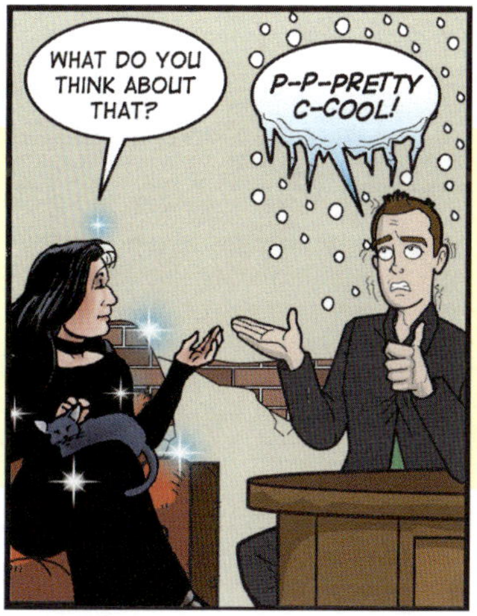
WHAT DO YOU THINK ABOUT THAT?
P-P-PRETTY C-COOL!

***Breaking The Ice* (Strip 91):** Jamie Robertson is a very talented artist and storyteller. I remember when we went to a bookstore café and began the thinking process of having Chelsea appear in *WAH*. I thought it would take all afternoon. But we clicked instantly, and story ideas poured out of us in no time. The comics the three of us created came out brilliantly. It was a real privilege for Paul and I to work with him.

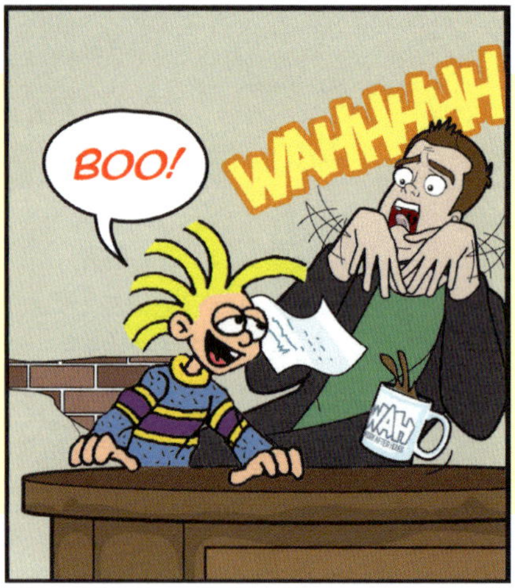
BOO!
WAHHHHH
WAH

He Screams The Name Of The Show When Frightened **(Strip 101):** George Ford really came through for us when Paul and I were in a bind. We had been working on guest strips with another artist, but he canceled on us two weeks before the comics were to be published. Despite juggling numerous balls in the air, George answered our desperate call for help. Almost overnight, he had drafted a bunch of ideas, and within a few days we had the entire arc laid out. He followed up by getting his art to Paul with time to spare. He was truly amazing.

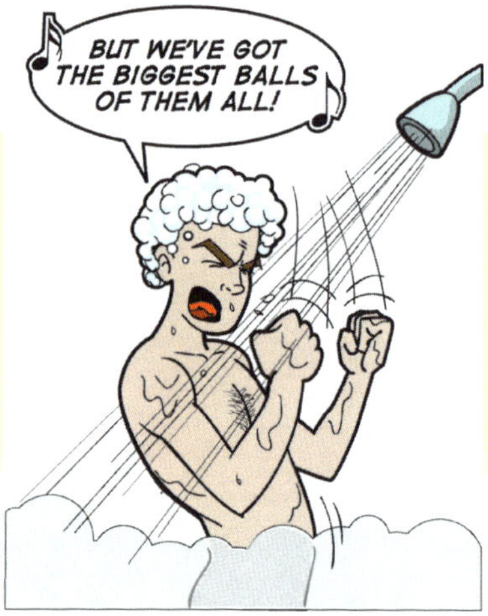
BUT WE'VE GOT THE BIGGEST BALLS OF THEM ALL!

It's an AC/DC Song, Honest **(Strip 116):** This is another one of my favorite strips. Not because of the childish euphemism, or that I let AC/DC do 95% of the writing, but because Paul just absolutely nailed Woody in the shower. Boy, that actually sounds really dirty. We should probably change that sentence before the book is published.

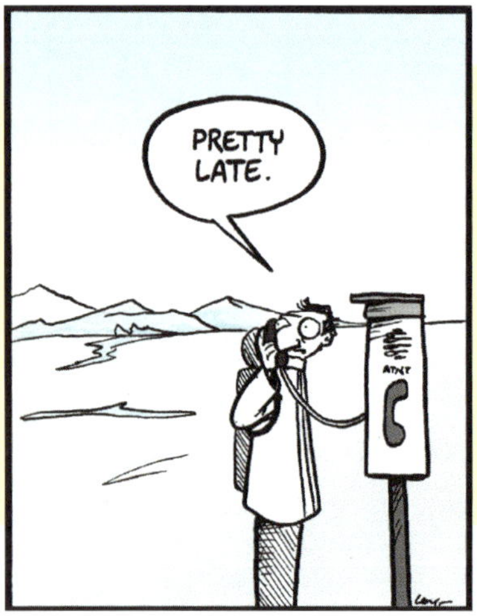
PRETTY LATE.

A Chilling Situation **(Strip 141):** Funny story about working with Dan Long; in an email to Dan I accidentally told him that the Edmund guest strips would start in February, when I really meant to type "January." Since he thought he had another whole month to turn in his artwork, we didn't have squat that cold January night before the first strip was to be published. Luckily for us Dan is a superb guy and agreed to adjust his very packed schedule in order to meet ours. Less than a week later Edmund was on and we were good to go.

Know Your Audience (Strip 150): Were you aware that you can purchase a cameo in a *Woody After Hours* comic? During our first year we were convinced no one else knew either. Then, one day, we were pleasantly surprised to learn that Raphael Hofer had fallen into our trap... er, I mean, taken the leap of faith. The result was a strip that did a nice job of blending our two cultures. We think it came out great. Switzerland, however, has officially forbidden us from visiting until we apologize.

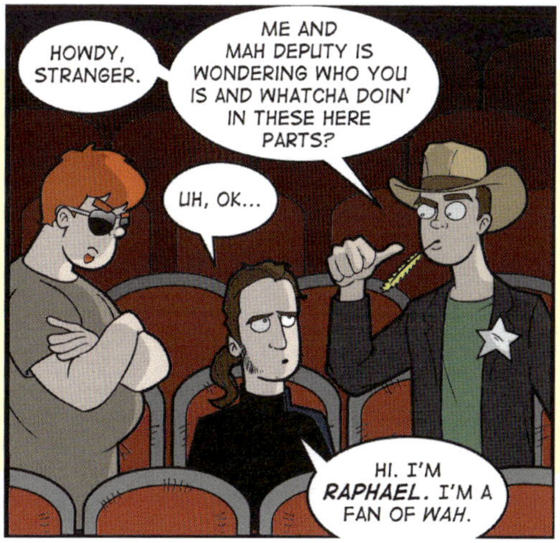
HOWDY, STRANGER.
ME AND MAH DEPUTY IS WONDERING WHO YOU IS AND WHATCHA DOIN' IN THESE HERE PARTS?
UH, OK...
HI. I'M *RAPHAEL*. I'M A FAN OF *WAH*.

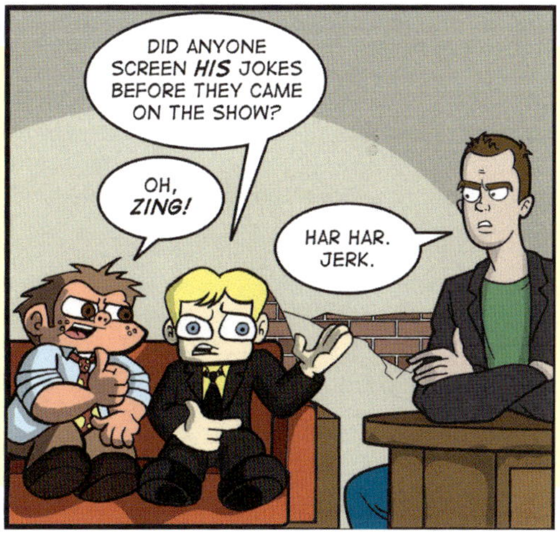
DID ANYONE SCREEN *HIS* JOKES BEFORE THEY CAME ON THE SHOW?
OH, *ZING!*
HAR HAR. JERK.

Ageism With A Lemon Twist (Strip 154): Tim Lai bailed us out of another predicament, this one self-inflicted. I had procrastinated finding Woody a guest to interview almost to the point in which it was too late for it to make sense in the storyline of that night's show. Fortunately, Tim stepped up to the challenge and helped us out. He brought some wonderful ideas, art and dialogue to the table, and together we created some terrific strips. We couldn't have asked for a better collaboration on such short notice.

OMG WTF (Strip 170): Paul had drawn 169 strips over 13 months and needed a break. Normally in this situation, a webcomic will ask other comic artists to draw filler strips. Instead, one of us (I'm not going to say who) thought that Paul's break was the perfect opportunity for me to try my hand at drawing the strip. Unfortunately, I have limited drawing skills. We lost 90% of our readership while Paul was on vacation. Years later they still haven't returned, despite our many offers of financial reconciliation.

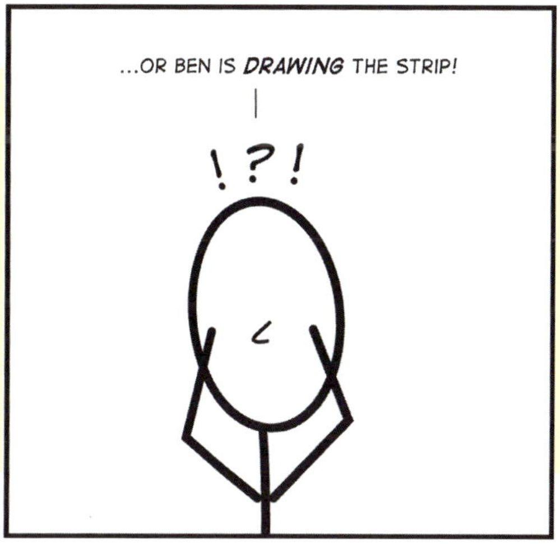
...OR BEN IS *DRAWING* THE STRIP!
!?!

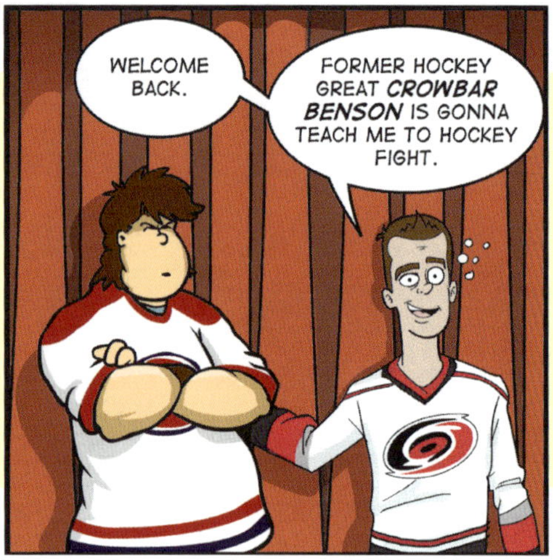
WELCOME BACK.
FORMER HOCKEY GREAT *CROWBAR BENSON* IS GONNA TEACH ME TO HOCKEY FIGHT.

Substitution Effect **(Strip 204):** When Paul informed me that Sandy Debreuil was interested in having Crowbar as a guest on *WAH,* I honestly wasn't sure it was going to work. First of all, Sandy is, well, to be blunt, Canadian. Second, his comic is about hockey. But after only a few minutes of talking with him and trading ideas, I knew our collaboration was going to be awesome. We asked a lot of Sandy, and he came through with great art, writing and friendliness. Together we published a record-breaking ten *WAH* guest strips over a month and a half.

Wherein The Host Pats The Fan **(Strip 208):** Up to this point, Paul and I knew all of the artists we collaborated with before their characters appeared in *WAH*. After seeing an ad for *Circuit* on our site, I blindly introduced myself to Luke Pola and asked if he'd like to work together. I'm really glad I took the chance. Luke is an excellent person with a fantastic sense of humor. He was a lot of fun to work with and get to know. I guess it just goes to show that advertising really does pay off.

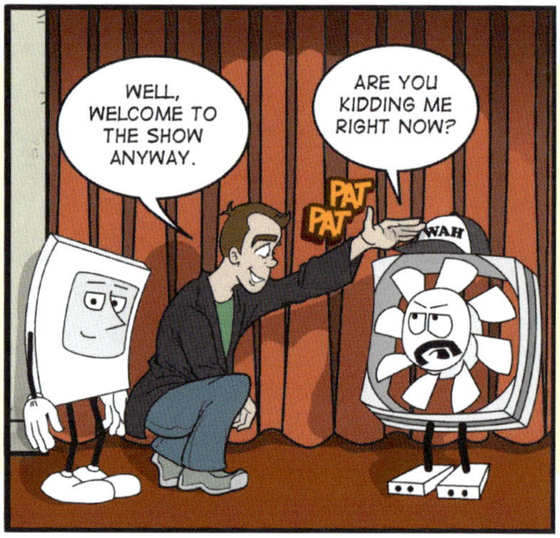
WELL, WELCOME TO THE SHOW ANYWAY.
ARE YOU KIDDING ME RIGHT NOW?
PAT
PAT
WAH

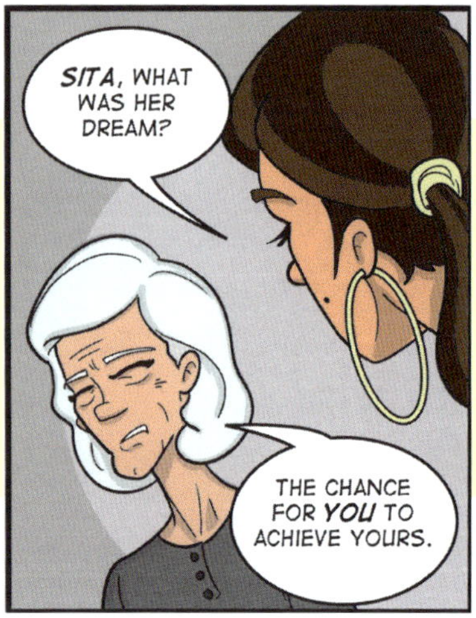
SITA, WHAT WAS HER DREAM?
THE CHANCE FOR *YOU* TO ACHIEVE YOURS.

Remembering A Person Who Made Life Possible **(Strip 235):** The story arc with Isabel and her grandmother's friend was a real challenge for me to write. Isabel and I are almost completely different people, so I have a difficult time relating to her under normal circumstances. Therefore, having her discuss her hopes and fears with someone who I have absolutely nothing in common with was a real struggle. In the end, however, I'm glad I challenged myself to complete it.

AND NOW LADIES AND GENTLEMEN

WE PROUDLY PRESENT, FOR THE FIRST TIME IN PRINT, The SENSATION Popular Enough to Crash YooTube: WOODY'S TRIBUTE TO

☆ ☆ ☆ ☆ ☆ ☆ ☆ ☆ ☆ ☆ ☆ ☆ ☆ ☆

MICHAEL JACKSON

(while under a Chelsea Chattan spell).

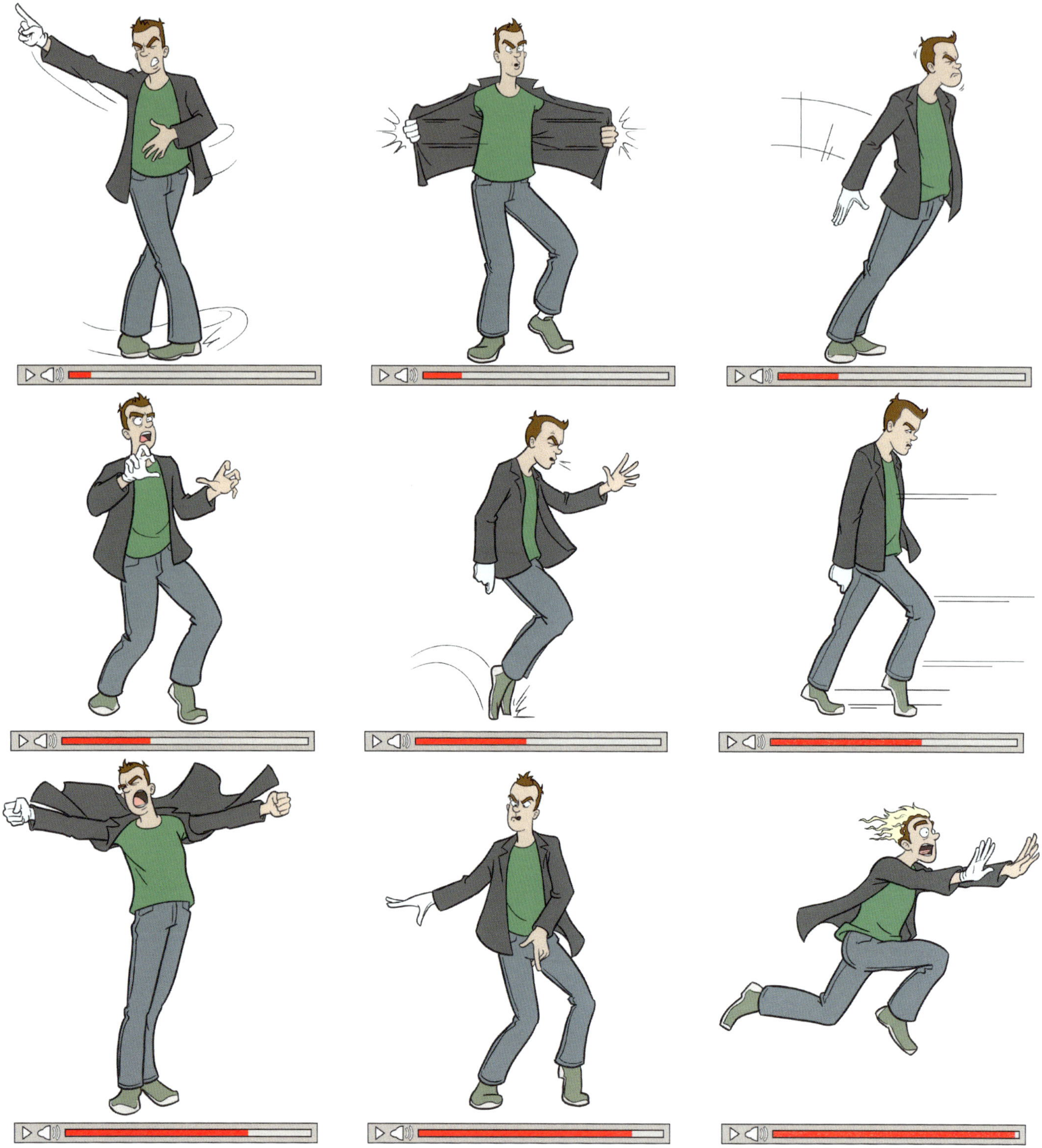

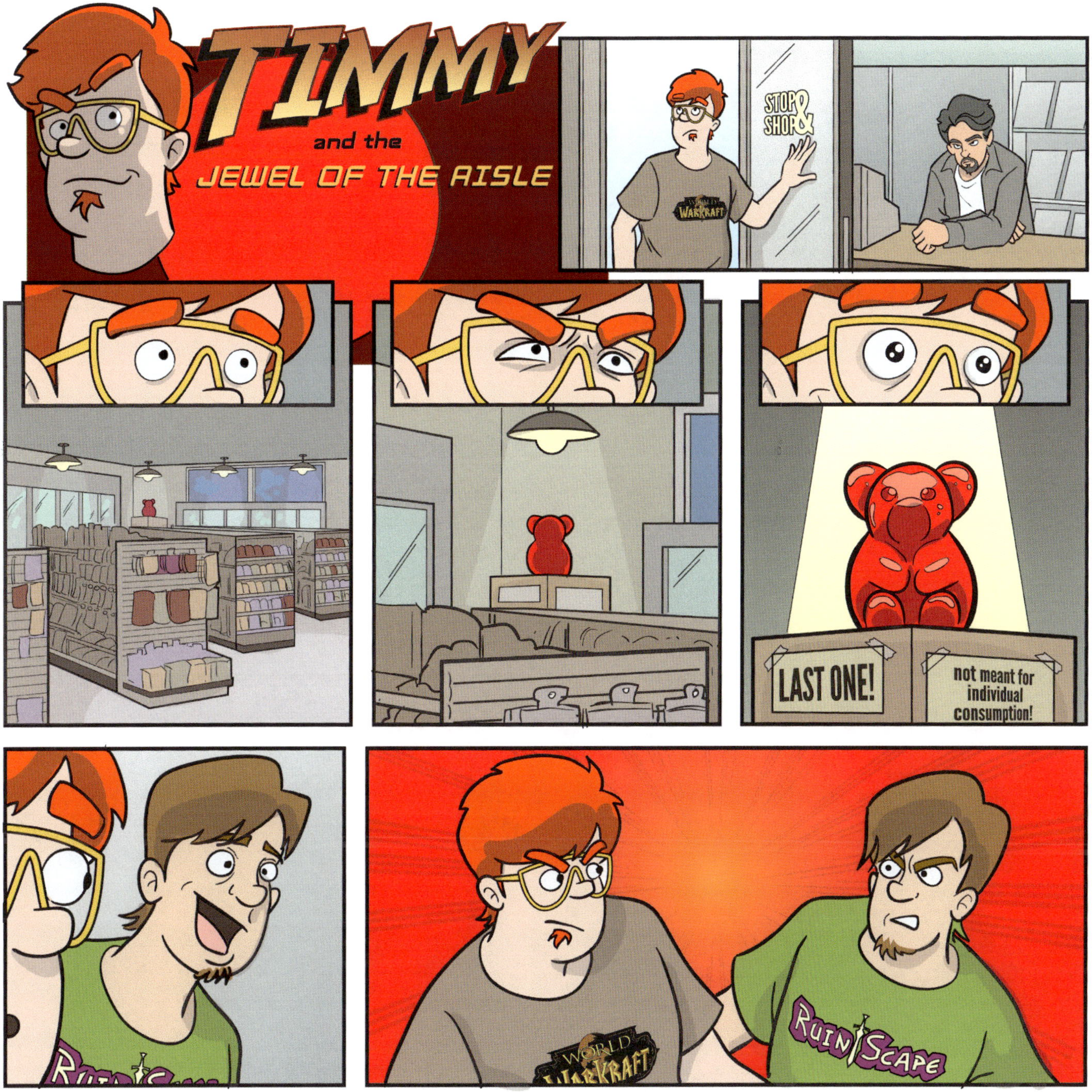
TIMMY
and the
JEWEL OF THE AISLE
STOP & SHOP
WORLD WARKRAFT
LAST ONE!
not meant for individual consumption!
RUIN SCAPE

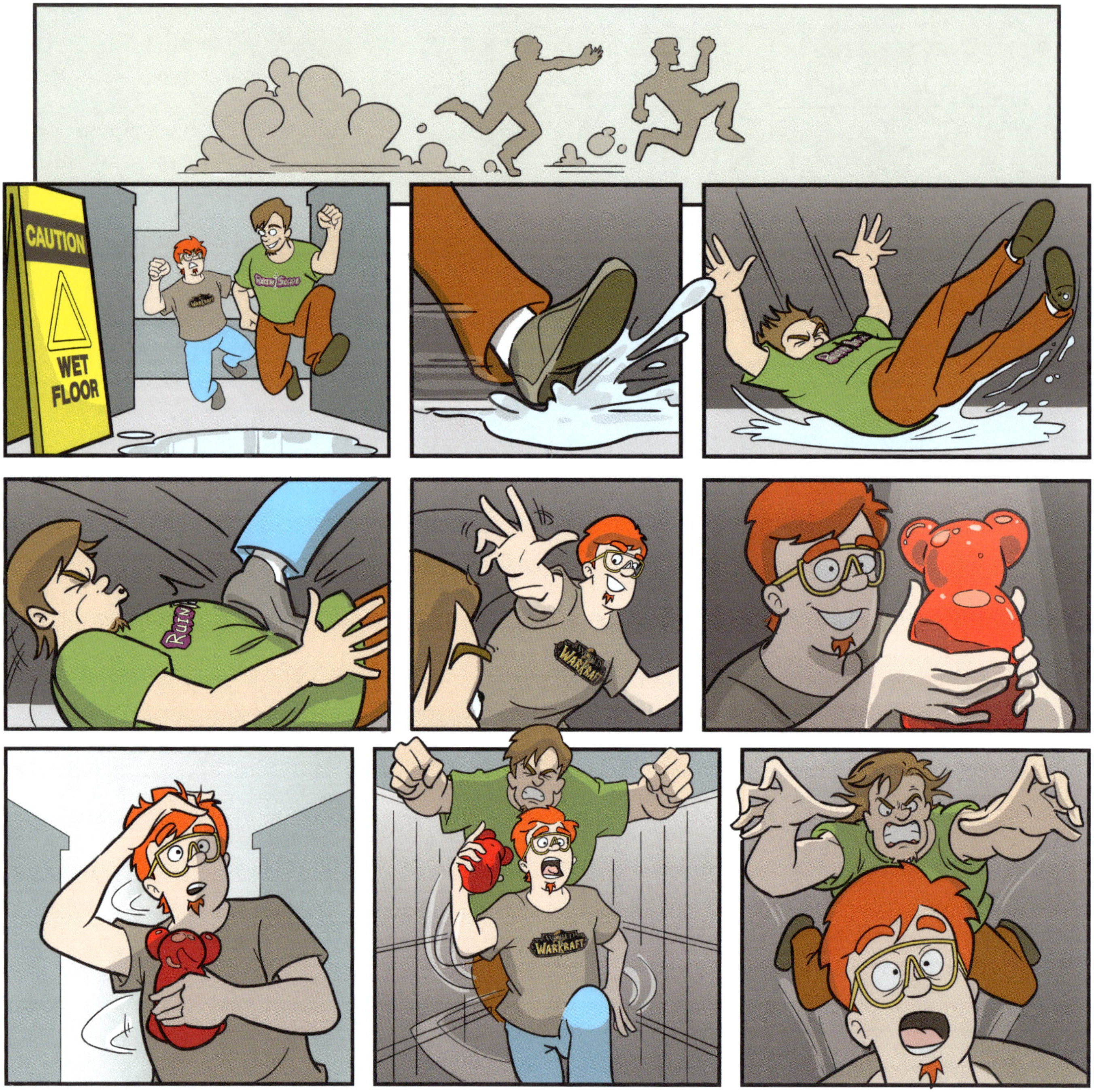
CAUTION
WET FLOOR

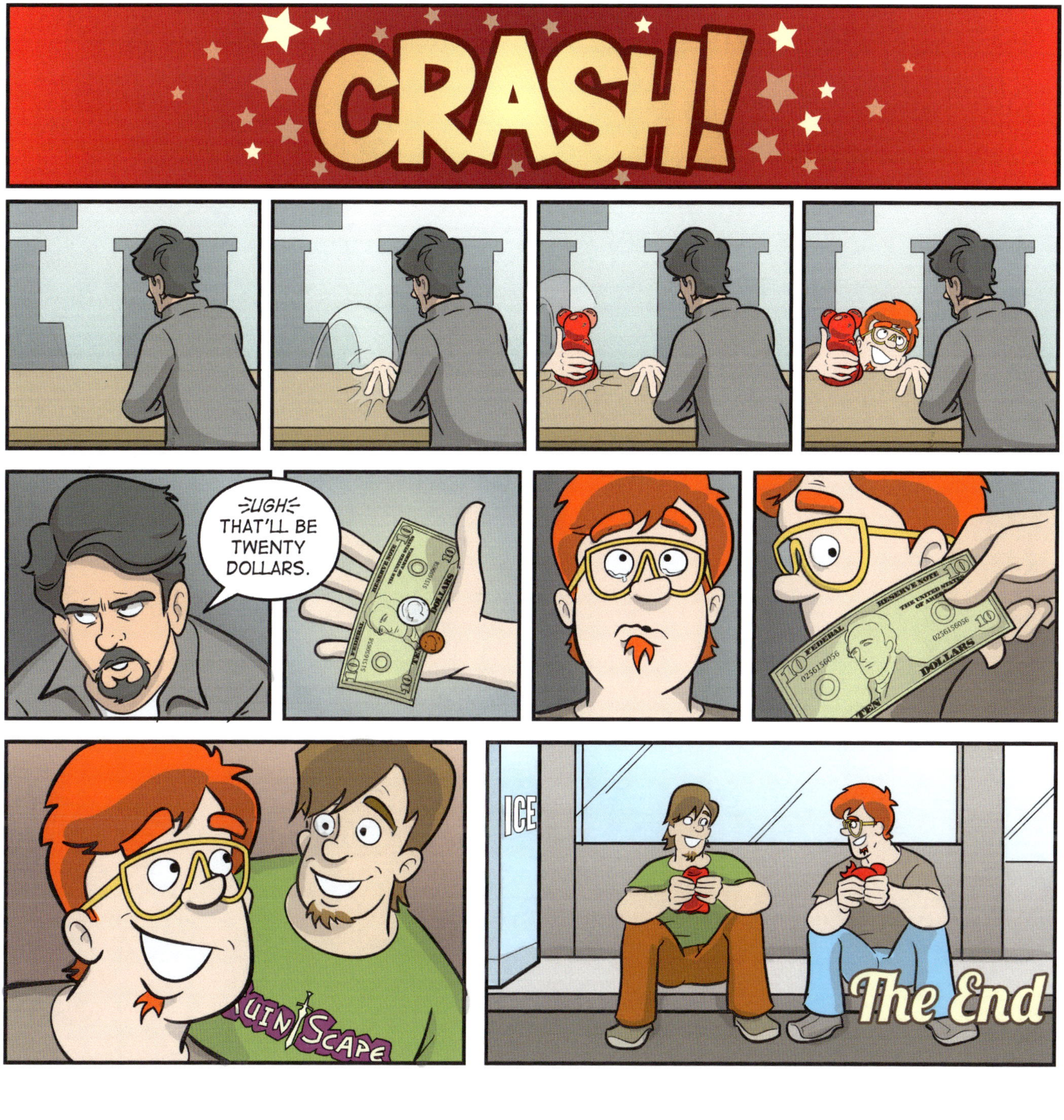
CRASH!
UGH
THAT'LL BE TWENTY DOLLARS.
ICE
The End

INDEX OF STRIPS (by title and release date)

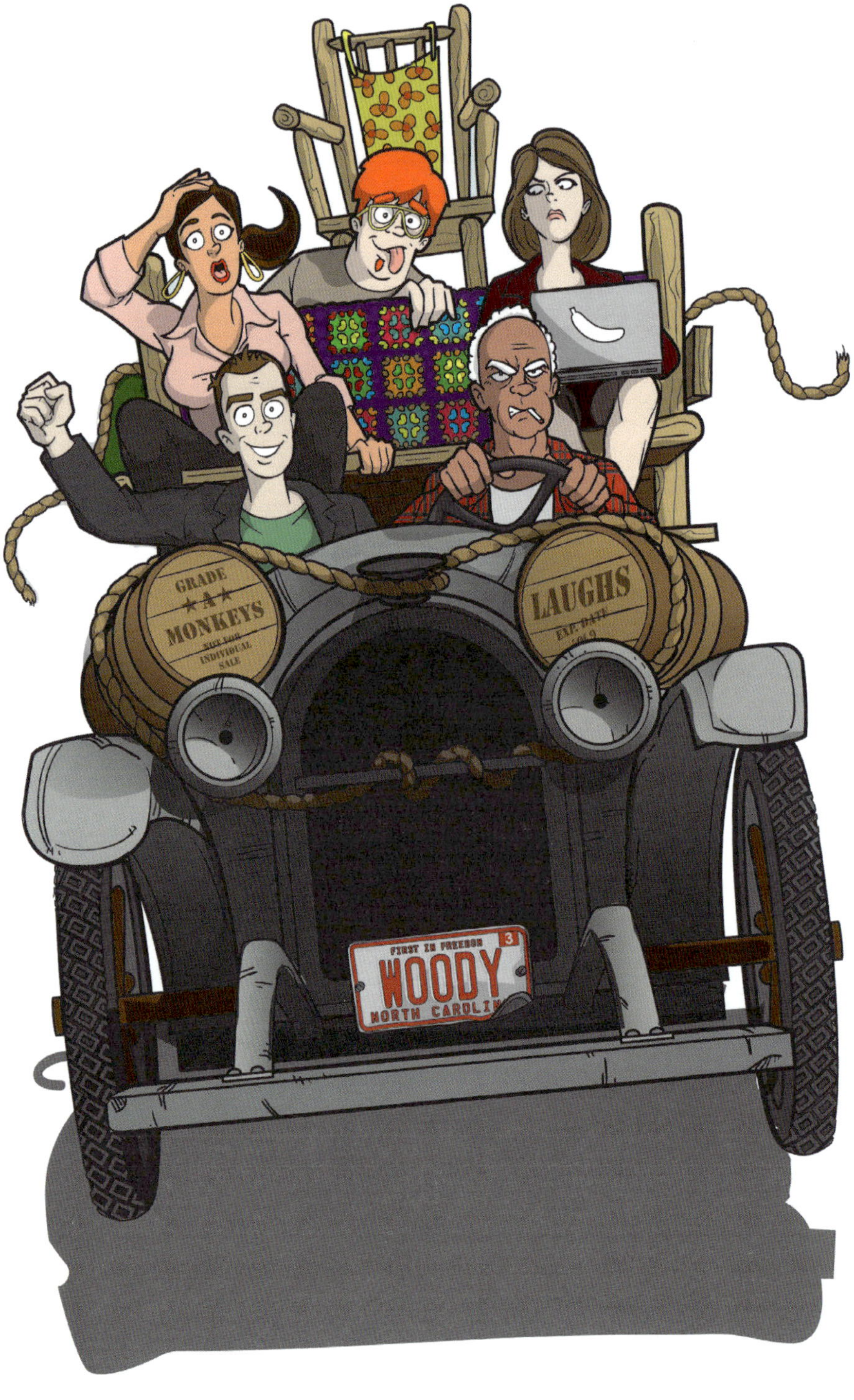
GRADE
★A★
MONKEYS
INDIVIDUAL
SALE
LAUGHS
EXP. DATE
FIRST IN FREEDOM
3
WOODY
NORTH CAROLIN

Made in the USA
Charleston, SC
15 February 2013